Z
678
.L374
2001

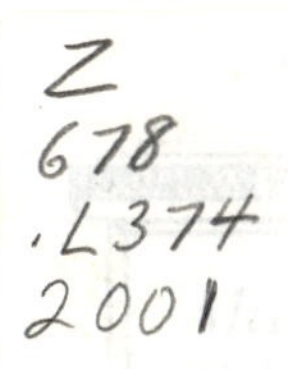

D0147485

D. Winston, MLS, PhD

Leadership i... ...ry and Inform... Pro... Theory ... a

Leadership in the Library and Information Science Professions: Theory and Practice has been co-published simultaneously as *Journal of Library Administration*, Volume 32, Number 3/4 2001.

Pre-publication REVIEWS, COMMENTARIES, EVALUATIONS . . .

"SUPERB. . . . From leadership development through cultural diversity to technology and evaluation models, this is a very complete, EXCELLENT FOUNDATION FOR STUDENTS AND PRACTITIONERS ALIKE."

Nancy Tessman
Executive Director
Library Leadership Institute at Snowbird
Director
Salt Lake City Public Library

RECEIVED
OCT 28 2002
MEMORIAL LIBRARY

More pre-publication
REVIEWS, COMMENTARIES, EVALUATIONS . . .

"A FINE VOLUME that would make a good textbook for a leadership course or could well serve as a source for supplemental readings in a general management course. Excellent chapters by Betty J. Turock on women and leadership and Stuart Glogoff on information technology in the virtual library are alone worth the price of the book. THOROUGH . . . Mark Winston's choice of authors is remarkable."

Jane B. Robbins, PhD
Dean and Professor
School of Information Studies
Florida State University
Tallahassee

The Haworth Information Press
An Imprint of The Haworth Press, Inc.

Leadership in the Library and Information Science Professions: Theory and Practice

Leadership in the Library and Information Science Professions: Theory and Practice has been co-published simultaneously as *Journal of Library Administration*, Volume 32, Numbers 3/4 2001.

The *Journal of Library Administration* Monographic "Separates"

Below is a list of " separates," which in serials librarianship means a special issue simultaneously published as a special journal issue or double-issue *and* as a "separate" hardbound monograph. (This is a format which we also call a "DocuSerial.")

"Separates" are published because specialized libraries or professionals may wish to purchase a specific thematic issue by itself in a format which can be separately cataloged and shelved, as opposed to purchasing the journal on an on-going basis. Faculty members may also more easily consider a "separate" for classroom adoption.

"Separates" are carefully classified separately with the major book jobbers so that the journal tie-in can be noted on new book order slips to avoid duplicate purchasing.

You may wish to visit Haworth's Website at . . .

http://www.HaworthPress.com

. . . to search our online catalog for complete tables of contents of these separates and related publications.

You may also call 1-800-HAWORTH (outside US/Canada: 607-722-5857), or Fax 1-800-895-0582 (outside US/Canada: 607-771-0012), or e-mail at:

getinfo@haworthpressinc.com

Leadership in the Library and Information Science Professions: Theory and Practice, edited by Mark D. Winston, MLS, PhD (Vol. 32, No. 3/4, 2001. *Offers fresh ideas for developing and using leadership skills, including recruiting potential leaders, staff training and development, issues of gender and ethnic diversity, and budget strategies for success.*

Off-Campus Library Services, edited by Ann Marie Casey (Vol. 31, No. 3/4, 2001 and Vol. 32, No. 1/2, 2001). *This informative volume examines various aspects of off-campus, or distance learning. It explores training issues for library staff, Web site development, changing roles for librarians, the uses of conferencing software, library support for Web-based courses, library agreements and how to successfully negotiate them, and much more!*

Research Collections and Digital Information, edited by Sul H. Lee (Vol. 31, No. 2, 2000). *Offers new strategies for collecting, organizing, and accessing library materials in the digital age.*

Academic Research on the Internet: Options for Scholars & Libraries, edited by Helen Laurence, MLS, EdD, and William Miller, MLS, PhD (Vol. 30, No. 1/2/3/4, 2000). *"Emphasizes quality over quantity. . . . Presents the reader with the best research-oriented Web sites in the field. A state-of-the-art review of academic use of the Internet as well as a guide to the best Internet sites and services. . . . A useful addition for any academic library." (David A. Tyckoson, MLS, Head of Reference, California State University, Fresno)*

Management for Research Libraries Cooperation, edited by Sul H. Lee (Vol. 29. No. 3/4, 2000). *Delivers sound advice, models, and strategies for increasing sharing between institutions to maximize the amount of printed and electronic research material you can make available in your library while keeping costs under control.*

Integration in the Library Organization, edited by Christine E. Thompson, PhD (Vol. 29, No. 2 1999). *Provides librarians with the necessary tools to help libraries balance and integrate public and technical services and to improve the capability of libraries to offer patrons quality services and large amounts of information.*

Library Training for Staff and Customers, edited by Sara Ramser Beck, MLS, MBA (Vol. 29, No. 1, 1999). *This comprehensive book is designed to assist library professionals involved in presenting or planning training for library staff members and customers. You will explore ideas for effective general reference training, training on automated systems, training in specialized subjects such as African American history and biography, and training for areas such as patents and trademarks, and business subjects.* Library Training for Staff and Customers *answers numerous training questions and is an excellent guide for planning staff development.*

Collection Development in the Electronic Environment: Shifting Priorities, edited by Sul H. Lee (Vol. 28, No. 4, 1999). *Through case studies and firsthand experiences, this volume discusses meeting the needs of scholars at universities, budgeting issues, user education, staffing in the electronic age, collaborating libraries and resources, and how vendors meet the needs of different customers.*

The Age Demographics of Academic Librarians: A Profession Apart, by Stanley J. Wilder (Vol. 28, No. 3, 1999). *The average age of librarians has been increasing dramatically since 1990. This unique book will provide insights on how this demographic issue can impact a library and what can be done to make the effects positive.*

Collection Development in a Digital Environment, edited by Sul H. Lee (Vol. 28, No. 1, 1999). *Explores ethical and technological dilemmas of collection development and gives several suggestions on how a library can successfully deal with these challenges and provide patrons with the information they need.*

Scholarship, Research Libraries, and Global Publishing, by Jutta Reed-Scott (Vol. 27, No. 3/4, 1999). *This book documents a research project in conjunction with the Association of Research Libraries (ARL) that explores the issue of foreign acquisition and how it affects collection in international studies, area studies, collection development, and practices of international research libraries.*

Managing Multicultural Diversity in the Library: Principles and Issues for Administrators, edited by Mark Winston (Vol. 27, No. 1/2, 1999). *Defines diversity, clarifies why it is important to address issues of diversity, and identifies goals related to diversity and how to go about achieving those goals.*

Information Technology Planning, edited by Lori A. Goetsch (Vol. 26, No. 3/4, 1999). *Offers innovative approaches and strategies useful in your library and provides some food for thought about information technology as we approach the millennium.*

The Economics of Information in the Networked Environment, edited by Meredith A. Butler, MLS, and Bruce R. Kingma, PhD (Vol. 26, No. 1/2, 1998). *"A book that should be read both by information professionals and by administrators, faculty and others who share a collective concern to provide the most information to the greatest number at the lowest cost in the networked environment." (Thomas J. Galvin, PhD, Professor of Information Science and Policy, University at Albany, State University of New York)*

OCLC 1967-1997: Thirty Years of Furthering Access to the World's Information, edited by K. Wayne Smith (Vol. 25, No. 2/3/4, 1998). *"A rich–and poignantly personal, at times–historical account of what is surely one of this century's most important developments in librarianship." (Deanna B. Marcum, PhD, President, Council on Library and Information Resources, Washington, DC)*

Management of Library and Archival Security: From the Outside Looking In, edited by Robert K. O'Neill, PhD (Vol. 25, No. 1, 1998). *"Provides useful advice and on-target insights for professionals caring for valuable documents and artifacts." (Menzi L. Behrnd-Klodt, JD, Attorney/Archivist, Klodt and Associates, Madison, WI)*

Economics of Digital Information: Collection, Storage, and Delivery, edited by Sul H. Lee (Vol. 24, No. 4, 1997). *Highlights key concepts and issues vital to a library's successful venture into the digital environment and helps you understand why the transition from the printed page to the digital packet has been problematic for both creators of proprietary materials and users of those materials.*

The Academic Library Director: Reflections on a Position in Transition, edited by Frank D'Andraia, MLS (Vol. 24, No. 3, 1997). *"A useful collection to have whether you are seeking a position as director or conducting a search for one." (College & Research Libraries News)*

Emerging Patterns of Collection Development in Expanding Resource Sharing, Electronic Information, and Network Environment, edited by Sul H. Lee (Vol. 24, No. 1/2, 1997). *"The issues it deals with are common to us all. We all need to make our funds go further and our resources work harder, and there are ideas here which we can all develop." (The Library Association Record)*

Interlibrary Loan/Document Delivery and Customer Satisfaction: Strategies for Redesigning Services, edited by Pat L. Weaver-Meyers, Wilbur A. Stolt, Yem S. Fong (Vol. 23, No. 1/2, 1997). *"No interlibrary loan department supervisor at any mid-sized to large college or university library can afford not to read this book." (Gregg Sapp, MLS, MEd, Head of Access Services, University of Miami, Richter Library, Coral Gables, Florida)*

Access, Resource Sharing and Collection Development, edited by Sul H. Lee (Vol. 22, No. 4, 1996). *Features continuing investigation and discussion of important library issues, specifically the role of libraries in acquiring, storing, and disseminating information in different formats.*

Managing Change in Academic Libraries, edited by Joseph J. Branin (Vol. 22, No. 2/3, 1996). *"Touches on several aspects of academic library management, emphasizing the changes that are occurring at the present time. . . . Recommended this title for individuals or libraries interested in management aspects of academic libraries." (RQ American Library Association)*

Libraries and Student Assistants: Critical Links, edited by William K. Black, MLS (Vol. 21, No. 3/4, 1995). *"A handy reference work on many important aspects of managing student assistants. . . . Solid, useful information on basic management issues in this work and several chapters are useful for experienced managers." (The Journal of Academic Librarianship)*

The Future of Resource Sharing, edited by Shirley K. Baker and Mary E. Jackson, MLS (Vol. 21, No. 1/2, 1995). *"Recommended for library and information science schools because of its balanced presentation of the ILL/document delivery issues." (Library Acquisitions: Practice and Theory)*

The Future of Information Services, edited by Virginia Steel, MA, and C. Brigid Welch, MLS (Vol. 20, No. 3/4, 1995). *"The leadership discussions will be useful for library managers as will the discussions of how library structures and services might work in the next century." (Australian Special Libraries)*

The Dynamic Library Organizations in a Changing Environment, edited by Joan Giesecke, MLS, DPA (Vol. 20, No. 2, 1995). *"Provides a significant look at potential changes in the library world and presents its readers with possible ways to address the negative results of such changes. . . . Covers the key issues facing today's libraries . . . Two thumbs up!" (Marketing Library Resources)*

Access, Ownership, and Resource Sharing, edited by Sul H. Lee (Vol. 20, No. 1, 1995). *The contributing authors present a useful and informative look at the current status of information provision and some of the challenges the subject presents.*

Libraries as User-Centered Organizations: Imperatives for Organizational Change, edited by Meredith A. Butler (Vol. 19, No. 3/4, 1994). *"Presents a very timely and well-organized discussion of major trends and influences causing organizational changes." (Science Books & Films)*

Declining Acquisitions Budgets: Allocation, Collection Development and Impact Communication, edited by Sul H. Lee (Vol. 19, No. 2, 1994). *"Expert and provocative. . . . Presents many ways of looking at library budget deterioration and responses to it . . . There is much food for thought here." (Library Resources & Technical Services)*

The Role and Future of Special Collections in Research Libraries: British and American Perspectives, edited by Sul H. Lee (Vol. 19, No. 1, 1993). *"A provocative but informative read for library users, academic administrators, and private sponsors." (International Journal of Information and Library Research)*

Catalysts for Change: Managing Libraries in the 1990s, edited by Gisela M. von Dran, DPA, MLS, and Jennifer Cargill, MSLS, MSed (Vol. 18, No. 3/4, 1994). *"A useful collection of articles which focuses on the need for librarians to employ enlightened management practices in order to adapt to and thrive in the rapidly changing information environment." (Australian Library Review)*

Monographic "Separates" list continued at the back

Leadership in the Library and Information Science Professions: Theory and Practice

Mark D. Winston, MLS, PhD
Editor

Leadership in the Library and Information Science Professions: Theory and Practice has been co-published simultaneously as *Journal of Library Administration*, Volume 32, Numbers 3/4 2001.

The Haworth Information Press
An Imprint of
The Haworth Press, Inc.
New York • London • Oxford

Published by

The Haworth Information Press®, 10 Alice Street, Binghamton, NY 13904-1580 USA

The Haworth Information Press® is an imprint of The Haworth Press, Inc., 10 Alice Street, Binghamton, NY 13904-1580 USA.

Leadership in the Library and Information Science Professions: Theory and Practice has been co-published simultaneously as *Journal of Library Administration*™, Volume 32, Numbers 3/4 2001.

© 2001 by The Haworth Press, Inc. All rights reserved. No part of this work may be reproduced or utilized in any form or by any means, electronic or mechanical, including photocopying, microfilm and recording, or by any information storage and retrieval system, without permission in writing from the publisher. Printed in the United States of America.

The development, preparation, and publication of this work has been undertaken with great care. However, the publisher, employees, editors, and agents of The Haworth Press and all imprints of The Haworth Press, Inc., including The Haworth Medical Press® and Pharmaceutical Products Press®, are not responsible for any errors contained herein or for consequences that may ensue from use of materials or information contained in this work. Opinions expressed by the author(s) are not necessarily those of The Haworth Press, Inc.

Cover design by Thomas J. Mayshock Jr.

Library of Congress Cataloging-in-Publication Data

Leadership in the Library and information science professions : theory and practice / Mark D. Winston, editor.

p. cm.

Co-published simultaneously as Journal of library administration, v. 32, nos. 3/4, 2001.

Includes bibliographical references and index.

ISBN 0-7890-1415-7 (alk. paper) — ISBN 0-7890-1416-5 (pbk. : alk. paper)

1. Library administration. 2. Information services--Management. 3. Leadership. 4. Organizational change--Management. I. Winston, Mark. II. Journal of library administration.

Z678 .L374 2001

025.1--dc21

2001039488

Indexing, Abstracting & Website/Internet Coverage

This section provides you with a list of major indexing & abstracting services. That is to say, each service began covering this periodical during the year noted in the right column. Most Websites which are listed below have indicated that they will either post, disseminate, compile, archive, cite or alert their own Website users with research-based content from this work. (This list is as current as the copyright date of this publication.)

Abstracting, Website/Indexing Coverage . . . . Year When Coverage Began

- *Academic Abstracts/CD-ROM* 1993
- *Academic Search: data base of 2,000 selected academic serials, updated monthly: EBSCO Publishing* 1995
- *Academic Search Elite (EBSCO)* 1993
- *AGRICOLA Database* 1991
- *BUBL Information Service: An Internet-based Information Service for the UK higher education community <URL: http://bubl.ac.uk/>* 1999
- *Business ASAP* 1993
- *CNPIEC Reference Guide: Chinese National Directory of Foreign Periodicals* 1995
- *Current Articles on Library Literature and Services (CALLS)* 1992
- *Current Awareness Abstracts of Library & Information Management Literature, ASLIB (UK)* 1998
- *Current Cites [Digital Libraries] [Electronic Publishing] [Multimedia & Hypermedia] [Networks & Networking] [General]* 2000
- *Current Index to Journals in Education* 1997
- *Educational Administration Abstracts (EAA)* 1991
- *FINDEX <www.publist.com>* 1999
- *FRANCIS.INIST/CNRS <www.inist.fr>* 1999
- *General BusinessFile ASAP <www.galegroup.com>* 1993
- *General Reference Center GOLD on InfoTrac Web* 1984
- *Higher Education Abstracts, providing the latest in research theory in more than 14 major topics* 1991

(continued)

- *IBZ International Bibliography of Periodical Literature* 1995
- *Index Guide to College Journals (core list compiled by integrating 48 indexes frequently used to support undergraduate programs in small to medium sized libraries)* 1999
- *Index to Periodical Articles Related to Law* 1991
- *Information Reports & Bibliographies* 1991
- *Information Science Abstracts* 1991
- *Informed Librarian, The <http://www.infosourcespub.com>* 1993
- *InfoTrac Custom <www.galegroup.com>* 1996
- *INSPEC <www.iee.org.uk/publish/>* 1991
- *Journal of Academic Librarianship: Guide to Professional Literature, The* 1995
- *Konyvtari Figyelo (Library Review)* 1995
- *Library & Information Science Abstracts (LISA)* 1991
- *Library and Information Science Annual (LISCA) <www.lu.com/arba>* 1991
- *Library Literature & Information Science* 1991
- *MasterFILE: updated database from EBSCO Publishing* 1995
- *OCLC Public Affairs Information Service <www.pais.org>* 2000
- *PASCAL, c/o Institute de L'Information Scientifique et Technique <http://www.inist.fr>* 1994
- *Referativnyi Zhurnal (Abstracts Journal of the All-Russian Institute of Scientific and Technical Information–in Russian)* 1991
- *Trade & Industry Index* 1991

Special Bibliographic Notes related to special journal issues (separates) and indexing/abstracting:

- indexing/abstracting services in this list will also cover material in any "separate" that is co-published simultaneously with Haworth's special thematic journal issue or DocuSerial. Indexing/abstracting usually covers material at the article/chapter level.
- monographic co-editions are intended for either non-subscribers or libraries which intend to purchase a second copy for their circulating collections.
- monographic co-editions are reported to all jobbers/wholesalers/approval plans. The source journal is listed as the "series" to assist the prevention of duplicate purchasing in the same manner utilized for books-in-series.
- to facilitate user/access services all indexing/abstracting services are encouraged to utilize the co-indexing entry note indicated at the bottom of the first page of each article/chapter/contribution.
- this is intended to assist a library user of any reference tool (whether print, electronic, online, or CD-ROM) to locate the monographic version if the library has purchased this version but not a subscription to the source journal.
- individual articles/chapters in any Haworth publication are also available through the Haworth Document Delivery Service (HDDS).

Leadership in the Library and Information Science Professions: Theory and Practice

CONTENTS

ABOUT THE EDITOR

Mark D. Winston, MLS, PhD, is a faculty member in the Rutgers University School of Communication, Information and Library Studies. He teaches courses in library management and leadership. In addition to his prior professional experiences in banking and auditing, he has held professional positions in academic libraries, including those of Assistant University Librarian (Assistant Director for Public Services), Coordinator of Instruction, and Business Undergraduate Services Librarian.

Dr. Winston's publications have included book chapters, journal articles, a book, and other publications on topics such as leadership, management, professional recruitment, collaboration between librarians and business school faculty, and diversity.

Dr. Winston is an Advisory Committee member for the W. K. Kellogg/Rutgers University Leadership Development Initiative Task Force, Mid-Atlantic Consortium. In addition, he is a member of the planning team for the Rutgers University/AT&T Organizational Quality Leadership program, which is developing an interdisciplinary undergraduate program in leadership theories and organizational quality.

ALL HAWORTH INFORMATION PRESS
BOOKS AND JOURNALS ARE PRINTED
ON CERTIFIED ACID-FREE PAPER

Introduction

Mark D. Winston

Leadership as a concept is difficult to define and is often equated with management, which is more narrow and often position specific. What is apparent is the need for those who can provide leadership in organizations, which face many challenges and which must accomplish a great deal in a highly competitive and dynamic environment. A significant number of organizational and societal issues highlight the need for increased focus on the issue of leadership in the library and information science professions. In the case of the more than 120,000 libraries in the U.S.,[1] these challenges include the demands of various publics and clients, related issues of accountability, a growing number of competitors, as well as an increasingly competitive environment in relation to financial resources and talent, growing expectations of employees for involvement in decision making, and the proliferation of information technology. In response to these issues, organizational changes have included increased examples of participative management, team-based decision making, flattened hierarchies, and matrix organizational structures. As a result, it has become apparent that there is the need for leadership at all levels in organizations.

Certainly, this challenging, competitive, and dynamic environment requires that organizations today and in the future identify, develop, and retain leaders who are able to make substantive contributions to the success of organizations. Thus, effective leadership is needed in terms of developing and promoting vision, fostering support for the organiza-

[Haworth co-indexing entry note]: "Introduction." Winston, Mark D. Co-published simultaneously in *Journal of Library Administration* (The Haworth Information Press, an imprint of The Haworth Press, Inc.) Vol. 32, No. 3/4, 2001, pp. 1-3; and: *Leadership in the Library and Information Science Professions: Theory and Practice* (ed: Mark D. Winston) The Haworth Information Press, an imprint of The Haworth Press, Inc., 2001, pp. 1-3. Single or multiple copies of this article are available for a fee from The Haworth Document Delivery Service [1-800-342-9678, 9:00 a.m. - 5:00 p.m. (EST). E-mail address: getinfo@haworthpressinc.com].

© 2001 by The Haworth Press, Inc. All rights reserved.

tion's mission and priorities, and making difficult decisions in ensuring the provision of information services for a changing, diverse, and increasingly technologically-savvy user population. These organizations will be in need of leaders who are knowledgeable, flexible, self-aware, collaborative, and forward-thinking.

However, ensuring this level of effective leadership is not easily accomplished, as the issues related to leadership are complex and multifaceted. Thus, it is critical that we are willing to ask the difficult questions and address difficult issues related to leadership. Certainly, this collection of writings is intended to make a substantive contribution to the scholarly and practical discussion of the leadership. These difficult issues related to leadership include the need to attempt to define leadership, to identify the types of knowledge that are needed by leaders in the global information age and an increasingly diverse world, and to determine how we can develop leadership at all levels in organizations, with increased competition, significant technological developments, and ever-expanding expectations of our organizations and professionals.

This collection of writings addresses a number of the most significant issues related to leadership by offering insight to inform practice and to further the understanding of leadership issues–priorities, which clearly must be addressed within the arena of library and information services in the future.

The authors have addressed many of the more difficult and substantive issues related to leadership, including the identification of the challenges to be faced and opportunities to be addressed in relation to the leadership in organizations, the importance of identifying and addressing the professional development needs of leaders and future leaders, including the determination of knowledge and competencies required of effective leaders in relation to information technology and financial management. In addition, the importance of leadership evaluation and assessment is addressed, as is the role of technology-related organizations in providing and helping to ensure effective leadership in the profession. As U.S. organizations address issues relating to the increasingly diverse and emerging global information society, the consideration of leadership from a broader perspective becomes increasingly important. As a result, the authors consider the relationship between feminist theory and leadership, diversity and leadership, and the concept of leadership as it is understood and applied in other countries.

One of the goals of this collection of writings is to address one of the most critical and timely issues that affects many professions. The authors provide thoughtful and well-documented analyses in consideration of this important area and help to further a discussion that will better define the issues and inform practice in a substantial way.

NOTE

1. "Libraries Today: Libraries Build Community." Chicago: American Library Association, 1.

The Crisis and Opportunities in Library Leadership

Donald E. Riggs

SUMMARY. Libraries will continue to undergo rapid change in the years ahead. People who work in libraries will have to learn how to lead change and to live positively with more ambiguity. For too long, libraries have been over-managed and under-led. If this practice continues, libraries are headed for big trouble! Leadership in libraries can no longer be pushed aside and ignored; it must be brought to center stage, and treated with a capital L. Without strong, dynamic, and visionary leadership, libraries are certain to drift backward into the future. However, before we begin thinking of doomsday for libraries, we should explore and enthusiastically implement action plans for promoting and learning more about this phenomenon known as "Leadership."
[Article copies available for a fee from The Haworth Document Delivery Service: 1-800-342-9678. E-mail address: <getinfo@haworthpressinc.com> Website: <http://www.HaworthPress.com> © 2001 by The Haworth Press, Inc. All rights reserved.]

KEYWORDS. Leadership, leading change, vision, management

INTRODUCTION

Throughout the world, leadership is generally perceived as something we need more of, while at the same time it is generally misunderstood. There are at least 100 definitions of leadership. The definitions include leadership styles, functional leadership, situational leadership, bureaucratic leadership, charismatic leadership, servant leadership, follower leadership, group-centered leadership, and so on. One of the best

Donald E. Riggs is Vice President for Information Services and University Librarian at Nova Southeastern University.

[Haworth co-indexing entry note]: "The Crisis and Opportunities in Library Leadership." Riggs, Donald E. Co-published simultaneously in *Journal of Library Administration* (The Haworth Information Press, an imprint of The Haworth Press, Inc.) Vol. 32, No. 3/4, 2001, pp. 5-17; and: *Leadership in the Library and Information Science Professions: Theory and Practice* (ed: Mark D. Winston) The Haworth Information Press, an imprint of The Haworth Press, Inc., 2001, pp. 5-17. Single or multiple copies of this article are available for a fee from The Haworth Document Delivery Service [1-800-342-9678, 9:00 a.m. - 5:00 p.m. (EST). E-mail address: getinfo@haworthpressinc.com].

© 2001 by The Haworth Press, Inc. All rights reserved.

definitions on leadership is found in James MacGregor Burns's definitive work entitled *Leadership*: "Leadership over human beings is exercised when persons with certain motives and purposes mobilize, in competition or conflict with others, institutional, political, psychological, and other resources to arouse, engage, and satisfy the motives of followers."[1]

It is common to confuse management with leadership; notwithstanding the fact that both are necessary, management and leadership are two separate hemispheres.

DISTINCTION BETWEEN MANAGEMENT AND LEADERSHIP

Owing to the confusion between management and leadership, it is necessary to distinguish the ways in which management and leadership are different. Library managers tend to work within defined bounds of known quantities, using well-established techniques to accomplish predetermined ends; the manager tends to stress means and neglect ends. On the other hand, the library leader's task is to hold, before all persons connected with the library, some vision of what its mission is and how it can be reached effectively. Like managers, there are leaders throughout the library. The head librarian is not the only leader in a library. This fact must be remembered and addressed during leadership development programs.

The contours of library leadership may stand out in clearest relief when compared with the nature of library management. In his book, *On Becoming a Leader,* Warren Bennis says that leaders "master the context" rather than surrender to it and makes the following distinction between managers and leaders:

- The manager administers; the leader motivates.
- The manager is a copy; the leader is an original.
- The manager focuses on systems and structure; the leader focuses on people.
- The manager relies on control; the leader inspires trust.
- The manager has a short-range view; the leader has a long-range perspective.
- The manager asks how and when; the leader asks what and why.
- The manager imitates; the leader originates.
- The manager accepts the status quo; the leader challenges.
- The manager does things right; the leader does the right thing.[2]

The above delineation should not imply that one cannot be both a good manager and a fine leader. Also, the delineation is not intended to demean managers. Competent managers are extremely important to our libraries. Many library leaders were first effective managers. Libraries are well managed, but many are under-led. It is quite obvious we must give greater emphasis to library leadership.

ARE WE HEADED FOR A LEADERSHIP CRISIS?

This author has been intrigued with "leadership" for many years. In 1982, his book, *Library Leadership: Visualizing the Future,*[3] became one of the first, if not the first, book(s) published on library leadership. During the research for this book, it was discovered that there was a noticeable scarcity of books and journal articles on leadership in librarianship. At the same time this research was being conducted, there were many articles and books written on and about leadership in other professions. Why do we librarians not like to talk or write about leadership?

Bennis believes that the signs of a world leadership crisis are alarming and pervasive. He argues that unlike the possibility of plague or nuclear holocaust, the leadership crisis will probably not become the basis for a best seller or a blockbuster movie, but in many ways it is the most urgent and dangerous of the threats we face today, if only because it is insufficiently recognized and little understood.[4] Is there really an unconscious conspiracy to discourage and suppress genuine leadership? Is there a fear of creative leadership? Is there truly a conspiracy lulling us into conformity, complacency, cynicism, and inaction toward leadership? Do we really fear risk taking and discourage people to stand up and be counted? If the answer to only one of these questions is "yes," then we are already in a leadership crisis. Who would want to be a leader with one or more of these circumstances already in place?

Bringing the above concerns closer home to libraries, it is puzzling why librarians do not write and talk more about leadership. How many library and information science books do you know that were published during the past five years that contain the word "leadership" in their titles? *Leadership and Academic Librarians,* by Terrence F. Mech and Gerard B. McCabe,[5] is an example of a fine library leadership book. Can you name three library and information science journal articles published during the past five years with the word "leadership" in their titles? Why does the *Journal of Library Administration* not change its title to *Journal of Library Leadership?* Why does *Library Administra-*

tion & Management not change its title to *Library Leadership?* Or, why does someone not begin a new journal entitled *Library Leadership?* Why does the Library Administration and Management Association (a division of the American Library Association) exclude the word "leadership" from its title? Why not change the organization's name to "Library Leadership and Management Association," or to some other name including the word "leadership"?

Few, if any, schools of information and library science are teaching leadership classes. These schools were teaching administration classes while business schools were teaching management classes; now SILS programs are teaching management classes while business schools are teaching leadership classes. Should we not expect more emphasis on leadership from the schools preparing our future library leaders?

The above observations and suggestions are not intended to be critical of the current environment and practices, but to illustrate how one could conclude that there is an unconscious conspiracy against library leadership. It is obvious that not enough has been done to prevent a library leadership crisis. The wake-up call has been received; now is the time to better understand leadership, take it seriously as part of our daily working lives, and become more conscious of the potential for a leadership crisis. We are not in a library leadership crisis yet, but must remember that as a person cannot function without a brain, the library world cannot function without leaders.

MYTHS

Numerous myths about leadership have been perpetuated during past centuries. One of the most common myths existing is that only one person in an organization can be the leader. This misperception is damaging to the advancement of an organization. In a given library, there are or should be several leaders. The head librarian is the one person normally perceived to be a leader; however, department heads should also be leaders. The department head should be cultivated and supported as a leader.

Due to the complexities of being a leader there is the myth that a leader cannot be trusted. This myth is so far off base that it borders on being foolish. To be successful as a leader, the trust factor is extremely important. Followers deserve a leader they can trust now and in the future; trust, as the emotional glue, binds leaders and followers together in a library. In addition to being consistent in action, the library leader must listen to followers and trust them. Trust is a two-way street and it should never be taken for granted.

It is often assumed that if one is an excellent leader in one library setting that person will do a comparable job in another library setting. This assumption may be far from reality. In essence, leadership is situational. Even though library skills are transportable from one location to another, the various complexities of a given library situation will require a leader of a specific temperament, focus, and charisma. Too many times, search committees for a new library leader do not precisely know what kind of person is best for the future of their library. They normally believe that if a person is successful in one library that person will do well in another setting.

The most dangerous leadership myth is that leaders are born. This belief centers on leadership coming from genes. This type of believing is purely fictional. Leaders are made rather than born. Physical and mental attributes are certainly important elements in the leadership equation, but they are not paramount. Leadership evolves from life and job experiences. Role models, mentors, difficult experiences, and leadership training institutes are a few examples of leadership development.

LEADING CHANGE

New technology has brought with it many changes in the worklife of librarians. They are now doing things much differently compared with practices and procedures of a few years ago. The mission of libraries has not changed due to technology, but the way the mission is achieved has changed dramatically. Building a commitment to, overcoming resistance to, acceptance of, and sustenance of change in libraries require dynamic and caring leadership. Human nature appears to resist change and prefers to continue functioning in established patterns; however, it is especially important for the library leader to recognize, accept, and adjust to the constantly changing environment in order to perform at the maximum level in promoting successful change. Effective library leadership is characterized in part by the ability to break away from established structures. One practical way of breaking away from current practices/procedures is to create a "stop doing task force." Libraries are noted for maintaining specific practices/procedures forever. The proposed task force would critically look at all current activities, and subsequently made recommendations for discontinuation or major redesign of some activities. A library, like any other organization, should constantly engage in continuous improvement.

Library leaders must create an environment that embraces change not as a threat but as an opportunity. Leaders must listen to–and act on–the multiple sounds around them. Leaders must encourage their organizations to dance to forms of music yet to be heard.[6] Due to scarce resources, libraries are not known for their risk taking. Library leaders must find ways to encourage their followers to engage in risk taking, at least calculated risk taking. Errors from experimentation must be encouraged and embraced by library leaders. It may be possible to realize some funds for research/development purposes via innovation by substitution (i.e., substituting a new activity for a current, ineffective activity).

Managing change is not good enough. We must anticipate, plan, and lead change. With the impact of the evolving library technology, some librarians who have been successful in the past may not be successful in the future if they continue doing things they have been doing in the past. Their learning process will have to change significantly; for example, they will have to talk with different people, listen to different people, and, in a sense, they will have to unlearn those activities that brought them success in the past. The "unlearning process" is normally difficult for librarians to handle. Margaret Wheatley offers an excellent perspective on the transition to the new way of viewing and doing things:

> I believe that we have only just begun the process of inventing the new organizational forms that will inhabit the twenty-first century. To be responsible inventors and discoverers, though, we need the courage to let go of the old world, to relinquish most of what we have cherished, to abandon our interpretations about what does and doesn't work. We must learn to see the world anew.[7]

Librarians who have successfully made the transition from forgetting past practices and learning new ones are quick to acknowledge the importance of the role of top leadership. The listening skills, empathy, emotional support, empowerment, and coaching skills of library leaders are certainly tested during this type of transition.

EXPECTED QUALITIES OF EFFECTIVE LEADERS

Library leaders come in various sizes, shapes, and dispositions–neat, sloppy, short, tall, fat, slim, young, and old. Some leaders may have similar attributes, but it is rare to find any two leaders who are somewhat identical. The following qualities, however, can be found in most leaders. These qualities are not presented in any semblance of priority of importance, nor are they inclusive.

Vision. Library leaders are not expected to see around corners, but they are expected to develop and sustain a compelling vision of the future. Burt Nanis describes a vision as being a realistic, credible, attractive future for an organization.[8] Vision is certainly one of the cornerstones of leadership. Without a compelling, achievable vision, there will not be much leadership. Leaders lead into the future and their effectiveness will be measured by their vision in advancing the library forward.

Dreams. Visions must be achievable! However, leaders should also be dreamers. Dreams allow leaders to imagine, hope, to enter a state of abstraction, and engage in a wild fancy about the library's future.

Creativity. It is commonplace to hear library colleagues complain about the large amount of their daily work being routine and pedestrian. Much of library work, unfortunately, does not require an MLS librarian. Library leadership should challenge the professional staff to stretch their minds in creating a more satisfying work environment. Successful leaders are generally creative people. Thus, the library leader has to create a work environment wherein the librarians' mental capacities are challenged via creative endeavors, and the leader must demonstrate creative skills in moving the library into the future.

Innovation and Entrepreneurship. Innovation follows creativity in the sense that development of new products and services come after the idea. An innovative strategy focuses on "new and different" approaches for delivering library services. Innovation means change. Innovation dates back to creative leadership, and the library world tends to view innovators initially with suspicion and, if the new product/service is successful, subsequently heaps praise and commendation on the innovator.

The entrepreneurial spirit is a rare attribute among library leaders. Entrepreneurs tend to be very focused on the completion of a new service or product. They do not adhere to established policies and procedures, and they sometimes are perceived as not working well with teams. Pinchot devised ten commandments for the entrepreneur:

1. Come to work each day willing to be fired.
2. Circumvent any orders aimed at stopping you.
3. Do any job needed to make your project work, regardless of your job description.

4. Find people to help you.
5. Follow your intuition about the people you choose, and work only with the best.
6. Work underground as long as you can–publicity triggers the corporate immune mechanism.
7. Never bet on the race unless you are running in it.
8. Remember it is easier to ask for forgiveness than for permission.
9. Be true to your goals, but be realistic about the ways to achieve them.
10. Honor your sponsors.[9]

Planning. It is difficult to think of a genuine library leader who is not a planner. Results-oriented library leaders employ the principles of strategic planning while determining future directions. Strategy is the "cat's meow" of strategic planning. A plan without strategies is not much more than a traditional planning document. Strategies delineate the "courses of action" for attaining the library's goals and objectives. The planning document will never be completed. It has to be a living document; it has to evaluate "What went right?" and "What went wrong?" on a regular basis, and it must be updated annually. Strategic planning offers the creative library leader the flexibility to address and implement various options for realizing the library's goals and objectives.

Courage. Leadership roles in libraries are not for the faint-hearted. Leaders, be they department heads or head librarians, must have the courage to call the shots. As mentioned earlier, the manager does things right, while the leader does the right things. Doing the right things can cause discomfort. Notwithstanding clear articulation of a proposal, there will be times when "doing the right thing" may not be accepted by the library staff. (They may not "buy in" to the planned endeavor.) Some library leaders choose to back off from these types of difficult decisions; however, in the long run the courageous leaders with strong (and correct) convictions thrive and come out on top. There are times when the leader finds himself or herself alone, ignored, or betrayed by other loyalties. To know when to stand valiantly alone and let time and circumstance justify his/her stand is essential to the library leader.

Getting the Truth. One of the biggest problems of a leader is that of getting the truth. Colleagues may not want to disagree with the leader for various reasons (e.g., job security) and subsequently the leader makes mistakes. There has to be an agreement between leaders and followers that they will jointly seek out and share the truth. To sustain credibility, the leader must get at the truth despite the pain and discomfort it may cause.

Trust. An obvious responsibility of a leader is to create a climate of trust. Trust has to be a two-way street. Integrity is closely tied to trust. Competence, by leaders and followers, goes a long way toward enhancing mutual trust. Respect, openness, and good listening practices are building blocks leading to an environment reflecting earnest trust.

Values. Values are the principles or standards that help libraries determine what is worthwhile or desirable. Collections, staff, and effective services are typically thought of when one thinks about a library's values. The vision of the library is based on its values. The organizational culture of the library is determined by values. Library leaders should understand their own values and how they conform with those of the library. It is the responsibility of the leader to refresh the library's values. New directions for the library may be hindered by long-standing (and deeply rooted) values.

Passion for One's Work. Leaders are normally very hard working people. They have high expectations for themselves and for their colleagues. If one desires to be a library leader, then one must expect to work long hours (the nature of the work goes with the territory). Generally speaking, most library leaders love their work and cannot wait to get to work each morning. This enthusiasm for work is often infectious and found among all leaders in a given library.

Caring for Colleagues (Followers). The more successful leaders are humanists. They truly care for their colleagues and make provision for them to be successful. Followers will "walk the extra mile" for the leaders they have confidence in and respect.

Librarians aspiring to become leaders should learn the importance of improving working conditions for colleagues, offering opportunities for improving job skills, and enhancing staff development capabilities.

Communicating. A leader is expected to have well-developed written and oral communication skills. These skills are especially important when the leader is articulating the vision of the library. E-mail has significantly enhanced communications throughout the library and among different libraries. Compressed video is an evolving means for further enhancement of information exchange.

Transforming. Transactional leadership is a step above management; it focuses on short term goals, budgeting, and various transactional based functions of the library. Transformational leadership, on the other hand, looks at the big picture, questions the status quo, reviews the vision statement, and seeks out ways to make a significant improvement in services. When one speaks of a change agent, the transformational leader is being described. We need more transformational leaders in the library profession. Moreover, we must acknowledge that participant-oriented change is based on the premise that the more people have to say about the form and direction which the change has to take, and the more they are involved with the decision making process, then the more likely they are to be committed to that process.[10]

Inspirational Motivation. The inspirational motivation of transformational leadership provides followers with challenges and meaning for engaging in shared goals and undertakings. The inspirational appeals of the authentic transformational library leader tend to focus on the best in people–on harmony, charity, and good works.[11] People like to work for inspirational leaders who can motivate them toward more and better work. Leading by example is an excellent way to inspire and motivate followers.

OPPORTUNITIES FOR LEADERSHIP DEVELOPMENT

Based on the current status of library leadership, there are many opportunities for developing leaders. The first hurdle to overcome is that of drawing a clear differentiation between "management" and "leadership." The differentiation cannot be overemphasized; our tendency to refer to a program or session as being related to "leadership" when it is clearly "management" is destructive to the advancement of leadership. The library profession cannot continue to avoid the important topic of leadership. Management is very important, but what we need now is more leadership. Now is the time to declare a library leadership manifesto!

Developing library leaders should begin with the local library; the head librarian must create a work environment that recognizes potential leaders and provides the resources for their leadership development. Local library consortia should include more programs on leadership development. Regional library networks can play a major role in presenting programs designed to prepare librarians to become leaders (or better leaders). National organizations have many opportunities for advocating library leadership; for example, the Library Administration and Management Association (LAMA) can and should serve a pivotal role in leadership development. It is unfortunate that LAMA's programs are generally geared for managers rather than leaders.

Commendations are in order for the designers of programs that teach and promote leadership. Such programs include the University of California at Los Angeles Senior Fellows Program, the Library Leadership Institute at Snowbird, and the Association of College and Research Libraries/Harvard Leadership Institute. These programs demonstrate the right intentions; however, upon examining the contents of these programs, there is much more emphasis on managerial aspects than on leadership. Nevertheless, these types of programs are an excellent beginning for advocating, promoting, and teaching library leadership. Within the next few years, there will likely be more programs/institutes focusing on library leadership. Only a few people can attend the national programs; thus, libraries and local library consortia must step up to the challenge of including more leadership training in their staff development and continuing education programs. Leadership development is too important to limit it to only a few librarians who can participate in national programs.

Current library leaders must continue to renew/reinvent themselves. The old style of leadership embodying bureaucracy, one-person control, predictability, and orderliness is not going to work anymore. Rapid change, ambiguity, leadership teams, and enabling technology call for a new style of leadership. Thus, numerous opportunities exist for reinventing our library leaders. Programs/institutes are needed to assist with reinventing leaders for the challenging roles in today's environment. Effective leadership requires a process of continuous renewal of leadership skills.

Learning to lead is an ongoing process. Warren Bennis and Joan Goldsmith wrote an interesting book on this topic: *Learning to Lead: A Workbook on Becoming a Leader.*[12] This work is recommended for anyone aspiring to be a library leader and for those serving in library leadership roles. Various exercises in the book enable the reader to better understand specific aspects of leadership. For example, chapter 3 provides exercises on the leadership crisis and chapter 4 offers a checklist for leaders to learn how to better understand themselves. Elwood N. Chapman, in his book entitled *Leadership,* presents various exercises, tests, and assessment forms that help readers weave what they learn into their respective leadership styles.[13] Someone should develop a workbook similar to these two for library leaders. There are so many opportunities for improving library leadership, but so few people are stepping up to this important challenge.

CONCLUSION

Are we in a library leadership crisis? Not yet, but if we continue to be passive, inert, and drift along without giving proper attention to this extremely important topic, the crisis will certainly occur.

The leadership crisis will come about more quickly if we do not learn the distinction between management and leadership. The common practice of referring to "management practices" as "leadership" has to stop immediately. Furthermore, we must stop ignoring the importance of strong, dynamic, and transformative leadership. Why are we not giving greater attention to, writing more about, and talking more about library leadership? This question deserves an answer now!

Opportunities for advancing library leadership are unlimited. The unpredecented changes in libraries are demanding more and better leaders. Renewal opportunities must exist for current leaders. New library leaders are expecting help from more experienced leaders. And the leadership story goes on and on.

According to Gary Heil, Tom Parker, and Rick Tate, no one is exempt from library leadership: "In tomorrow's organization, there will be no non-leaders. To label a person (or even think of them) as such will be to limit unnecessarily their ability to contribute."[14]

NOTES

1. James MacGregor Burns, *Leadership* (New York: Harper & Row, 1978), 1.

2. Warren Bennis, *On Becoming a Leader* (Reading, Mass: Addison-Wesley, 1989), 45.

3. Donald E. Riggs, *Library Leadership: Visualizing the Future* (Phoenix, AZ: Oryx Press, 1982).

4. Warren Bennis, *Managing People Is Like Herding Cats* (Provo, UT: Executive Excellence Publishing, 1997), 21.

5. Terrence F. Mech and Gerard B. McCabe, *Leadership and Academic Librarians* (Westport, CT: Greenwood Press, 1998).

6. Bennis, *Managing People Is Like Herding Cats*, 161.

7. Margaret Wheatley, *Leadership and the New Science* (San Francisco: Berett-Koehler, 1992), 5.

8. Burt Nanus, *Visionary Leadership: Creating a Compelling Sense of Direction for Your Organization* (San Francisco: Jossey-Bass, 1992), 8.

9. Gifford Pinchot, *Intrapreneuring* (New York: Harper & Row, 1985), 22.

10. Rachid Zeffane, "Dynamics of Strategic Change: Critical Issues in Fostering Positive Organizational Change," *Leadership & Organization Development Journal* 17, 7 (1996):36-43.

11. Bernard Bass and Paul Steidlmeier, "Ethics, Character, and Authentic Transformational Leadership Behavior," *The Leadership Quarterly* 10 (summer 1999):181-94.

12. Warren Bennis and Joan Goldsmith, *Learning to Lead: A Workbook On Becoming a Leader* (Reading, Mass.: Addison-Wesley, 1994).

13. Elwood N. Chapman, *Leadership* (Englewood Cliffs, NJ: Prentice Hall, 1989).

14. Gary Heil, Tom Parker, and Rick Tate, *Leadership and the Customer Revolution: The Messy, Unpredictable, and Inescapably Human Challenge of Making the Rhetoric of Change a Reality* (New York: Van Nostrand Reinhold, 1995), 7.

Recruitment Theory: Identification of Those Who Are Likely to Be Successful as Leaders

Mark D. Winston

SUMMARY. The theoretical basis for leadership in organizations includes the consideration of many factors, including the qualities of successful leaders, the development of those qualities, and the relationship between effective leadership and organizational success. Another aspect of leadership theory is the study of the relative importance of factors associated with the identification of individuals who are likely to be successful as leaders and to contribute to organizational success. The development of this theoretical discussion is based on the results of a number of relevant research studies, including those involving segments of the information professions for which recruitment is particularly challenging. The research, thus, indicates the importance of factors that can form the basis for effective recruitment strategies in the profession, as well as in various professional specialities. *[Article copies available for a fee from The Haworth Document Delivery Service: 1-800-342-9678. E-mail address: <getinfo@haworthpressinc.com> Website: <http://www.HaworthPress.com> © 2001 by The Haworth Press, Inc. All rights reserved.]*

KEYWORDS. Leadership theory, recruitment theory, business librarians, science and engineering librarians, children's librarians

INTRODUCTION

In the increasingly global economy of the year 2000 and beyond, the information profession, like many other professions, will face many

---

Mark D. Winston, PhD, is Assistant Professor at Rutgers University, School of Communication, Information and Library Studies.

[Haworth co-indexing entry note]: "Recruitment Theory: Identification of Those Who Are Likely to Be Successful as Leaders." Winston, Mark D. Co-published simultaneously in *Journal of Library Administration* (The Haworth Information Press, an imprint of The Haworth Press, Inc.) Vol. 32, No. 3/4, 2001, pp. 19-34; and: *Leadership in the Library and Information Science Professions: Theory and Practice* (ed: Mark D. Winston) The Haworth Information Press, an imprint of The Haworth Press, Inc., 2001, pp. 19-34. Single or multiple copies of this article are available for a fee from The Haworth Document Delivery Service [1-800-342-9678, 9:00 a.m. - 5:00 p.m. (EST). E-mail address: getinfo@haworthpressinc.com].

© 2001 by The Haworth Press, Inc. All rights reserved.

challenges and experience a multitude of changes. One of the major issues facing organizations in the 21st century will relate to the need for effective and proactive leadership. Although there has been increased emphasis on leadership in the LIS literature of late, the discussion of the theoretical basis for the successful leadership of organizations is not new. This discussion, which provides a conceptual framework for the consideration of issues of leadership, includes theoretical constructs such as situational leadership, transformational leadership, leader-member exchange theory, contingent reward leadership, administrative conservatorship, ecovision, among others.

One issue which is of great importance in relation to the discussion of leadership relates to development of knowledge, competencies, and self-awareness among those who will fulfill leadership roles in organizations–an issue, which is addressed elsewhere in this volume.[1] An issue that is related to leadership development is the consideration of the ways in which we can identify those who are likely to be successful as leaders. As a sub-theme of leadership theory, recruitment theory is the theory associated with the identification of individuals who are likely to be successful and to contribute as leaders in organizations and professions, and is based upon the literature of library and information science, as well as that of other disciplines. As is often the case with theory, the discussion of leadership theory in and of itself is not necessarily of value for those in library and information science, without consideration of the application of the theoretical constructs in the profession. This article will address the development and importance of this theoretical discussion, as well as the results of a number of relevant research studies, in the context of the leadership of library and information service organizations.

THEORY ASSOCIATED WITH IDENTIFICATION OF POTENTIAL LEADERS

Recruitment theory relates to the relative importance of various factors in the career decisions of individuals, as those factors relate to the ability to recruit those individuals, who are likely to be successful as leaders, in various professions. The research conducted in library and information science, as well as that conducted in numerous other disciplines provides a basis for identifying those factors, which have an impact on the decisions of the individuals to choose a particular profession and/or professional specialty. Many researchers have contributed to a body of literature that might be described as "recruitment theory," which relates to the identification of the documented factors, which have an impact on career choices of individuals and the relative importance of those factors, in a broad range of professions, at various educational levels, and in a number of demographic categories. These categories include various medical specialties,[2] education majors and educators,[3] counseling, school administration, various library and information science specialties, as well as high school, college, technical school, graduate students, men and women, and members of minority groups. [4] Across these professions, educational and demographic categories, many common themes emerge with regard to the relative importance of individuals, such as professors, teachers, counselors, parents, friends, and other role models, and activities, experiences, and other factors, such as interesting academic courses, work experience, expected salary and benefits, ethnicity and gender, in the career decision-making process. The recruitment factors identified in the literature of other professions correspond closely with those related to recruitment of librarians in general and in various LIS specialties. Certainly, one premise of this research is that recruitment theory, or what is known about the reasons why individuals have chosen their professional specialties, provides a worthwhile basis for the development of recruitment strategies because there are similarities between those who are currently employed in a given profession and those who are likely candidates for recruitment into that profession. This premise is valid based on the findings in the published research. It should also be noted that career assessment instruments, used by career counselors and others, often are designed to measure the extent to which responses and preferences are similar to those of individuals in various professions and to those who are happy in their professions, based on the assumption that similar responses and preferences are likely to correlate with similar professional preferences. It also follows that there are likely to be similarities between those who have been successful in the profession and those who are likely to be successful, particularly as systematic assessment of the factors affecting recruitment choices and leadership activities is undertaken.

Numerous researchers have characterized the list of factors affecting the recruitment of individuals into professions in terms of either the individuals or the activities that affect career choices. The individuals who have an impact on the career decision-making process include family members,[5] friends and peers,[6] teachers,[7] counselors,[8] and other role models.[9] The activities and other factors that influence the process include "interesting" academic courses and curricula,[10] course grades,[11] extracurricular activities,[12] work experience, including internships,[13] the desire to make a contribution,[14] expected salary and benefits,[15] ethnicity, and gender.

The published research addresses the issue of the relative importance of the factors, in terms of providing explanations regarding the factors that appear to be most important to those who are making career decisions. The recruitment factors that have been rated most highly, generally, are the influence of teachers, interesting courses, grades, work experience, the desire to make a contribution, and expected salary and benefits. Other factors were not rated highly in some instances. For example, the importance of family members was noted by young people who are selecting a career field, but this was not the case for older individuals in all instances. The role of ethnicity and gender in career decision making appears to be in dispute. Some researchers have found that gender and ethnic background lead to differences in career choices for men and women[16] and minorities and non-minorities. Others have found that gender and ethnicity do not have such an effect.[17]

LIS recruitment literature includes writings by Buttlar and Caynon,[18] and de la Pena McCook and Geist,[19] who address the factors affecting the recruitment of minorities into the profession. Other writings that add to the theoretical framework regarding LIS recruitment include those by Vazakas and Wallin,[20] Paskoff,[21] Brown,[22] Hudson,[23] Heim and Moen,[24] and Alire.[25] Thus, current recruitment theory indicates that the factors, which cause individuals to be recruited into the library and information science profession include personal desire to enter the profession of librarianship,[26] information provided by role models and/or "the influence of role models"[27] on individuals to consider librarianship as a profession,[28] availability of financial aid and scholarships,[29] prior paraprofessional or student assistant library work experience, which, in turn, motivated them to consider the profession[30]; an appreciation for the work in which the professionals are engaged, which has encouraged them to consider the profession as a career[31]; an appreciation for "the environment of library work"[32]; interest in entering "a service position" or a service profession[33]; availability of professional positions in the field[34]; the image of the profession or the specialty[35]; salaries paid to library and information professionals[36]; the influence or input of parents or other family members; and, the influence or input of friends or peers.

While further discussion of the implications of the recruitment theory to the LIS profession is presented elsewhere,[37] the results of a number of research studies provide further insight into issues of the identification of those who are likely to be successful as leaders.

TESTING RECRUITMENT THEORY IN THE PROFESSION–ACADEMIC LIBRARIES

In order to test recruitment theory in relation to a number of specific segments of the library and information science community, the relationship between the factors that have had an impact on the decisions of science and engineering librarians, and business librarians in colleges and universities, and children's librarians, to be recruited into the professional specialties, and the extent to which they have been involved in leadership activities, formed the basis of three research studies. The studies were intended to help to define more fully the populations of academic science/engineering and business librarians and children's librarians, with a focus on the issues of recruitment and leadership, in light of the challenges associated with the roles of those in these specialties, the recruitment challenges associated with these specialties, as well as the other professional opportunities that are available to those with backgrounds in the sciences, engineering or business.

In the instances of science/engineering and business, these are library and information science specialties for which those with educational or professional backgrounds or interest in the sciences, engineering, or business are likely to consider other career fields, which may be more lucrative, or are likely to be unaware of the opportunities that exist in library and information science for those with such backgrounds. Based on what is known about the roles and responsibilities of academic librarians in these specialties, it is clear that there are significant professional challenges, with regard to the nature of the scholarly record in the disciplines and with regard to the expectations of researchers in these disciplines. Thus, there are specific demands associated with the collection development and the provision of information services in these areas, often leading to the suggestion that a background in the sciences or business and an understanding of the nature of the literature, terminology, and work of professionals in the sciences or the private sector are important components in the successful performance of librarians in these specialties. Thus, the recruitment challenges are compounded for administrators, particularly with regard to recruiting individuals who are likely to take on leadership roles in the specialties, the profession, and within their organizations.

In order to address the issue of their recruitment into the specialties, the respondents in the research studies were surveyed to determine the extent to which a number of factors were important in their decisions to enter the specialties within the profession. The factors that were mentioned most frequently as being primary factors in the decision to enter the academic science or engineering library specialty were: an interest in science or engineering as a subject (53.3%), a personal desire to enter the professional specialty of academic science or engineering librarianship (48.9%), an appreciation for the environment of academic science or engineering library work (36.7%), an appreciation for the work in which academic science or engineering librarians are engaged (32.2%), interest in entering a service position (25.6%), and the availability of professional positions (22.2%). Factors which were mentioned least often as primary factors in the decision-making process included: taking the position because no one else on the staff was willing to take it (1.1%), the professional image of academic science or engineering librarians (3.3%), and salaries paid to academic science or engineering librarians (3.3%).[38]

The results of the study of academic business librarians indicates that the factors identified most often by respondents as primary factors in their choice of professional specialty were: "interest in business as a subject," "interest in entering a service position," "a personal desire to enter the specialty," the fact that a business library position was the "only position available at the time," the "availability of professional positions," "an appreciation for the work done by academic business librarians," an appreciation for the environment in which academic business librarians work, the influence of/information provided by role models, and paraprofessional and student assistant library work experience. (See Table 1.)

As it was important to address the issue of the recruitment in these areas, it is particularly important to consider the recruitment of those who are most likely to be successful and to take on leadership roles. In the context of this research, leadership was defined on the basis of those factors which are correlated with success in the academic environment–namely, research and scholarly publications and presentations, service, and teaching or performing the primary responsibilities of the position. As leadership is generally defined in relation to influencing the behavior or attitudes of others, particularly in the achievement of organizational or larger goals, research and the dissemination of the results of such research, as well as service, are designed to have an impact on behavior or practice and to inform the thinking and perceptions of the audiences for the research results. Service certainly relates to influencing the direction of the organization or profession of which one is a part. In addition, the primary work responsibilities can be considered in relation to the measures of success, in terms of earning tenure or a tenure equivalent, if such an option is available in the institution in question, as well as in terms of longevity in the position and in the specialty.

In relation to the level of participation in service and scholarly activities, including professional associations and college/university committee activities and scholarly presentations and publications, the respondents in both studies were shown to be professionally active in relation to nearly all measures addressed.

TABLE 1. Factors Affecting Recruitment Decisions: Business and Science/Engineering Librarians

Recruitment Factor (Identified as a primary factor)	Business Librarians (% of total)	Science/Engineering Librarians (% of total)
Interest in business **or** Interest in science or engineering as a subject	38.3%	53.3%
Interest in entering a service position	35.9%	25.6%
Personal desire to enter the specialty	21.5%	48.9%
Only position available at the time	21.3%	10.0%
Availability of professional positions	19.0%	22.2%
An appreciation for the work	15.2%	32.2%
An appreciation for the environment	14.1%	36.7%
Information/Influence of Role Models	11.4%	15.6%
Paraprof./Student Assistant Positions	8.9%	11.1%
No one else willing to take the position	7.6%	1.1%
Information/Influence of Peers/Friends	3.8%	6.7%
Information/Influence of Parents/Family	2.5%	5.6%
Availability of Financial Aid	2.5%	6.7%
Professional Image	1.3%	3.3%
Salaries	0.0%	3.3%

There are a number of factors which may have been correlated with significant differences in the level of professional activity in relation to publication, presentations, and committee activities. Thus, consideration was given to factors such as that of job title, tenure status, tenure eligibility for librarians in the employing institution, educational background in relation to science and engineering at the undergraduate and graduate levels, coursework completed in relation to science and engineering resources in the MLS program, as well as age, gender, ethnic background, and the amount of time employed as science or engineering librarians, in relation to the measure of professional activity in terms of one important measure of professional activity in the academic environment–journal articles authored or co-authored. Only two factors–the amount of time employed as a science or engineering librarian and the completion of other science or academic library related courses in the masters of library and information science program–yielded results, with chi squares approaching statistical significance, representing differences in terms of journal publications. In addition, statistical analysis was undertaken in order to help to define the relative importance of the various factors and the relationship to success/leadership activities.

For the science and engineering librarians, there were no instances in which the importance placed upon the various recruitment factors was correlated with significant differences in the level of professional activity. In other words, the reasons identified as the basis for the selection of the professional specialty were not shown to be correlated with the number of journal articles published. However, there are a number of differences associated with recruitment, which suggests that the value placed upon various recruitment factors would necessitate multi-faceted recruitment strategies which target more than one population of potential science and engineering librarians.

For the business librarians, those recruitment factors which were shown to correlate with the level of professional activity included interest in business as a subject, only position available at the time, information provided by role models, the influence of friends or peers, and paraprofessional or student assistant positions. However, only the factor related to the only position available at the time was correlated with differences in the level of activity related to publications, as opposed to the other types of leadership activity. Generally, the results suggest that those who did not intend to become academic business librarians, as characterized by the factors that affected their choice of a professional specialty, are somewhat less involved in leadership activities.[39] Thus, while there are distinctions between these two studies of segments of the academic library community, implications emerging in relation to the evolution of recruitment theory and the development of recruitment strategies are important to consider.

TESTING RECRUITMENT THEORY IN THE PROFESSION–PUBLIC LIBRARIES

While the inclusion of multiple perspectives appears to enhance the learning experiences of children, gender underrepresentation is quite pronounced in relation to the professional specialties, which involve work with children, as is racial/ethnic underrepresentation in science/engineering and business librarianship. While similar recruitment factors were considered in the study of children's librarians, there are certainly differences in relation to the leadership activities that are valued for the population of children's librarians in the public library setting. The LIS literature dealing with leadership and public libraries has addressed the type of leadership activities that are valued in public libraries.[40] However, the issue of leadership, as it has been addressed in terms of public libraries, has related mainly to the study of those who are currently in leadership positions in public libraries.

Effective leadership in the public library has been addressed in the literature, often in relation to its role as a public institution. According to Reed Osborne, "Libraries, like other public organizations, require effective leadership in order to provide quality service. The library is arguably one of the most heavily used public services in any community, and this level of use only continues to grow."[41] However, the issue of leadership, as it has been addressed in terms of public libraries, has related mainly to the study of those who are in senior positions. In some instances, these individuals have been surveyed in order to determine their perceptions regarding factors such as the role of mentorship in their career development,[42] or "public library change and where public libraries are heading in the last decade of the twentieth century."[43] In addition, those who report to these leaders have been surveyed, as well. It is interesting to note that the issue of identifying the leaders in public libraries is not easily accomplished. Joan Durrance and Connie Van Fleet address this issue in their research based on "a public library leadership survey conducted in 1990."[44] They have indicated that "selecting the leaders of the field is fraught with dangers for the researcher."[45] Thus, they refer to the identification of public library leaders in research conducted by Alice Gertzog[46] and by Linda Crismond and Anthony Leisner[47] and consider such factors as the leadership positions held by individuals in public libraries, as well as other factors, including their professional associations activities, such as membership on the American Library Association Council and the Public Library Association Board in their research. While the importance of the study leadership as it relates to those in clearly-defined leadership positions is apparent in the success of libraries, the leadership role of those who have other responsibilities should not be underestimated.

"In Public Library Leadership: Meetings and Mechanics of Growth," William Knott notes that "it should be clear to even the most calloused observer that libraries seem to be uncommonly well-led."[48] However, he emphasizes that effective leadership abilities are not only needed by those in senior managerial positions, but by all of those in public libraries. "Leadership is not the work of some steely-eyed CEO, sitting in isolation and issuing ex-cathedra pronouncements. The work applications are for the entire library community and are a necessary part of the work of us all."[49] As this discussion relates to the issues of leadership activities undertaken by those in public libraries, it is interesting to note that Durrance and Van Fleet found that, with regard to their activities, the leaders that they identified in their research "do more public speaking than writing. Some lament that they have not had enough time to write."[50] The fact that public library leaders themselves have focused on other leadership activities, such as active participation in professional associations and presentations, suggests that these activities are more appropriate measures of leadership among public librarians than are writing and publishing, for example, as is the case in academic libraries. In addition, those in clearly-defined leadership positions are more likely to value these activities in those who are in earlier stages of their careers or in other positions, such as those related to children's services.

In relation to the issue of the recruitment of children's librarians, a factor related directly to the nature of the work, that is, interest in working with children, was identified as a primary factor in the decision to enter the specialty by the largest percentage of the respondents (77.8%). (See Table 2.) Additionally, a personal desire to enter the specialty of children's services and an appreciation for the work in which children's librarians are engaged were each identified as primary factors by more than sixty percent of the respondents.

While paraprofessional or student assistant positions provided greater motivation for those who have chosen to become academic business or science/engineering librarians, it certainly may be the case that there are a greater number of such positions in the college and university environment for those who are completing graduate programs in library and information science and making professional choices. While this may be consistent with the fact that only half of the respondents in this study completed an internship in children's services during their Masters of Library and Information Science (MLS) programs, it may be the case that those who completed the internships or held other student assistant positions had already determined that their professional career direction would be that of children's services, on the basis of other factors that preceded this student employment situation.

The role of friends and peers was not overwhelming in influencing the decision-making process, as was the case in terms of the influence of parents and other family members. However, for approximately 25.0% of the respondents, information provided by, or the influence of,

TABLE 2. Factors Affecting Recruitment Decisions: Children's Librarians

Recruitment Factor	Primary Factor	Partial Factor
Interest in Working with Children	77.8%	20.7%
A Personal Desire to Enter the Specialty of Children's Services	70.2%	23.7%
An Appreciation for the Work in which Children's Librarians are Engaged	63.1%	32.3%
An Appreciation for the Environment of Children's Services Work	51.5%	36.9%
Interest in Entering a Service Profession	32.8%	38.9%
Information Provided by/ Influence of Role Models to Consider the Specialty	27.8%	34.8%
Interest in Serving as a Role Model for Children	27.3%	48.0%
Availability of Positions in Children's Services	16.7%	34.3%
Paraprofessional or Student Assistant Position(s) Which Motivated Them to Consider Children's Services	13.6%	22.2%
Information Provided by/ Influence of Friends or Peers to Consider the Specialty	8.6%	25.3%
Information Provided by/ Influence of Parents or Other Family Members to Consider the Specialty	6.1%	23.7%
Only Position Available at the Time	6.1%	10.1%
Position Constituted a Promotion or Was Likely to Lead to a Promotion	4.5%	11.6%
The Professional Image of Children's Librarians	4.0%	21.2%
The Availability of Financial Aid or Scholarships to Complete the MLS Program	3.5%	12.1%
No One Else was Willing to Take the Position	1.0%	4.5%
Salaries Paid to Children's Librarians	0.5%	9.6%

peers to consider the specialty was a partial factor, as was the case with nearly 25.0% in relation to their parents or other family members.

Few of the respondents indicated that factors such as the fact that a children's services position was the only position available at the time they were searching, that the position represented a promotion or was likely to lead to a promotion, the professional image of children's librarians, the availability of financial aid or scholarships to complete the MLS program, the fact that no one else on the staff was willing to take the position of children's librarian, or salaries paid to children's librarians were important considerations in their choice of professional specialty.

The additional factors that the respondents identified as being important in their decisions to enter children's services included an interest in children's literature, the desire to promote literacy, the opportunity to exhibit creativity, variety in terms of responsibilities and duties, and the fact that they possess talent or skill that relates to the role of the children's librarian. As considered on the basis of gender, there were no significant differences in relation to the factors which had an impact on the career choices of men versus women, in a specialty in which men are underrepresented.

In consideration of recruitment, it is important to note factors which were correlated with differences in importance of various recruitment factors for the children's librarians. There were a number of instances in which significant differences were noted on the basis of whether or not the respondents had prior work or volunteer experience with children. As represented by various levels of significance, differences in relation to the importance of the recruitment factors reflect that those who have had prior experience working with children identify factors involving an interest in working with children and in the specialty itself as more important than those who have not had such experience. Conversely, those who have not worked with children indicated that factors relating to position availability were of greater importance for them than was the case for those who have worked with children in the past.

CONCLUSION

In conclusion, there is the need for research and study of the recruitment of those who are likely to be successful as leaders in the profession.

One purpose of the research studies discussed was to provide more comprehensive information regarding the nature of the population of the professional specialties of academic science/engineering and business librarians and children's librarians, as a part of considering the issue of recruitment theory and identifying individuals who are likely to be successful as leaders in their specialties. Certainly, these national studies address important segments of the library population, which face many professional challenges and for which issues of recruitment present particular challenges. However, considering recruitment theory in these demanding contexts further informs our understanding as we consider leadership in the profession more broadly. One significant finding resulting from each of the three studies relates to the documented and primary importance of interest in the content of the specialty (either science, engineering, business, or work with children) in the recruitment decisions of individuals. Certainly, this finding helps to inform recruitment strategy and to identify individuals who might be targeted for recruitment.

Certainly, further research is needed in order to define more fully the nature of the distinctions in the relative importance of factors, such as the fact that the position in the specialty was the only position at the time of the job search. The results of the studies do not provide all necessary clarification in this regard. However, as we test and refine theory in a discipline which has a direct relationship to professional practice, original research, particularly that involving practitioners and pertinent professional issues, helps to ensure the relevance of theory to practice.

NOTES

1. Becky Schreiber and John Shannon, "Developing Library Leaders for the 21st Century," *Journal of Library Administration*. 32:3/4 (2001): 35-57.

2. S. Redman et al., "Determinants of Career Choices Among Women and Men Medical Students and Interns," *Medical Education* 28 (September 1994): 361-71; Frederick S. Sierles, "Decline of U. S. Medical Student Career Choice of Psychiatry and What to Do About It," *American Journal of Psychiatry* 152 (October 1995): 1416-1426; Landy F. Sparr, "Recruitment of Academic Psychiatrists: Applicants' Decision Factors," *Academic Psychiatry* 16 (Fall 1992): 141-146.

3. Jerry B. Davis, "A Look at Those Who Have Decided to Teach," *High School Journal* 77 (April-May 1994): 274-279; N. Ribak-Rosenthal, "Reasons Individuals Become School Administrators, School Counselors, and Teachers," *School Counselor* 41 (January 1994): 158-164.

4. Sabrina Hope King, "Why Did We Choose Teaching Careers and What Will Enable Us to Stay? Insights From One Cohort of the African American Teaching Pool," *Journal of Negro Education* 62 (Fall 1993): 475-492.

5. Richard J. Noeth, Harold B. Engen, and Patricia E. Noeth, "Making Career Decisions: A Self-Report of Factors That Help High School Students," *Vocational Guildance Quarterly* (June 1984): 244; Maduakolam Ireh, Ernest Savage, and Larry O. Hatch, "Factors Influencing the Career Choices of Technical College Students," *Journal of Studies in Technical Careers* 15 (1995): 114, 120; Alire, Camila, "Mentoring on My Mind: It Takes a Family to Graduate a Minority Library Professional," *American Libraries* 28 (November 1997): 41.

6. Judith D. Emmett and Carole W. Minor, "Career Decision-Making Factors in Gifted Young Adults," *Career Development Quarterly* 41 (June 1993): 354; Noeth, Engen, and Noeth, "Making Career Decisions," 245; Ireh, Savage, and Hatch, "Factors Influencing the Career Choices of Technical College Students," 119.

7. Noeth, Engen, and Noeth, "Making Career Decisions," 244-45.

8. Ibid., 244.

9. Ireh, Savage, and Hatch, "Factors Influencing the Career Choices of Technical College Students," 119; Kermit R. Davis, Jr., Hubert S. Field, and William F. Giles, "Recruiter-Applicant Differences in Perceptions of Extrinsic Rewards," *Journal of Employment Counseling* 28 (September 1991): 89; Sonia M. Goltz, "Recruiter Friendliness and Attraction to the Job: The Mediating Role of Inferences About the Organization," *Journal of Vocational Behavior* 46 (February 1995): 109-18; Daniel B. Turban, "Factors Related to Job Acceptance Decisions of College Recruits," *Journal of Vocational Behavior* 47 (October 1995): 193-213.

10. Noeth, Engen, and Noeth, "Making Career Decisions," 244; Ireh, Savage, and Hatch, "Factors Influencing the Career Choices of Technical College Students," 119; Nancy B. Kaltreider, "Student Education and Recruitment in Psychiatry: A Synergistic Proposal," *Academic Psychiatry* 18 (Fall 1994): 154-61.

11. Noeth, Engen, and Noeth, "Making Career Decisions," 245.

12. Ibid., 244.

13. Davis, Field, and Giles, "Recruiter-Applicant Differences in Perceptions of Extrinsic Rewards," 89.

14. Emmett and Minor, "Career Decision-Making Factors in Gifted Young Adults," 358; Edward D. Bewayo, "What Employees Look for in First and Subsequent Employers," *Personnel* (April 1986): 54.

15. Ireh, Savage, and Hatch, "Factors Influencing the Career Choices of Technical College Students," 119; William J. Kassler, "Why Medical Students Choose Primary Care Careers," *Academic Medicine* 66 (January 1991):41-43; Emmett and Minor, "Career Decision-Making Factors in Gifted Young Adults," 354.

16. Consuelo Arbona and Diane M. Novy, "Career Aspirations and Expectations of Black, Mexican American, and White Students," *Career Development Quarterly* 39 (March 1991): 238; Ireh, Savage, and Hatch, "Factors Influencing the Career Choices of Technical College Students," 119.

17. Arbona and Novy, "Career Aspirations and Expectations of Black, Mexican American, and White Students," 237-238; Noeth, Engen, and Noeth, "Making Career Decisions," 246.

18. Lois Buttlar and William Caynon, "Recruitment of Librarians into the Profession: The Minority Perspective," *Journal of Library & Information Science Research* 14 (1992): 270-275.

19. Kathleen de la Pena McCook and Paula Geist, "Diversity Deferred: Where Are the Minority Librarians?" *Library Journal* 118 (November 1993): 35-38.
20. Susan M. Vazakas and Camille Clark Wallin, "Where Are All the Science Librarians?" *College & Research Libraries News* 53 (March 1992): 166-71.
21. Beth M. Paskoff, "Recruitment for Special Librarianship," in Librarians for the New Millenium, eds. William Moen and Kathleen Heim (Chicago: ALA Office for Library Personnel Resources, 1988), 57-64.
22. Lorene B. Brown, "Recruiting Science Librarians," in Librarians for the New Millenium, eds. William Moen and Kathleen Heim (Chicago: ALA Office for Library Personnel Resources, 1988), 65-71.
23. Phyllis J. Hudson, "Recruitment for Academic Librarianship," in Librarians for the New Millenium, eds. William Moen and Kathleen Heim (Chicago: ALA Office for Library Personnel Resources, 1988), 72-82.
24. Kathleen M. Heim and William E. Moen, "Information Services Recruitment: The Challenge of Opportunity," RQ 29 (Summer 1990): 562-66.
25. Alire, "Mentoring on My Mind: It Takes a Family to Graduate a Minority Library Professional," 41-42.
26. Paskoff, "Recruitment for Special Librarianship," 57; Buttlar and Caynon, "Recruitment of Librarians into the Profession: The Minority Perspective," 272; Heim and Moen, "Information Services Recruitment: The Challenge of Opportunity," 566.
27. Buttlar and Caynon, "Recruitment of Librarians into the Profession: The Minority Perspective," 272.
28. Vazakas and Wallin, "Where Are All the Science Librarians," 166; Hudson, "Recruitment for Academic Librarianship," 79.
29. Buttlar and Caynon, "Recruitment of Librarians into the Profession: The Minority Perspective," 272; Paskoff, "Recruitment for Special Librarianship," 60; McCook and Geist, "Diversity Deferred," 36.
30. Buttlar and Caynon, "Recruitment of Librarians into the Profession: The Minority Perspective," 272; Brown, "Recruiting Science Librarians," 69.
31. Paskoff, "Recruitment for Special Librarianship," 58; Brown, "Recruiting Science Librarians," 69; Buttlar and Caynon, "Recruitment of Librarians into the Profession: The Minority Perspective," 274.
32. Buttlar and Caynon, "Recruitment of Librarians into the Profession: The Minority Perspective," 274.
33. Ibid., Heim and Moen, "Information Services Recruitment: The Challenge of Opportunity," 563.
34. Buttlar and Caynon, "Recruitment of Librarians into the Profession: The Minority Perspective," 274; Brown, "Recruiting Science Librarians," 65.
35. Paskoff, "Recruitment for Special Librarianship," 59; Buttlar and Caynon, "Recruitment of Librarians into the Profession: The Minority Perspective," 275.
36. Hudson, "Recruitment for Academic Librarianship," 77; Buttlar and Caynon, "Recruitment of Librarians into the Profession: The Minority Perspective," 275; Brown, "Recruiting Science Librarians," 68.
37. Winston, Mark. "The Role of Recruitment in Achieving Goals Related to Diversity," *College & Research Libraries* 59 (May 1998): 242-245.
38. Mark Winston, "Academic Science and Engineering Librarians: A Research Study of Demographics, Educational Backgrounds, and Professional Activities," *Science & Technology Libraries* 19:2 (2001): 3-24.

39. Mark D. Winston, "The Recruitment, Education and Careers of Academic Business Librarians" (Ph.D. diss., University of Pittsburgh, 1997): 125-128, 149.

40. Mark D. Winston and Teresa Y. Neely, "Leadership Development and Public Libraries," *Public Library Quarterly* 19(3) (2001). In press. Joan Durrance and Connie Van Fleet, "Public Libraries: Adapting to Change," *Wilson Library Bulletin* 67 (October 1992): 31. Alice Hertzog, "An Investigation into the Relationship Between the Structure of Leadership and the Social Structure of the Library Profession," (Ph.D. diss., Rutgers, The State University of New Jersey, 1989). Linda Crismond and Anthony Leisner, "The Top Ten Public Library Leaders: A Survey," *Public Libraries* 27 (Fall 1988): 122-124.

41. Reed Osborne, "Evaluation of Leadership in Ontario Public Libraries," *Canadian Journal of Information and Library Science* 21 (September-December 1996): 21.

42. Elfreda Chatman, "The Role of Mentorship in Shaping Public Library Leaders," *Library Trends* 40 (Winter 1992): 492-512.

43. Joan Durrance and Connie Van Fleet, "Public Libraries: Adapting to Change," *Wilson Library Bulletin* 67 (October 1992): 31.

44. Joan Durrance and Connie Van Fleet, "Public Libraries: Adapting to Change," *Wilson Library Bulletin* 67 (October 1992): 31.

45. Durrance and Van Fleet, "Public Libraries: Adapting to Change," 31.

46. Alice Hertzog, "An Investigation into the Relationship Between the Structure of Leadership and the Social Structure of the Library Profession," (Ph.D. diss., Rutgers, The State University of New Jersey, 1989).

47. Linda Crismond and Anthony Leisner, "The Top Ten Public Library Leaders: A Survey," *Public Libraries* 27 (Fall 1988): 122-124.

48. William Knott, "Public Library Leadership: Meetings and the Mechanics of Growth," *Colorado Libraries* 23 (Summer 1997): 30.

49. Knott, "Public Library Leadership," 30.

50. Durrance and Van Fleet, "Public Libraries," 32.

Developing Library Leaders for the 21st Century

Becky Schreiber
John Shannon

SUMMARY. The transformation in library and information services demands intrepid leadership. Within the profession, we see excitement for boundless possibilities, mingled with apprehension about which directions to pursue. There is enthusiasm for implementing new systems, residing uncomfortably close to nostalgia for the old days. The library leaders we serve are eager to test their competence in managing these diverse reactions within themselves and their staff, while occasionally having their own fears about being up to the task.

This article presents our rationale for focusing on library leadership at this point in time, core beliefs guiding our approach to leadership development, leadership traits we try to develop in training and consulting, and the conceptual framework we use to design training experiences. We also include strategies administrators can use to develop leadership within their libraries.
[Article copies available for a fee from The Haworth Document Delivery Service: 1-800-342-9678. E-mail address: <getinfo@haworthpressinc.com> Website: <http://www.HaworthPress.com> © 2001 by The Haworth Press, Inc. All rights reserved.]

KEYWORDS. Leadership development, leadership training, leadership traits, self-awareness

---

Becky Schreiber and John Shannon are partners in Schreiber Shannon Associates, a New Mexico-based, change management consulting firm serving private and public organizations in high tech, industrial, and service sectors since 1973. They have been consulting to libraries since 1983, and are best known in the field for their work in leadership institutes, team development, executive and staff retreats, and strategic planning.

[Haworth co-indexing entry note]: "Developing Library Leaders for the 21st Century." Schreiber, Becky, and John Shannon. Co-published simultaneously in *Journal of Library Administration* (The Haworth Information Press, an imprint of The Haworth Press, Inc.) Vol. 32, No. 3/4, 2001, pp. 35-57; and: *Leadership in the Library and Information Science Professions: Theory and Practice* (ed: Mark D. Winston) The Haworth Information Press, an imprint of The Haworth Press, Inc., 2001, pp. 35-57. Single or multiple copies of this article are available for a fee from The Haworth Document Delivery Service [1-800-342-9678, 9:00 a.m. - 5:00 p.m. (EST). E-mail address: getinfo@haworthpressinc.com].

© 2001 by The Haworth Press, Inc. All rights reserved.

RATIONALE

Why is it critical to develop leadership within the library profession at this particular time? While leadership within the profession has always been important, the hyper speed of changes in information services now demands libraries that are *lean, mobile, and strategic*. They must be *lean* to meet expanding customer expectations within the confines of limited budgets; *mobile* to move quickly and easily with technological and other innovations; and *strategic* to anticipate and plan for market changes.

As we consult with libraries across this country and internationally, we see some trends which seem to be gaining force and speed. The expectations of customers are expanding and becoming more diverse–new careers for aging baby boomers, the proliferation of home-based and small businesses, the cultural diversity of our communities and academic institutions, patrons on both sides of the digital divide–all are looking to libraries for additional, improved, and faster services. Technology is driving decisions, as libraries struggle to balance budget allotments between traditional services and digital resources. Staffing issues of recruitment, training, and deployment are putting pressure on budgets and management policies. Our goal is to support libraries and their leadership as they maintain their relevance at the core of their communities, campuses, and businesses.

Building responsive organizations demands leadership which moves away from the bureaucratic paternal/maternal model of the past to a more fluid, engaging, and collaborative one. The speed of change requires action-oriented initiative from all staff members, not just those at the top of the organization. For those who have always embraced the concept of encouraging leadership from every position in the organization, and for those who are trying to make the transition from their own traditional roots, we applaud your efforts, and hope this article will offer support.

We began helping individuals and organizations respond to a rapidly changing environment more than twenty-five years ago, believing that individual employees working at full capacity have the most to offer their organizations and the customers they serve. Our life's work has become: helping individuals realize their full potential within healthy organizations that respond effectively to their customers.

In 1983, we were invited into the world of libraries through the front door of the Baltimore County Public Library in Maryland where we were then living. We immediately recognized an affinity with the values libraries hold–individual and community development, intellectual freedom, and life-long learning. We also became aware that the skills we teach–managing the chaos of change to strategic advantage–were desperately needed in libraries transforming themselves to meet client needs in the information age. While we continue to consult in a variety of other industries, libraries have a special place in our hearts.

When Dennis Day, along with Margaret Chisholm, Brooke Sheldon, Bill Summers, Paul Sybrowsky and Nancy Tessman asked us to take up the banner of library leadership in 1989, we added a leadership focus to our background in organization development for organizations in transition. Design of the Library Leadership Institute at Snowbird gave us a forum to make a clear distinction between management and leadership, and enabled us to apply our teaching techniques to the personal growth of individuals who have chosen to lead within their libraries.

The concept of "leading from any position" has always been core to our organization development consulting practice. We have always encouraged our clients to take the path of participative management and teamwork, and to recognize the advantages of inclusion. A few years ago, Ira Chaleff wrote *The Courageous Follower* which supports our approach to leadership–that it needs to come from each individual in the organization.[1] What he calls courageous followership, we call leading from any position. The concepts are the same–to become a leader, you must first be a good follower; that is, you must be loyal, ethical, proactive, and constructively confrontive, leading from your current position.

And how do we define leadership? For the purposes of this article, we will discuss "those who have insight and initiate action in an effort to inspire others to positive action." We want to support the success of all leaders–those who lead from official positions of power and those whose leadership comes through informal influence. We particularly want to support library leaders to act on their values, courageously confronting the critical issues facing libraries in the 21st century.

CORE VALUES AND BELIEFS GUIDING OUR DESIGNS FOR LEADERSHIP TRAINING

A leadership focus to our work forced us to confront our beliefs and values about how ethical leadership can exert positive and productive energy toward strategic results for libraries. What follows are the beliefs we bring to leadership training design, and what we hope is transferred to our participants. When we do leadership institutes, we expect the nominated participants who attend to be good at leading. Our intention is to make them better. For some, "getting better" means letting go of personal fears that hold them back–feeling their personal sense of confidence grow beyond bounds. For many, it is glimpsing a personal vision of what might be, with some good ideas on how to get there. In our programs, we create an intense and supportive learning environment; so while no one has to travel their road alone, leadership development is a personal journey for each participant. Thus, it should be noted that self-awareness is an important component of leadership development.

Leading Is Organic

It is a discovery process. Each new dilemma we encounter informs us about what we need to learn next. Leaders need to cultivate a welcoming attitude toward leadership problems. There are models and theories to guide each person's development, but ultimately each of us must learn to lead by analyzing a situation, developing a plan, and getting into action. We learn from the results of our attempt to exert influence. Experience *is* the best teacher. It is from our magnificent failures that we learn the most valuable lessons. The library leaders we most respect are those who have been bold enough to have some failures, and who are willing to share the lessons they have learned.

Involvement Leads to Commitment

This is such common good sense that leaders can easily overlook its guidance, and often do. As consultants, we always build in opportunities for involvement; and, as leadership trainers, we design experiential learning into every program. The core belief is that involving individuals in decisions that directly impact their lives opens the door to their sense of professionalism, accountability, and commitment to succeed. At our programs each participant is expected to define his or her personal learning goals, and pursue them to successful conclusion.

There is research to support our belief in inclusion. As early as 1936, Roethlisberger and Dickson, studying the Western Electric Hawthorne factory, discovered that environmental factors were not as important as the workers being involved in controlling their work lives. When asked what would improve working conditions at the Hawthorne Plant, the workers identified brighter lights. Brighter lights were installed and production went up. When asked again later, the workers said the lights were too bright and the lights were returned to previous levels or below. Production went up. Clearly, one of the keys to the increased production was the simple act of asking workers for their input in a change situation, *and* then making it happen. The results of this early experiment became known as the Hawthorne Effect and the relevance remains with us today.[2] To have an empowered workforce, one must involve them in designing, analyzing, and creating the results of their labor. Time and again we have seen committed library employees working with a poor plan surpass another group that has a great plan, but low commitment.

The following example demonstrates how we use this belief in consulting. Years ago, we facilitated resolution of a bitter conflict within a county library system by involving all staff in finding the solutions. We interviewed the major players, asking how the conflict could be resolved. We shared the various perceptions with everyone interviewed and helped them identify what could be resolved and what needed to be let go. As a result of this open group sharing, the staff clarified a number of misunderstandings, let go of some old resentments, recommitted to traditional *and* innovative goals, and developed a plan of implementation. It was seen by the new director, the patrons, the local press, and the library board as a 180° turnaround. Involvement led to commitment and, in this case, revived a good system that had become mired in deep conflict.

We encourage leaders in our institutes and in our consulting practice to trust the process of involvement–to not omit it for efficiency's sake or for fear of losing control. It is one of the most powerful tools a leader can use to build, change, or turn around an organization.

Sharing Power Builds Strategic Partnerships

These ideas of sharing power and involvement include the library's partners as well. When a colleague of ours assumed the directorship of a large municipal library, she reached out to establish a close working relationship with the mayor and city government. The new relationship led to exciting results for all involved. The library's bond issue passed with the support of the city government, and they are now building a spectacular new main library that will anchor redevelopment of the city center. While this professional relationship cannot be given complete credit for all that came after its establishment, it was a critical first step toward something great for the library, its patrons, and the city.

This is an example of "out of the box" thinking in strategic partnerships between systems. In Ohio, a city library and next-door county library system are sharing a branch that serves a fast-growing neighborhood that straddles their common boundary. Independently, neither had sufficient capacity to support this branch easily, and the patrons did not neatly fit the geographic jurisdictions. As we understand it, the city library built and maintains the branch while the county system staffs it. The library systems and communities can be justly proud of a solution these two directors found by working together for common advantage.

Within library systems, there are numerous examples of librarians crossing traditional boundaries of organizational infrastructure to create new partnerships–action teams, job sharing, and the blurring of professional/paraprofessional boundaries. Although non-traditional relationships may create anxiety, the leaders of tomorrow must see them as opportunities to create the next step in their library's evolution. We support leaders who continually look for opportunities to build strategic partnerships that go beyond the easy win-win to encompass the needs of the whole community they serve and create a collective result for all stakeholders.

Systems Thinking Is Essential

Conventional organization development wisdom says "everything is connected to everything else." This sweeping statement informs us that when one part of an organization is manipulated, all other parts will feel the impact. This makes sense; yet, how many times do managers focus only on their particular responsibility, without considering the consequences for those in other parts of the organization? A holistic, systems approach has enormous strategic importance when attempting to exert influence and lead organizations through a chaotic change process. We rely on our leaders to avert disaster, and one of the best ways to do so is to look beyond the bits and pieces of the change to maintain a system-wide awareness of the nature of the impact of change–a concern for the interconnectedness of the whole system. To do this, leaders must rely on their network of employees, or form change management teams that will hold a system's view–to see the necessary system-wide changes through the eyes of their organization's values and purpose.

Start Where the System Is

This belief is a leadership strategy that builds on the previous ideas of involvement and systems thinking. Before leaping into action, effective leaders need to understand the structures, the staff and their currently-held perceptions of themselves, traditional history, and the organization's place in the community. This understanding should suggest where and where not to begin. We do not urge caution, but the development of a respect for what is already in place.

One of our participants tells the humorous story of how he, when first hired to supervise a tech services group, let his enthusiasm for quick improvements run away with him. Over a weekend, when his staff was not around, with efficiency on his mind, he moved desks, tables, and stacks of material. He streamlined what he saw as random, chaotic piles of materials and, quite pleased with the new system, could not wait for Monday morning to see the grateful expressions on his new staff members' faces. He was stunned by their negative reaction and, as he laughingly tells it, was quite lucky to escape with his hide in one piece. Sure, he screwed up, but more importantly, he learned a valuable lesson. Start where the system is, and involve those affected in identifying what must change and how to implement.

While many think that they would never make a mistake like this one, think again. We have seen many organizations reconfigured by new leadership who were unaware or unconcerned that a restructuring had recently preceded them. And how many "crash and burn" experiences could have been avoided by leaders not starting too far ahead, leaving everyone behind. So, we design this important leadership value into our leadership programs.

Build Capacity for Learning Wherever You Go

Organizations that are curious about where they are going and what might be possible are the ones defining the future for the profession. Learning organizations do not just happen. They are developed by leaders who value the opportunity to learn for themselves and encourage this same opportunity for those around them. They create innovative organizations through formal and informal structures, partnerships, and teams that learn from their experience. Employees within learning organizations are encouraged to have conversations at all levels and across boundaries to problem solve, think out of the box, and generate innovative solutions.

In our consulting, we shift the focus from right-wrong, fault-finding to modeling continuous learning-expecting organizational sharing of how results were achieved.

Enhance Your System by Leaving Your Skills Behind

As consultants, we sometimes quip that our responsibility is to work ourselves out of a job. We try to transfer knowledge and experience to build organizational capacity to operate more effectively when we are gone. For leaders, this value should be true as well. Few professions have as well-traveled senior leaders as the library profession. Building the organization's competency base through training, mentoring, coaching, and power sharing–in each job you hold–is part of the leader's job. In our institutes, we encourage participants to build the leadership skills of those around them in the organization, even those above them. If the participants could "do it better," as we so often hear, we ask them to help their manager do just that. We assert that "every person has something to learn and something to teach." No one is irreplaceable or should be. We need to share our knowledge and skills to ensure the success of the organization.

Amidst All the Innovation, Be Practical

Thus far we have said leaders should involve others, take a systems approach, build relationships, welcome problems, and probably have enormous personal charisma . . . and then, a reasonably good, practical plan that just might work.

Bill Cosby tells the hilarious tale of his Temple University football coach whipping the team into a frenzy to win the game, only to find out they are locked in the locker room. Leading means having a plan to get the team out of the locker room and onto the playing field to make things happen. A pragmatic approach is the ability to formulate how to organize people and resources in realistic ways.

Our bias as consultants or trainers is to insure a level of practicality in whatever we are doing. We like to anchor learning and practice new skills in "real time" work–work that will make a difference to individuals within the organization, and to the customers they serve. People are more likely to commit their energies to projects that are the "right" thing to do, and within the resources and abilities of those tasked to do them. A well-crafted vision statement should inspire, but also be concrete enough to be seen in practice. A task force should have lofty goals *and* a project plan with measurements at key intervals. A leader's ability to clearly define and broadly communicate a practical plan is as fundamental as knowing where they are going. It is critical for employees to believe that they have a decent chance of success.

Express an Optimistic Bias

An optimistic bias means giving straight messages with an optimistic style. The message is, "we can do this and this is how." Expressing confidence in yourself and others' ability to succeed is part of it. We coach participants to be "realistic Pollyannas." During the chaos of change, some will voice their fears and doubts. While it is important to create the forum for such natural hesitation, it is equally important to counter balance the situation with realistic optimism. Leaders must learn to use specific past experiences to demonstrate the reasons for their current confidence.

The corollary to this value is also true. At times everyone, even the most powerful, feels a need to express their frustrations. The smart leader does not express his or her powerlessness publicly, but finds ways of bolstering the flagging confidence with an active support network. People trust those who stay focused on the goal, and are not disabled or side-tracked from the goal by a temporary setback.

Expressing an optimistic bias is the final belief we bring to the development of leadership. To make our own optimism about library leadership for the future a reality, we also support the development of six critical leadership behavior traits in the leaders we serve–from the enthusiastic young leadership participant to the seasoned senior administrator facing new challenges.

SIX CRITICAL LEADERSHIP TRAITS

We believe that leadership starts with some innate tendencies, but we agree with Brooke Sheldon, Warren Bennis, James Kouzes, Barry Posner and others, that leadership skills can be developed. Brooke Sheldon writes in *Leaders in Libraries,* "all of our students have some measure of leadership ability, and this ability can be identified, nurtured, and strengthened in the process of attaining the first professional degree."[3] Bennis says in *Leaders,* "Leadership seems to be the marshaling of skills possessed by a majority but used by a minority. But it is something that can be learned by everyone, taught to everyone, denied to no one."[4] In *The Leadership Challenge,* Kouzes and Posner state, "by viewing leadership as a nonlearnable set of character traits, a self-fulfilling prophecy has been created that dooms societies to having only a few good leaders. If you assume that leadership is learnable, you will be surprised to discover how many good leaders there really are."[5]

We have been teaching leadership skills for many years, and have seen the difference learning these skills can make in the lives of those who attend our workshops. The evidence can be seen in career decisions made, committees chaired, and challenges well met. So what are the skills critical to effective leadership?

At various times during the evolution of our consulting practice, we have defined five to ten leadership traits. They have not changed significantly, but have been grouped to meet design demands. The following six are leadership capabilities we encourage, whether we are serving courageous followers or senior administrators. In each section, we will share how we encourage development of these traits in our institutes, and suggest how library administrators can support development of each trait at all levels of their organizations.

Self-Awareness

> *Leaders who know themselves are able to maximize their strengths, learn new skills, and know when to get out of the way of those who can do it better.*

Generally, administrators know how difficult it can be to find people who will give you direct feedback, the best tool for self-awareness. Unless the administrator has consciously encouraged staff to do so, they are reluctant to share negative information about the administrator's performance, to tell the emperor he or she has no clothes. It is often more rare for the administrator to hear appreciative acknowledgment of a job well done. The staff simply supposes that he or she does not want to hear bad news, and that the administrator knows when he or she performs well.

Acknowledgment of strengths and weaknesses, and asking for help with them, can be a powerful way to engage all staff in supporting each other's success. If one "owns" that she is not expecting herself to perform perfectly, the staff may be willing to help one to be a better leader, and the organization can commit itself to the improvement of every staff member, including the senior administrators. We once worked with a tough-minded chief executive officer of a major hospital who was making his first speech to his top 65 managers as the new CEO. His ascension to the post was not universally popular because he had had to make some hard decisions to make the organization profitable. We suggested that he include in the speech his strengths and weaknesses, and how he would need the help of this group to be successful. After getting over the shock that we had seen some weaknesses and delineated the same, he acquiesced and did a beautiful job talking to his managers. He was astounded by the standing ovation he received, and learned that a leader sharing his humanity can be very powerful in building support for his own success.

In our workshops, we use self-assessment instruments like the Myers Briggs Type Indicator or the Enneagram to help participants examine their styles of leadership, and to suggest developmental strategies. All of our experiential activities are designed to help participants gain personal insight on practical matters of leadership. Our goal is to create opportunities for exerting leadership in a safe learning environment. Being challenged is certainly part of the program, but equally important is the analysis of what occurred during that challenge. Understanding what happened and why is the key. Were the desired outcomes achieved? Whose support did I gain or lose? Were there new opportunities generated by our activities? Did we stay focused on the goal? Did we build trust and teamwork? Such questions produce critical learning, and may define the next steps in a learning process or in an organization's future. We have yet to meet an effective leader who has stopped analyzing the moves he or she makes–learning more about themselves and the dynamics of leadership. We try to foster this inquisitiveness and value of life-long learning in all our programs.

In our consulting, we encourage leaders in any position in the organization to ask for performance evaluation, and support the development of a strong appraisal system. If leaders are not getting feedback, they need to figure out how to get it, and make sure they are doing their part by providing information to others to help them to be successful. Leading from any position means supporting 360° feedback–up, down, and across the chain of command–and supporting the success of every employee, including the boss.

We encourage administrators to set the tone for self-awareness in the organization. If one is willing to look for personal insight using self-assessment instruments and share the results (warts and all), staff will be more open to learning about themselves. With an effective performance appraisal system, with regularly scheduled, two-way assessment, systematic feedback and coaching, staff, including managers, will get used to sharing constructive feedback with each other. By setting aside a generous share of the budget for training and attending conferences, the administration sets the expectation of career-long improvement for the staff.

Embracing Change

> *Leaders must convince others that change is normal and, recognizing that each person deals with change differently, must guide them through the chaos.*

Library administrators know all too well that the pace of change continues to accelerate. Managing change may be the single most important leadership skill to learn for now and the foreseeable future. Peter Vaill, of George Washington University School of Business and Public Management, describes the chaos of change as permanent white water.[6] We gratefully acknowledge and freely use this analogy to help leaders understand their role in navigating the white water of change. The most critical task of the leader is to help employees see the quickening pace and volume of changes as normal. If they are waiting for "things to get back to normal" or "settle down," they are missing the opportunities inherent in the change. They may even think you are a poor leader to let these things happen to them!

In developing leaders, we use their own professional situations to illustrate how layers of organizational changes produce the white water effect and how to use a transition model to make the right interventions at the right time within each change. For example, the third stage of our transition cycle is "The Pit." It is a time of emotional turmoil when employees get disheartened and lack the will to proceed. Staff is often labeled as "resistant" at this point, and leaders get impatient. It is critical at this stage for leaders to create forums for honest discussion of concerns and fears. Organizational soul searching will enable genuine issues to emerge, optimistic realism to be heard, and self-confidence to return. This is also the time for keeping the goals and a plan to get there in front of people. A good leader will also make a keen distinction between staff who are in the Pit because they are temporarily discouraged, and the more permanent, but few people in some organizations we call Pit Dwellers. Appropriate leadership responses to the two groups are entirely different.

To keep up with the pace of changes, leaders must build a critical mass of support to implement each change, not wait until everyone has bought into them. Consensus is often confused with unanimity, and waiting for unanimity can paralyze movement toward goals. We have seen this taken to the extreme in some library systems where a minority of one effectively has veto power. If we don't all agree, we won't move! That is shifting participation into democracy–not a viable way to lead.

In our workshops, we also share individual reactions to change, based on the Myers Briggs Type Table, to help leaders develop strategies to move themselves and others through the transition. Once again, self-awareness and awareness of others can transform a leader's effectiveness in managing change, reduce the amount of effort needed, and shorten the time to accomplish the goals.

For administrators managing a transition, it is helpful to possess the insights we have mentioned and to then communicate constantly with staff. In the chaos of change, opportunities for communication must be deliberate and frequent. The new rule of "share what you know as soon as you think you know it" replaces communicating on a "need to know" basis. It is important to treat people with respect by keeping them in the loop. The grapevine is quicker than official memos, and since people always imagine the worst, administrators must figure out how to manage rumors. One of our clients created the "Restroom Reader" to get out breaking news. Enough said? Make sure communication goes in all directions–up, down, and across the organization. Putting the systems in place to find out what staff thinks and providing opportunities to share great ideas on how to break down barriers to reaching goals are worthwhile tactics. Resistance to change is often overcome by having a conversation with staff around three questions: Why are we doing this? What will it look like when we get there? How will it affect me?

Customer Focus

> *Leaders know it is important for the organization to be strategic, not just reactive.*

This leadership trait speaks to why libraries exist–for their customers. It answers the question, "Why are we doing this?" During times of rapid change, it is easy to become self-focused, concerned about how we as individuals or the organization will survive. It is enlightened self-interest for leaders to keep their focus on customers–as a way to ensure customer satisfaction *and* individual and organizational relevance. If one accurately anticipates and intelligently responds to customer needs, the organization can be positioned to take advantage of major trends.

In our leadership institutes and in our consultation with libraries, we encourage leaders to identify customer expectations, current and potential competitors, professional innovations, core capabilities, national and international trends, funding changes, and other factors–to create a map of their current environment. We often have them take a look back as well, to identify core values and lessons learned from the past. This builds a context for strategic planning. Without it, planning is being done in a vacuum. Then one can evaluate the library's current response to its environment and values with an analysis of strengths, weaknesses, opportunities, and threats, to determine strategic directions.

When the Borders bookstore chain first burst onto the scene, libraries saw them first as irrelevant, then only as competition. Now libraries are coordinating story times, piggy-backing on book signings, and finding other ways to serve the same customers, while building a broader customer base for both organizations. Leaders of libraries must clarify the market niche of their organizations in relation to competitors and potential partners. Traditionally, this was the planning activity of identifying the library's roles. In the new *Planning for Results*, by Himmel and Wilson, what we call your market niche is described as "what a library does for, or offers to, the public in an effort to meet a set of well-defined community needs," or service responses.[7]

An intimate knowledge of customer expectations and professional practices takes the guesswork out of planning. Library restructures, capital projects, beginning new services and ending old ones–all should be in response to accurate and frequent communication with customers and colleagues in the field. Strategies for meeting customer demands within limited budgets need to be shared more consistently throughout the profession. One of the pleasures of our consulting practice is sharing good ideas among clients. We like linking those clients who have an experience that might be helpful to another client so that all do not have to start from scratch. We would like to see even more publication of successes *and* failures to enhance the learning opportunities within the profession.

Administrators know that polling of internal customers helps with continuous improvement and smoother teamwork. Accurately measuring the quantity and quality of internal work processes enables libraries to enhance services within the existing budget and staff limitations. We are always amazed at the efficiencies employees find when given the opportunity to analyze their own work flow, and at the teamwork created by seeing other departments as suppliers and customers.

Stands to Take in the Future

> *Leaders put their stakes in the ground. Based on core personal and organizational values, they create a shared vision to pull the organization into the future.*

Leaders see the present through eyes of the future. Some do it through data gathering and analysis to project logically into the future. Others intuitively see what lies ahead, always thinking in future tense and have difficulty staying in the present very long. Whatever direct or circuitous road they take, leaders must be able to imagine the future in sufficient detail to plot the route for others. They must determine which traditional values and practices will go unscathed into the future, and which must be altered to enter into a new era.

The Cheshire cat told Alice "If you don't know where you're going, any road will take you there." Particularly in a time of multiple transitions, leaders must create a shared vision with their followers. A clear sense of "where the organization is going" is a beacon leading the way into an unfamiliar port, the North Star to weary travelers. The more compelling and widely held the vision, the more drawing power it has. It must create the critical tension needed to stimulate action. In the eyes of staff, the destination must be worth the effort of the journey.

When we do strategic planning with libraries, we pull together as many stakeholders as possible to work together to create an organizational vision–that is, where they would like the library to be in 3-5 years, in response to its customers and environmental context. We do the same thing in our institutes, but with a focus on libraries as a whole rather than on one system. We ask people in both situations to take time out to imagine the possibilities, without limitations of time and money. There is plenty of time to do reality checks later; this is the time to dream. We want people to imagine the best they could be as an organization; then write what they see in concrete, compelling, credible, confronting, and easily communicated language. We are always encouraged by the excitement that is generated, and the creativity explored, as notes are compared and integrated into an organizational vision. The other steps of strategic planning follow. Strategic directions are defined, goals are prioritized, activities are initiated, and the whole organization moves the vision toward reality.

We encourage administrators to explore the power of engaging the entire staff and other stakeholders in organization-wide planning. There are several guides to further understand the process. Marv Weisbord and Sandra Janoff present a process in *Future Search: An Action Guide to Finding Common Ground in Organizations & Communities,* complete with sample flip charts.[8] In *Preferred Futuring,* Lawrence Lippitt encourages us to *Envision The Future You Want And Unleash The Energy To Get There.*[9] Large group facilitation is a challenging business, but "getting everyone in the room" can have a profound effect on motivating change and gaining commitment to organizational goals. It then becomes the administrator's job to make sure the vision is constantly guiding decisions at every level of the library–to make course corrections for a safe and timely arrival.

Collaborative Spirit

> *Leaders build relationships and coalitions; they commit themselves to support the success of others.*

This trait is so core to our beliefs about leadership, it sends waves into every other trait. Theodore Friend III, past president of Swarthmore College, defines leadership as "heading into the wind with such knowledge of oneself and such collaborative energy as to move others to wish to follow."[10] Yet, in the real world of competition–for limited dollars, for personal accolades, for staff and customers–it is difficult to keep a big-picture, long-term, collaborative view. As we said earlier, we are realistic optimists. We believe in abundance–that there are more money, unlimited praise, enough staff, and customers to be created. We just have to figure out how to get people to work together to create those possibilities. We have already described specific examples of these strategic collaborations in the section on strategic partnerships.

Based on our belief that involvement leads to commitment, we encourage leaders to involve followers at every opportunity. Why do so many managers believe they must do it alone? Too many believe it is a sign of weakness to ask for help, pride themselves on their independence, or arrogantly believe only they can do it "right." All of us like to be asked for advice and suggestions. Being asked demonstrates a leader's faith in employees' opinions. Great leaders surround themselves with good people, then use them well, ask for their advice. Leaders recognize they can bask in the reflected light of others' success, and thereby comfortably assume the role of servant leader defined by Robert Greenleaf.[11] Rather than being threatened or diminished by their followers' success, they are delighted by it and proud to be supportive.

In our workshops, we ask leaders to evaluate their work relationships, looking for defining characteristics of both the good and bad. We define steps for initiating new relationships and suggest strategies for enhancing or fixing existing ones. We involve senior library leaders as mentors in our programs–to share their examples of building collaboration in their organizations, and to expand the possibility thinking of the less experienced participants. Their stories and our own experience convince us that the long-term relationship is often more important than the victory immediately in front of us. The critical task of leaders is to make that determination.

In leadership institutes, we also discuss and practice the use of influence without power at all levels within and beyond the library. Often, all that is necessary for collaborative relationships and the potential to exert influence is letting go of the constraints of traditional management practice and reaching out to others with a good idea and an offer of sharing the rewards and the load, both at the institutes and back in the library. Being honorable, ethical, and consistently reliable authenticates the offers. Continually scanning for the right partners and the right opportunity is a leadership practice we hope becomes the norm for library leaders at all levels of the organization.

Encouraging collaborative work relationships is a primary responsibility for administrators, and modeling the way is probably the most effective strategy. To shift one's approach from a more traditional hierarchy, executive or management coaching might be helpful. Organizational agreement on common ground rules (norms for how you want to work) is a powerful tool because one can anticipate trouble spots and plan for them. But ground rules are only effective if one is willing to confront violations in straightforward, but compassionate ways. Administrators who hold themselves and others accountable to a higher standard, and institutionalize ground rules in all-level performance appraisal and reward systems, will see a collaborative spirit emerge.

Bias for Courageous Action

> *Leaders believe that individual acts of courage recreate organizations. Leaders act with passion and courage, and encourage others to take risks.*

A stated core value of a client we serve is "inventiveness to infinity," which they define as "boundless creativity." Exciting to consider, is it not? Also exciting to work in such an organization? But how can leaders support such exuberant risk taking? Leaders in that client organization have encouraged initiative by eliminating fault-finding, using mistakes and missteps as learning opportunities. They also reward risk taking with a rather substantial monthly and yearly "spirit award." The tangible rewards are not money, but premium parking spaces, extra vacation, and such.

Richard Senge describes some strategies for encouraging action in *The Fifth Discipline,* as he defines a learning organization.[12] Systems thinking, personal mastery, commitment to a shared vision, team learning–all are concepts leaders must embrace to encourage action. At a local microchip plant, managers and staff use a daily "all-hands" meeting to track progress, share ideas, and learn from mistakes. At a national laboratory, projects are not complete until a final "lessons learned" session is documented. Within our client systems, we use the Synectics, Inc., process of creative problem solving within team meetings to encourage positive treatment of individual ideas. One method from that process provides for evaluating ideas in an even-handed way. The "Itemized Response" forces us to first consider the merits of an idea–what we like about it–and then use concerns about the ideas as springboards to innovative thinking. It enables a work team to get away from killing ideas because one small part won't work and avoids the usual litany of "They'll never let us . . . , It will cost too much . . . , We don't have the staff . . . ," and the multitude of other reasons that stop ideas before they have a full hearing. The "how could we . . . " phrase moves us to more creative thinking. [13]

Courage can be defined as "choosing to act in the face of fear." We have seen many examples of courage in the library administrators we've served. Mentors at our leadership institutes tell amazingly candid stories of risks taken, spectacular successes and equally fabulous failures. We hear inspirational stories from individuals who continuously put their fears aside to venture into the unknown. We worked in a library which was moving from a traditional chain of command to a more participative management style. The director was insightful enough to know that his style was more traditional and was courageous enough to back off and allow his management team to lead the way. He enabled the transition to occur and supported the results, demonstrating self-awareness and courage.

J. Paul Getty said, "Without the element of uncertainty, the bringing off of even the greatest business triumph would be a dull, routine, and eminently unsatisfying affair."[14] Administrators know that most decisions are made with inadequate information–that the best you can do is take calculated risks. Rewarding staff when they take reasonable risks is a powerful tool in creating an organization with a bias for action. One can encourage initiative by creating "action teams" to solve problems, implement programs or re-design work processes. It is important to make sure the teams know their parameters and have progress checks, so they can be supported and their recommendations implemented.

We ask developing leaders to step up to the challenge in our institutes by leading their learning groups, evaluating their past risk-taking performance, and participating in activities to test their courage. The pattern is clear. After taking initiative in the institutes, participants are energized and enthusiastic about finding opportunities to do it again. They learn that the best way to develop courage is to be courageous.

In this field, we have found that interpersonal confrontation is often experienced as an opportunity for courageous action, that learning confrontive diplomacy is a challenge many want to avoid. Administrators can support leadership in their libraries by taking a personal stand based on principle, encouraging others to do the same, then listening well, and working toward resolution.

DESIGNING LEADERSHIP TRAINING

When designing leadership training programs that transfer the leadership values and traits outlined above, we try to balance abstract concepts with experiential activities. We believe both are necessary for integrated learning on the three attributes that enable a person to perform at a high competency level: *knowledge; attitude;* and *skill.* These three attributes are like a stool with three legs. If one leg is too short you will fall over. For example, a recent MLS graduate may have plenty of knowledge and a positive attitude, but needs real-world skill before becoming a consummate professional. A long-term employee may have knowledge and a great attitude but may need some new skills to perform well.

We also take into account that everyone has a different preferred learning style. In the National Training Laboratory Institute's *Reading Book For Human Relations Training,* David Kolb's model of adult learning is described in the article titled "Hands-On or Head Trip, How Do You Learn Best?"[15] Kolb describes the learning process as a four-step model.

He states that each of us has a preferred way of learning, enters the model from any of the four positions, then proceeds around the circle in the direction of the arrows. For instance, one may prefer to learn by first having a concrete experience. One would then reflect upon what happened. Out of this reflection one would form generalizations about the situation, then test generalizations in a new situation. Thus, the subject is now learning from a concrete experience of his or her own making, and so on around the circle. So, in our design of training programs, we challenge the participants on all three attributes, using both conceptual learning and experiential activities with time to reflect and test. Ultimately, the goal is for the participants to successfully apply their new learning–in all three areas of knowledge, attitude, and skill–when they return to their real world lives.

Our Design Model

The process of actually designing the training is a seven-step process from design, through delivery, to the participants applying their learning.

Our responsibility ————————→ Participant's Responsibility

Our responsibility starts at the bottom of the arrow, setting learning objectives based on the traits, values, and beliefs we want the participants to develop. We then adapt concepts or models that support the learning objectives. The structure, process and timing of events creates the overall workshop design. Each activity should build on the learning of those which preceded, and the pace should allow for both action and reflection. At the fourth step, we cross over the arrow as we engage the participants in co-creating experiential learning. There are many opportunities for feedback, but participants must take an active role in requesting and absorbing the feedback they receive. It is primarily their responsibility to develop conclusions from the information they receive, transforming that into new beliefs and models. While we help with action planning, the final and most important step is taken when they return home to apply the lessons learned.

STAGES OF LEADERSHIP DEVELOPMENT

We have presented our rationale for focusing on library leadership, core beliefs guiding our approach to leadership development, leadership traits we try to develop in training and consulting, and the conceptual framework we use to design training experiences. We included specific workshop approaches and strategies administrators can use to develop leadership within libraries.

The first stage of Courageous Follower is borrowed from Ira Chaleff.[16] We can support those in this stage by teaching them early on that they can lead from anywhere in the organization and that their inexperience can be used to ask the naïve question in challenging the status quo.

Stage 2 is Mastery, when the normal job is mastered, and there is confidence in the person's ability to perform at a high level. We can support this employee by encouraging professional sharing, publishing, and training of less experienced staff.

Stage 3 is one of Exerting Influence, going beyond the day-to-day job to have an influence in the rest of the organization. They may be doing that from the beginning, but in this stage, it should be a central focus. These stages are additive, not exclusive. In other words, in Stage 3, they don't stop asking questions or performing masterfully, they add the span of influence. To support Exerting Influence, an administrator simply needs to set the expectation, then assign responsibilities which fit that role. If they have not yet moved into positions in the hierarchy of the organization, they should be encouraged to do so, or find informal opportunities for influence.

As a Stage 4 Mentor, experienced leaders go beyond the sharing of basic skills to take several employees under their wing, grooming them to accept a hand-off of the leader's former responsibilities. Many administrators are in this stage, thinking actively about succession planning. Once again, succession planning should be an earlier consideration as well, but now it should be a central focus.

And finally, Stage 5 is the Sage. A wonderful freedom comes with this stage. It is a time for final influence, and re-creation of themselves, for finding new ways to support the profession while incorporating other passions of their lives. Our favorite story of this stage is of Margaret Chisholm, who after retiring from the library and information science profession, indulged her passions: books, travel, and shopping. She invented a position with a cruise line, doing book talks while traveling the world, shopping at international ports. Now that's a Sage!

We view leadership development as a life-long endeavor, which needs different kinds of support for different stages of our lives. While the stages of leadership development are overlapping and never as neat as a model might demonstrate, we think the concepts are useful in planning that support. The reader may want to consider in which stage she sees herself functioning right now and how to continue her own development.

FINAL THOUGHTS

We'd like to dedicate this article to Margaret and another esteemed leader we served, Dennis Day. It was a privilege to be inspired by and learn with them. We admire their vision in seeing the need for library leadership development back in 1989, and their willingness to take action with the creation of the Leadership Institute at Snowbird.

We also acknowledge that any good work we do with libraries is immeasurably enhanced by our association with our consulting clients, and the mentors and participants of our institutes. Our own leadership learning continues through their willingness to allow us to grow with them.

NOTES

1. Chaleff, I. (1995). *The Courageous Follower: Standing Up To and For Our Leaders*. San Francisco, CA: Berrett-Koehler.

2. Roethlisberger, F.J., and Dickson, W.J. (1936). *Management and the Worker*. Cambridge, MA: Harvard University Press.

3. Sheldon, B.E. (1991). *Leaders in Libraries*. Chicago and London: American Library Association, 71.

4. Bennis, W. (1985). *Leaders: The Strategies for Taking Charge*. New York: Harper, 27.

5. Kouzes, J. and Posner, B. (1987). *The Leadership Challenge*. San Francisco: Jossey-Bass, 314.

6. Vaill, P. (1996). *Learning as a Way of Being*. San Francisco: Jossey-Bass, 10.

7. Himmel, E. and Wilson, W.J. (1998). *Planning for Results: A Public Library Transformation Process*. Chicago and London: American Library Association.

8. Weisbord, M.R. and Janoff, S. (1995). *Future Search: An Action Guide to Finding Common Ground in Organizations & Communities*. San Francisco, CA: Berrett-Koehler.

9. Lippitt, L.L. (1998). *Preferred Futuring: Envision the Future You Want and Unleash the Energy to Get There*. San Francisco, CA: Berrett-Koehler.

10. Bennis, W. (1985). *Leaders: The Strategies for Taking Charge*. New York: Harper, 44.

11. Greenleaf, R.K. (1991). *Servant Leadership*. New York: Paulist Press.

12. Senge, P.M. (1990). *The Fifth Discipline: The Art and Practice of The Learning Organization*. New York: Doubleday/Currency.

13. Synectics, Inc. is an engineering firm which has become well known for its innovative problem solving processes.

14. We saw this quote on a plaque in a client's office.

15. Colantuono, S. (1982). "Hands-On or Head-Trip, How Do You Learn Best," *Reading Book For Human Relations Training*. National Training Laboratory Institute for Applied Behavioral Science. 300 North Lee Street, Suite 300, Alexandria, Virginia 22314.

16. Chaleff, *The Courageous Follower*.

Information Technology in the Virtual Library: Leadership in Times of Change

Stuart Glogoff

SUMMARY. Information technology is transforming society, education, business and the economy. Library administrators must understand these changes in order to position their organizations to flourish in the networked environment. This article describes the impact of this transformation on libraries, users, and library competitors. Restructuring organizations for adaptability and rapid decision-making, taking advantage of opportunities possible with advances in networked information, integrating the values of the "Net Generation" into the library organization, and adopting appropriate emerging technologies will allow libraries to continue to compete in the information marketplace. *[Article copies available for a fee from The Haworth Document Delivery Service: 1-800-342-9678. E-mail address: <getinfo@haworthpressinc.com> Website: <http://www.HaworthPress.com> © 2001 by The Haworth Press, Inc. All rights reserved.]*

KEYWORDS. Information technology, leadership, change, virtual libraries, networks, the Internet

INTRODUCTION

Change today is driven by technology, and not by policy.[1] (Barry Munitz, President and CEO, J. Paul Getty Trust)

Stuart Glogoff is Assistant Dean, Library Information Systems, University of Arizona.

[Haworth co-indexing entry note]: "Information Technology in the Virtual Library: Leadership in Times of Change." Glogoff, Stuart. Co-published simultaneously in *Journal of Library Administration* (The Haworth Information Press, an imprint of The Haworth Press, Inc.) Vol. 32, No. 3/4, 2001, pp. 59-80; and: *Leadership in the Library and Information Science Professions: Theory and Practice* (ed: Mark D. Winston) The Haworth Information Press, an imprint of The Haworth Press, Inc., 2001, pp. 59-80. Single or multiple copies of this article are available for a fee from The Haworth Document Delivery Service [1-800-342-9678, 9:00 a.m. - 5:00 p.m. (EST). E-mail address: getinfo@haworthpressinc.com].

© 2001 by The Haworth Press, Inc. All rights reserved.

For over one hundred years, library supporters have described libraries with values such as "intrinsic to democracy," the "heart of the university," "community centers for K-12," and "crucial resource for self-improvement." As computers were developed to support scientific computation and inventory control, libraries used them to automate paper routines, create searchable databases, and connect to worldwide networks.[2] At the beginning of the new millennium, library administrators must understand technology more than ever before, to continue positioning libraries as critical resources for their institutions and communities. Technical jargon such as client/server, high speed networks, intranets and extranets, disintermediation, metadata, e-business, portals, wireless, thin clients, and technology refresh are evidence of a profound transformation. A result is that libraries are facing real threats from private sector entrepreneurs.[3] What must library administrators know to position their organizations to use information creatively and efficiently, thereby maintaining viability?

To begin with, it is important to understand the impact of this technological revolution on libraries. In their 1998 book *Blur: The Speed of Change in the Connected Economy,* Stan Davis and Christopher Meyer explain that new organizational models are emerging that are driven by the rapid changes dictated by working in a digital economy. Successful organizations are re-structuring in ways that promote adaptability.[4] Davis and Meyer explain that the role of the organization as "go-between" is diminishing because individuals now have a greater ability "to participate directly in the large sphere of economic activity."[5] E-commerce sites, such as Amazon.com, E*TRADE℠, and eBay™ demonstrate the enormous growth of e-business and the integration of e-commerce into previously static web sites. E-business sites, such as electronic publishers and bookstores, may pose a threat to publicly funded libraries' revenue-base. Furthermore, intuitive and comprehensive online search services such as AltaVista® and Ask Jeeves diminish the need for individuals to consult with library staff as "go-between." There is no reason to believe that these electronic services will not continue to improve and flourish, diminishing further the need for mediated services, as users are empowered to find answers to questions and research materials virtually and forego visiting "brick and mortar" libraries. The threat to the librarian, as mediator to information, is significant.

> *There is always the chance that a future technological breakthrough will facilitate the transformation of the wilder technological dreams into reality.*[6] (George Basalla)

In the Afterword[7] to his 1989 novel *Earth,* author David Brin observed that individuals who lived from 1939 to 1989 experienced nearly unfathomable changes in their lives. Yet as they lived through those 50 years, the changes seemed to occur normally. We can all look back on ideas that must have seemed startlingly unrealistic when first presented. Consider the likely response when Post-It[RM] note pads and automatic teller machines (ATMs) were first suggested. How many people anticipated the impact that the World Wide Web would have on education, teaching, training, research, and scholarship, much less that it would spark an economic transformation? The point is that external forces, such as the Web, exemplify the rapid change possible today. The Web's impact on technology is significant because it is an enabler as much as a conduit to resources. Most products today use a Web browser as the front-end interface to the various applications and data contained therein. Looking back at progress spanning the past five years, this evolution seems logical. Administrators, therefore, should ask "what if?" and "why not?" when evaluating new ideas and possibilities. What follows is designed to give library administrators a sound understanding of how information technology is driving changes influencing society, education, business, and the economy.

THE NETWORK GENERATION AS AGENTS OF CHANGE

> *We don't want to be like the leader in the French Revolution who said, There go my people. I must find out where they are going so I can lead them.*[6] (John Fitzgerald Kennedy)

> *There isn't a digitally illiterate 10-year-old in the US. Even if they only play Sega or Gameboy, they are used to the technology.* (Professor Nicholas Negroponte, Massachusetts Institute of Technology (from a speech at the Edinburgh Television Festival), August 1997)

Not long ago I attended a regional meeting where the lunchtime thread turned to an experience shared, interestingly, by library technologists from several institutions. Each recounted attending a meeting where colleagues shared their visions of how libraries will deploy technology in the future. Instead of being engaged in discussing the significant impact of the enabling technologies on their constituencies, our colleagues spoke of essentially the same mission and services as practiced today. Recurring themes included helping library users find information, digitizing collections, creating finding aids, and selecting print and non-print materials. One senior member of a colleague's staff reportedly spoke in near diatribe tones of the negative impact of the Internet on society. Will library service remain essentially the same in the face of aggressive societal transformation and rapidly changing technology? What insights can we acquire by understanding the differences in learning and communication styles among today's middle and high school students from previous generations?

Let's begin with a review of Don Tapscott's excellent book *Growing Up Digital: The Rise of the Net Generation.* Tapscott identified four key factors indicative of a "new generation gap." Library administrators should remember these when establishing policies and outlining a strategic plan.

1. The older generations are uneasy about the new technology–which kids are embracing.
2. Older generations tend to be uneasy about new media–which are coming into the heart of youth culture.
3. Old media are uneasy about new media.[8]
4. The digital revolution, unlike previous ones, is not controlled by only adults.[9]

The generational differences regarding the acceptance of new technology are not surprising. It is consistent with principles of adult learning theory. Adult learning theory states that adults learn best through a complex process that includes references to past experiences, acceptance of the value of the learning, involvement in directing the process, and hands-on experimentation in a non-threatening environment.[10] Many librarians and staff also struggle to accept new technologies. Because computer technology was not directed initially to the consumer marketplace, many did not begin to use computers until they were introduced in their work environment. For many of these adults, there is little past history to draw upon, making adoption an uneasy experience.

At the heart of the Network Generation culture is interactivity. Tapscott reports that children today increasingly are participants not viewers, and are incited to discourse.[11] Contrary to fears that students are hurt by time spent on the Internet and in chat rooms, he finds that

> Digital kids are learning precisely the social skills which will be required for effective interaction in the digital economy. They are learning about peer relationships, about teamwork, about being critical, about how to have fun online, about friendships across geographies, about standing up for what they think, and about how to effectively communicate their ideas.[12]

Renowned futurist George Gilder also sees people deriving positive interactions from using computer networks. In *Life After Television* he wrote that "computer networks respond to all the human characteristics that TV networks defy."[13] His premise is that television as a medium is doomed because it is essentially only a broadcast medium and will be surpassed by wireless communications with virtually endless bandwidth and highly interactive design. In an article in *Barron's* in November 1999,[14] Lauren R. Rublin reported that children and teenagers are spending less time watching television than did their counterparts a decade ago. Rublin wrote that "TV faces growing competition from high-tech entertainment sources, namely video games, personal computers, and, of course, the Internet."[15] She notes that " . . . studies show that kids under 12 are logging on an average of almost 10 hours a month, while Internet usage among 12-17-year-olds tops 12 hours a month."[16] In addition, she cited a report by Juniper Communications that found that most children and teenagers are using the Internet for e-mail, search engines, homework help and games.

The U. S. Census Bureau has collected computer use data in October of 1984, 1989, 1993 and 1997 as a supplement to the Current Population Survey (CPS). In a detailed report[17] released in October 1999, the Bureau reported on children's computer and Internet use in 1997.

- Half of all children had a computer at home compared with 32 percent in 1993.
- About 71 percent of children enrolled in school used a computer at school.
- Of the 14 million children using the Internet, 9 million did so at school and 7 million at home.
- Among all children, regardless of computer ownership, 27 percent of those in households with family incomes above $75,000 used the Internet from home, compared with 2 percent of children in households with family incomes below $25,000.
- Children who used the Internet at home used it to find government, business, health or education information (76 percent); to send and receive e-mail (58 percent); to participate in chat rooms (32 percent); and to look for news, weather and sports (28 percent).

The upsurge in wireless communications over the next few years will find an enthusiastic audience among the Net Generation. If there are opportunities to seize, libraries should initiate services that create value between their products and services and a constituency whose skills have been honed by exploiting the Internet. Bear in mind, however, that a result of the Internet is also disintermediated services.[18] Competition from Internet portals and e-commerce sites may present formidable challenges.

The importance of understanding the behavioral patterns of Net-Geners exceeds merely appreciating that they are comfortable working online. Tapscott highlights what he labels the "Eight Shifts of Interactive Learning," finding that Net-Geners prefer interactive learning environments. The eight shifts are:

1. From linear to hypermedia learning
2. From instruction to construction and discovery
3. From teacher-centered to learner-centered education
4. From absorbing material to learning how to navigate and how to learn
5. From school to lifelong learning
6. From one-size-fits-all to customized learning
7. From learning as torture to learning as fun
8. From the teacher as transmitter to the teacher as facilitator[19,20]

An intrinsic part of librarianship has been its commitment to service and to function as a conduit between its users and vast warehouses of knowledge. The Internet has introduced a serious threat to this traditional role by providing people, such as Net-Geners, with direct access to information. Arguments about the quality and quantity of that information carry little merit to users who are satisfied with their results. In the end, these people see little need for the traditional mediated services that librarians have for decades relied upon as their *raison d'être*. Libraries need to evaluate how to transform services to match the preferences of these library users or they will attempt to satisfy their information needs elsewhere.

TRANSFORMING LEARNING

A number of important reports have been released in the past few years that forecast significant changes in education, instruction, and lifelong learning. Traditional methods of teaching and library service are being questioned nationally at public levels. For example, Peter Drucker was quoted as saying that "thirty years from now big university campuses will be relics." He attributed this to "totally uncontrollable expenditures without any visible improvement in either the content or the quality of education."[21] The rising costs associated with residential colleges and universities, coupled with the persistent finger-pointing by legislators and voters that public funds are not being applied in the most responsible manner, gives credence to alarmist forecasts. Another popular argument that predicts the decline of residential education is the expectation that distance learning will displace residential campuses and that much of the instructional content will come, not from traditional educational models, but instead from commercial endeavors. Fueling these arguments is the fact that technology has changed how we deliver instruction, what delivery mechanism students choose when afforded the choice, and where continuous learning takes place.

In 1996, *Buildings, books and bytes: libraries and communities in the digital age,*[22] a report sponsored by the W. K. Kellogg Foundation, was released. The findings reported that important segments of the public perceive libraries as being only marginally involved in the digital information marketplace. In fact, the 18-24 age group (college age) was the least enthusiastic. How can library administrators challenge staff to deliver services in new ways, engage students and faculty beyond the library's walls, develop partnerships with allies as well as competitors, and re-direct resources where they have the greatest impact on the user community? Developing a shared vision of the library's role as we begin the 21st century is a prerequisite to success. This vision should be developed with the active participation of the community, thereby validating the library's role in using enabling technologies.

The CIO for Chicago Public Schools, Richard Koeller, has undertaken a program to overhaul the school system's information technology infrastructure and expand its use of technology in the classroom. Koeller's workplan is to: (1) create a technology and policy infrastructure providing state-of-the-art technical support for all staff and students in the 600-school district; (2) educate teachers and school administrators so they can make the best use of IT; and (3) improve computer literacy for the more than 430,000 students by adding computers to each school, [and] connecting them to the Internet.[23] Each item in this action plan invites active participation with the school system's librarians. The libraries that succeed will be those that respond quickly, share a common vision for the future, and invest in the human infrastructure as well as the technical. Opportunities abound for librarians to contribute as well to policy design, curriculum development, and content integration. Certainly, there is much that can be accomplished under the proper leadership.

IMPACT OF NETWORKED INFORMATION

"Networked information does not require that physical collections be located near users, and the requirements for its organization and preservation are very different from print collections."[24] In one of the most provocative articles in the library professional literature in recent years, David W. Lewis advanced the thesis that because libraries are artifact-bound, their value will greatly diminish. Technology, he notes, underlies the communication and storage of knowledge, which has migrated from being paper-based to electronic.[25] Because libraries continue to commit significant resources to maintaining large print inventories–essentially "information artifacts"–their importance is declining. Furthermore, arguments that libraries are expanding their value by purchasing subscriptions to electronic text from publishers and aggregator services are only valid so long as the library's role in subsidizing information access continues. For Davis, this prompts the question of "whether libraries are the only, or even the best, means of making information easily and conveniently available."[26]

Consider the economic model that e-business on the Web has created. Is there a reason that students and community members need to go through the library to access information when it is available to them directly online? David R. Majka posits that the introduction of full-text electronic resources has resulted in a profound change in the delivery model for periodical-based information. In the old model, information flowed from publishers to libraries and then to library users. In his new model, publisher/aggregators disseminate directly to patrons through the Web, for example through portals such as Yahoo. This limits the library's role to providing on-site access of print and electronic resources.[27]

One of the leading vendors in the library marketplace is now marketing resources directly to faculty at middle and high schools, community colleges, and universities. This vendor also is offering value-added services that replace services performed by librarians. Faculty members are lured to the product because it allows them to create course packs of primary source materials, newspaper, magazine, and journal articles from thousands of online resources. It is a scalable venture for faculty because they may easily adapt article collections already prepared in their subject areas or complement existing material with new. This vendor has already secured copyright clearance and added features for attaching comments that students may view online. There are additional value-added features possible, such as links to related Internet sites, background information, interpretations, and references to other resources. Faculty and students utilize these resources online via the Web, facilitating integration with the faculty member's course delivered via the Web. For institutions that are struggling to deliver resources to distance learners, this product is a practical solution. While discussing this product at a recent conference, the vendor representative acknowledged that delivering the online resources to which his company has the rights via Internet portals is planned for the future.

Can libraries compete in this marketplace? Majka opined that libraries "have not captured the public imagination due to manifest deficiencies in leadership, technology (in some cases), and business skills."[28] A key for survival in the digital economy, as Davis and Meyer explained in *Blur,* is the need for a speedy response. "The need for speed of response in today's business environment puts a premium on systems that can operate in 'real time.' Rather than acting on historical experience or expectations about the future, these systems capture the reality of what's happening now and function 'on the fly.' "[29] Furthermore, Davis and Meyer emphasize that an outcome of operating in a digital economy is the merging of products and services. Library administrators, therefore, must see scenarios like the one described in this section as competition and find new ways to remain crucial to their clientele. Leadership qualities, such as innovation and risk-taking, are of paramount importance.

Another major area in which networked information has changed the way libraries operate is in delivering intellectual work. At a basic level, library administrators have observed an increasing percent of their budgets committed to purchasing online subscriptions to electronic text, whether through aggregating services, individual projects, or in-house development. Networks have changed the way intellectual content is delivered and, increasingly, how it is constructed. Traditional modes of scholarly publishing are breaking down and being replaced by digital-only options that present authors with the opportunity to reach larger audiences much faster, and at far less cost. A researcher can garner feedback on ideas quickly and make changes immediately. The emergence of the network is so important to delivering information that Malcolm Getz commented in his April 1999 presentation at ACRL's national conference that "it is at least imaginable that materials not delivered by network will become as if invisible."[30]

Consistent with the alternative forms of access to electronic resources identified above, Getz observed that when library users are invited or required to purchase online resources these users will "vote with their dollars for the services they value most."[31] Can libraries adapt? It will not be easy. Getz cites an article published in the Fall 1997 issue of *The Quarterly Review of Economics and Finance* reporting that "innovations in libraries and computing in higher education take about 10 years for full adoption . . . "[32] His conclusion is that when library users' personal decisions drive them to purchase information via networks, commercial publishers are better positioned to respond quickly and seize their market share from libraries.

One of the leading researchers on the transformation of scholarly publishing is Andrew Odlyzko.[33] Although librarians are exploring methods to insert themselves into the scholarly publishing process with efforts such as the Association of Research Libraries SPARC[34] initiative, Odlyzko is not convinced that libraries will succeed. He predicts, instead, that because of cultural, economic, technical and legal issues " . . . it will be the publishers who will come out ahead."[35] His reasons for this viewpoint are: (1) size–there are fewer publishers than libraries which makes it easier for publishers to realize economies of scale; (2) competition–publishers are used to competition and libraries are not; (3) rights issues–publishers already own the material; (4) funding–publishers will be attracted to tapping into library coffers. Odlyzko already sees this transformation in practice in the demise of the print journal. He writes that "most established publishers have already created or are creating electronic versions of their scholarly print journals. Often, they offer these digital editions at no extra cost to subscribers of the print versions. In some cases, institutions that forego the print version receive a modest discount."[36] Closely tracking market activity is important. A recent example of this trend occurred in the Fall of 1999 when Bell & Howell, an aggregator service, acquired Chadwyck-Healey, a publishing firm, for its "rich information resources to create unparalleled depth, opportunity for new products."[37]

Administrators also will be interested in learning of other predictions Odlyzko makes that focus on the impact of this technology-driven transformation. Because there will be so much more information to collect, classify and navigate, new roles for information specialists will surface, although there will be more competition for these positions. He suggests that less-skilled positions in circulation areas, such as checking out and re-shelving print materials, will be among the first jobs lost. Odlyzko predicts growth areas for professional positions in negotiating electronic-access licenses and serving as the "enforcer of access restrictions."[38] Understanding the many issues and significant changes networked information is bringing will help library administrators make the requisite organizational adjustments.

While traversing the changing paradigms and opportunities possible with advances in networked information, one should not loose sight of severe bandwidth limitations outside of major cities. One recent article stated that 86% of the Internet delivery capacity in the United States is concentrated in the twenty largest cities.[39] Consider, then, the impact this has on libraries located in rural areas. It may limit the ability of those libraries to provide the types of services described in this article and cause them to be only warehouses of print materials, unable to add value to services. Similarly, small businesses in these areas lacking sufficient connectivity will not look to the library as a partner in its future. Besides rural communities, poor suburban and inner city neighborhoods are at risk because high-speed networks are most often concentrated in business districts. As economic development suffers, so too will many communities because these communities will "miss out on developing high-speed home uses, such as telemedicine, distance learning and telecommuting."[40] Library administrators have a responsibility, therefore, to promote universal service concepts to lessen creating a class of electronic have-nots.

THE WORKPLACE

> *It's not about technology. It's about what we do with technology.* (José-Marie Griffiths, CIO, University of Michigan)

Technology has dramatically challenged and transformed our work processes and interactions with users. As discussed earlier in this article, it has not always engendered staff confidence. Still greater changes loom on the horizon, particularly as the Network Generation enters the workforce. Administrators will observe differences when hiring Net-Geners–first as they perform entry-level work and later as seasoned employees. The Xerox Corporation is an example of a major corporation that "takes N-Geners seriously, [by] routinely partnering with them to help invent the future, and incorporating lifelong learning into its corporate culture."[41] Will Net-Geners passively accept traditional organizations? Are libraries prepared to accept and adapt to the requisite cultural changes to attract and retain quality workers? Consider Tapscott's list of themes regarding the Net Generation's culture. These are the traits that will transform the library workplace into one that accepts and encourages: intellectual openness, collaboration, *internetworking* intellect for organizational consciousness, a culture of innovation, expectations for mature behavior, investigation, immediacy and the real-time business structure, corporate skepticism, and a culture of trustworthiness and trust.[42]

In addition to the impact of the Network Generation on library staffing, administrators must be cognizant of how technology is validating and transforming the basic tenets of the learning, teaching, and research communities. Collaboration technologies, enhanced by the increased capabilities and the Internet's reliability, are providing people with new ways to merge their skills, arrive at insights, and exchange resources. Dr. José-Marie Griffiths, the University of Michigan's CIO, has written that technology is creating a new social fabric[43] which she describes as virtual "knowledge communities." Knowledge communities are noteworthy not simply because they have evolved due to the enabling technologies but because they have activated a new dynamic in how people communicate and collaborate. Within this framework lie many opportunities for libraries to participate.

Griffiths identifies knowledge communities in terms of a number of concurrent characteristics. She explains that knowledge communities may function within both a formal or informal structure. Secondly, she emphasizes the importance of interdependent processes among knowledge communities and how these processes attract people of similar interests. While engaged in these processes, knowledge community members analyze information to develop new understandings, and create new knowledge or rediscover the old. Finally, knowledge communities may be spawned from interests as diverse as intellectual discourse, artistic endeavors, social interactions, or physical activities.[44] As participants become engaged in a respective knowledge community, they use new technologies in ways that support each other. Within this framework, administrators will find opportunities to involve staff. As repositories of knowledge, libraries can draw upon abundant resources and serve as conduits between knowledge community members. By building on strengths and by using computer networks effectively, libraries can facilitate connecting people and contributing to knowledge creation.

Administrators should recognize that the information technologists on their staff play important roles in assuring the library's place in knowledge communities. In the 30 years since the first ARPANET node was sketched[45] at the University of California, Los Angeles (UCLA), the information technologist's role has evolved from tactical to strategic.[46] It is as true for libraries as it is for businesses that the organization's IT unit is responsible for delivering its products and services to its users. IT units understand infrastructure requirements and the crucial role the network plays in facilitating relationships among people within the organization, as well as externally. Bob Evans, formerly editor-in-chief of *InformationWeek,* one of the most widely circulated IT trade magazines, wrote that people who manage technology in business also manage the corporate culture. "Those people are forging new human and technical links between accounting and manufacturing, between operations in Southeast Asia and marketing in Paris, between glitzy but still-unformed Web businesses and 100-year-old organizations with tens of billions in assets."[47] Library administrators who have not yet acknowledged this role must begin doing so immediately by involving the IT staff in strategic planning and front line activities. In the process, administrators should identify their expectations for IT staff and dialogue on what steps should be taken to build a shared understanding among the library staff.

THE EMERGING TECHNOLOGIES

> *This 'telephone' has too many shortcomings to be seriously considered as a means of communication. The device is inherently of no value to us.* (Western Union internal memo, 1876)
>
> *Trust in Allah, but tether your camel.* (Arab proverb)

Scarcely a day passes without an announcement extolling the promise of one of the many exciting new technologies appearing over the horizon or emerging in the marketplace. While it is often hard to separate hope from hype, trends driving new technologies are in motion. Among these are

- better methods of delivering information and data to the desktop
- constant extension of the World Wide Web to homes, education and the workplace
- realization of ubiquitous computing

This article can not do justice to preparing library administrators for many of the important new tools that will come into use in the next two to three years. Certainly, volumes could be written describing these emerging technologies. What follows instead is an attempt to highlight a select few and comment on their relevance.

An important book for library administrators to read is Tim Berners-Lee's *Weaving the Web: The Original Design and Ultimate Destiny of the World Wide Web by Its Inventor.* The reason is simple–the World Wide Web has revolutionized technology. It is, perhaps, the single most important factor in freeing our networks from proprietary protocols so that *intranets,*[48] local area networks using the Internet's open standards protocols, could develop. It has fostered document delivery and collaboration and led to the acceptance of the Web browser as the single interface to most of the software applications delivered over any network.

In *Weaving the Web,* Berners-Lee tells not only the story of how the World Wide Web was created and developed, but shares his vision for the future. He sees the Web as the universe of all accessible information, whether stored locally or remotely. This is important to library administrators because libraries traditionally have duplicated each other's collection development efforts. Our most prestigious libraries are often still rated by the quantity of their physical holdings. Such evaluation is more akin to a numerology cult. With the Web, local holdings are not as important. Among Berners-Lee's early vision was that "where information was physically stored should be made invisible to the user."[49] Therefore, it is incumbent upon us to move our thinking from ownership and size of collections to access to information anytime/anyplace. *Weaving the Web* also addresses Berners-Lee's vision for the future. He reviews the Web in relation to topics such as collaboration, interactivity and social implications, as well as hardware and software advances such as XML, VRML, and scalable vector graphics. It serves as an excellent foundation for the near future.

Thin client technology[50] may be a technology that administrators utilize to manage delivering resources in-house. Current configurations in libraries with sizable capital investments in PCs require a concomitant investment in technical staff to install, maintain, and upgrade the hardware, software and networking required to operate those PCs. With thin client technology, instead of each staff member operating duplicate software versions on the same computer, all of the computing is performed and stored on centralized, shared machines. All a staff member needs, therefore, is a keyboard, mouse, a monitor, and input/output devices for audio. Of course, this is as true for the scores of computers dedicated to public access. Thin clients can offer information systems staff great time savings. The seemingly endless array of Web browser plug-in upgrades, for example, can be done once on the server, instead of on each machine in the organization.

A Gartner Group[51] report estimated that thin clients are 26 percent to 39 percent less expensive to operate.[52] Interestingly, as this section was being drafted, a story on *InternetWeek Online* reported that Amazon.com was adding thousands of thin client terminals to its customer service and distribution operations for the 1999 holiday season. The explanation of why it opted for thin client terminals over PCs was that "it would have been impossible for Amazon.com to deploy desktop PCs quickly enough to meet its holiday demand."[53] At this time expectations are high for thin client technology. A recent article in *Computerworld* cited two reports in which estimates ranged from 6 million new thin clients by 2003 to a customer base of 30 million thin client machines by 2002.[54] Look for thin client technology to have a major impact on libraries in the next two to three years.

> *So let's begin our thinking about a new world by imagining one in which a computer screen is available whenever we want it.*[55] (Tim Berners-Lee)

Library administrators remember "portability" as a technology issue previously associated with the capability of carrying the library's database from one vendor's local library system to another. Because library holdings records adhered to the MARC standard, it was possible to abandon one vendor's system for a different one with relative ease. Today, "portability" carries a different meaning, as suggested by Berners-Lee in the above quote. Berners-Lee is expressing his vision of ubiquitous computing. It is an environment in which computer technology is no longer a physical location but is instead available wherever we may be. Indeed, we are on the threshold of realizing this with smart cards, advances in wireless communications, and the infrastructure built from the Internet's location-independent design.

Take for example, Sun Microsystems' new ultra thin client, the Sun Ray.[56] What adds value to the Sun Ray is its integration with smart card technology. A "smart card" is essentially a plastic identification or credit card containing an embedded integrated circuit that stores information. Smart cards make information always instantly accessible. They are being used by organizations as diverse as the military, where they can be embedded in a soldier's dog tags, to hospitals for storing patient medical record information. Colleges and universities find them useful as electronic money, enabling students to pay for services such as dining hall meals, bookstore purchases, items in vending machines, and at omnipresent photocopy machines. Consistent with the smart card's application for personal identification, it is an asset for access to secured areas, such as residence halls and computer labs. By factoring into the equation the capability to enter borrower privileges, administrators can see how smart cards will provide user authentication within circulation systems, replacing magnetic stripe and barcode identification systems. Other uses may include a user's reading preferences, account information, and volunteer profile.

The Sun Ray integrates networked computing with a smart card so that one is able to leave an active computer session in the server's memory by removing the smart card, then move to a different Sun Ray, insert the smart card, and immediately restore the session. This is possible anywhere on the network. A logical next step is to envision an environment where large computing networks are accessed by any number of small, portable devices, replacing the desktop computer as the center of the computing universe. This is a logical extension in the corporate world, where high-speed Internet connections allow companies to rent software applications over the Web from application service providers rather than pay constantly to upgrade in-house software and hardware packages. With the extension of powerful wireless devices such as phones, handheld computers, and pagers to access and update data stored at remote locations, the portability needed to support truly ubiquitous computing is nearer.

Portability and ubiquitous computing are driven today by the enormous advances made over the past few years in wireless computing. As product announcements touting new wireless products fill our e-mail in-baskets, library administrators should examine them for standards and applicability. WAP, Wireless Application Protocol, is "an open, global specification that empowers mobile users with wireless devices to easily access and interact with information and services instantly."[57] This standard is applicable to handheld digital wireless devices such as mobile phones, pagers, two-way radios, smartphones and communicators, and is designed to work with most wireless networks.

What sorts of wireless computing applications can libraries anticipate? Consider *Wireless Andrew,* a project at Carnegie Mellon University designed to "demonstrate the potential of ubiquitous access to information through the use of portable, online computing devices. It will provide high-bandwidth access to personal, group, and Internet information resources anytime, anywhere, by anyone in the Carnegie Mellon community."[58] *Wireless Andrew* clearly supports extending library resources along with a myriad of other online resources. If the library is a student's principal gateway to Internet resources, it will continue as the student's primary access point from wireless, handheld devices. Carnegie Mellon administrators see *Wireless Andrew*'s potential to facilitate new levels of integration, communication and knowledge sharing across the entire university community. This demonstrates the potential to integrate wireless communications in the knowledge community setting. Library administrators can help staff by encouraging them to adopt handheld devices as learning and working tools.

CONCLUSION

> *At LCS, we believe that technology is an inseparable child of humanity and that for true progress to occur, the two must walk hand in hand, with neither one acting as servant to the other.* [59](Michael L. Dertouzos, Director of the MIT Laboratory for Computer Science)

Technology is a means of achieving the library's service mission. It is also driving change in society, the economy, how we learn, and how we communicate with each other. In a report released in September 1999, the U. S. Department of Labor projects that the "use of computers and the Internet in workplaces will become more pervasive and the functions performed using computers will dramatically increase."[60] Technology's influence will go beyond new equipment and faster communications, as work and skills are redefined and reorganized. The Internet has garnered as many accolades for what it can accomplish as the negative hype heaped on it by sensationalists and persons intimidated by change. Library administrators need only review their own profession's history to find success stories and failures.

In 1971, Ellsworth Mason, then Director of Library Services at Hofstra University, wrote an article published in *College & Research Libraries,* extolling the vices he associated with librarians embracing technology. Mason's research, which was sponsored by the Council on Library Resources, led him to conclude that "after talking at length with some of the finest computer experts in the library world and probing the thinking behind more than forty computerized library operations, it became clear that the application of computers to library processes is a disaster, and that no one is willing to admit it."[61] Mason saw a conspiracy on college campuses starting at the highest administrative levels promoting " . . . the new campus ecology, now polluted by technologists." He concluded with a series of truths, the first of which was that "the computer has involved librarians in greater and more prolonged agonies than anything in recent history . . . "[62] Such thoughts would seem harmless today were it not, as reported earlier, still popular among some librarians to view technology as a threat rather than an asset.

Much has been ballyhooed about entering the "new Millennium." Remembering the lessons David Brin shared, it is likely that we will look back on the next twenty years of librarianship as having evolved in a logical path. That path, however, does not guarantee that libraries will retain the esteem traditionally held for them by the public. It requires skillful leadership from administrators to pilot a course through the enormous challenges looming ahead. Changing the library's "corporate culture," while one of the most daunting tasks a library administrator faces, is an essential component for future success.

Changing that culture starts with an appreciation of what technology brings at the organization's highest level. Seek out opportunities for your library to participate in exciting new electronic initiatives, be open to changes in the organizational structure that invite new ideas and promote organizational adaptability, and build an infrastructure that positions the library as an active participant in knowledge communities. If library administrators do this, then the profession will not be driven by technology but, instead, will be viewed as the driver.

NOTES

1. Barry Munitz, "Education As Competitive Industry: A Wave of Profound Change," *EDUCAUSE '99: Celebrating New Beginnings*, Long Beach, CA, October 29, 1999.

2. For a review of the transition from "paper library" to "automated library," see chapters 2 and 3 of Michael Buckland's *Redesigning Library Services: A Manifesto* (Chicago and London: American Library Association, 1992): 9-23.

3. An excellent book explaining this scenario is Stanley M. Davis and James W. Botkin, *The Monster Under the Bed: How Business Is Mastering the Opportunity of Knowledge for Profit* (New York: Simon & Schuster, 1994).

4. Stan Davis, and Christopher Meyer, *Blur: the Speed of Change in the Connected Economy* (Reading, MA: Addison-Wesley, 1998): 120.

5. Ibid., 162.

6. George Basalla, *The Evolution of Technology* (Cambridge: Cambridge University Press, 1988): 73.

7. David Brin, *Earth* "Afterword" (New York: Bantam Books, 1990): 665-667.

8. That is to say, for example, that traditional publishers are uneasy about publishing via electronic media.

9. Don Tapscott, *Growing Up Digital: The Rise of the Net Generation* (New York: McGraw, Hill, 1998): 48-50.

10. Stuart Glogoff, and James P. Flynn, "Developing a Systematic In-house Training Program for Integrated Library Systems," *College & Research Libraries*, 48 (November 1987): 530.

11. Tapscott, *Growing Up Digital*, 78.

12. Ibid., 107.

13. George Gilder, *Life After Television: The Coming Transformation of Media and American Life*, revised edition. (New York & London: W. W. Norton & Company, 1994): 16.

14. Lauren Rublin, "Tuning Out," *Barron's* LXXIX #45 (November 8, 1999): 37-38, 40.
15. Ibid.
16. Ibid.
17. See U.S. Census Bureau, Population Division, Education and Social Stratification Branch, "Computer Use and Ownership," at <http://www.census.gov/population/www/socdemo/computer.html>.
18. "Disintermediation" is a term more often associated with customers purchasing products through Internet-based businesses on the Web rather than going through traditional retail channels. Because Internet companies can often sell products faster and at less cost than retailers, the Internet has the capability of changing the dynamic of how people shop. This is analogous to the disconnect that libraries could feel to a great extent when their users turn to the Internet for their information rather than coming to traditional reference service points.
19. Tapscott, *Growing Up Digital*, 142-148.
20. This transformation is already being observed in higher education in the United States. See David L. Marcus, "The Big Are Getting Better: Research Universities Are Working to Put Undergraduates First," *U. S. News & World Report* (August 30, 1999): 66-68.
21. Robert Lenzner, and Stephen S. Johnson, "Seeing Things As They Really Are," *Forbes Magazine* (March 10, 1997 at http://www.forbes.com/forbes/97/0310/5905122a.htm>.
22. *Buildings, books, and bytes: Libraries and communities in the digital age.* 1996. Washington, DC: Benton Foundation at <http://www.benton.org/Library/Kellogg/buildings.html>.
23. Rick Saia, "A Day In the Life of a CIO," *ComputerWorld* (September 20, 1999) at <http://www.computerworld.com/home/print.nsf/all/990920c176>.
24. David W. Lewis, "What If Libraries Are Artifact-Bound Institutions?" *Information Technologies and Libraries* (December 1998): 193.
25. Ibid., 191.
26. Ibid., 192.
27. David R. Majka, "Of Portals, Publishers, and Privatization," *American Libraries* (October 1999): 46.
28. Ibid., 49.
29. Davis, *Blur*, 22.
30. Malcolm Getz, "Academic Publishing: Networks and Prices," ACRL National Conference, Detroit, MI, April 10, 1999, at <http://www.ala.org/acrl/getz.html>.
31. Ibid.
32. Ibid.
33. Andrew M. Odlyzko's home page may be found at <http://www.research.att.com/~amo/>.
34. SPARC: Scholarly Publishing & Academic Resources Coalition, is an alliance of libraries that fosters expanded competition in scholarly communication. See <http://www.arl.org/SPARC/> for more information.
35. Andrew M. Odlyzko, "Competition and Cooperation: Libraries and Publishers in the Transition to Electronic Scholarly Journals," *The Journal of Electronic Publishing*, 4 (June 1999) at <http://www.press.umich.edu/jep/04-04/odlyzko0404.html>.
36. Ibid.
37. "Bell & Howell Acquires Chadwyck-Healey," at <http://www.umi.com/hp/PressRel/990929.html>.

38. Odlyzko, "Competition and Cooperation."

39. David Lieberman, "America's Digital Divide," *USA Today Tech Report* (October 11, 1999) at <http://www.usatoday.com/life/cyber/tech/ctg382.htm>.

40. Ibid.

41. Connie Kafka, "Partnering With the Net Generation," *DocuWorld* (Fall 1998): 56.

42. Tapscott, *Growing Up Digital*, 211-216.

43. José-Marie Griffiths, "Knowledge Communities: Tradition, Technology and Transformation in Higher Education" at <http://www.cio.umich.edu/pubs/office/knowcom/index.html>.

44. Ibid.

45. An image of this important historical artifact may be viewed at <http://www.cybergeography.org/atlas/historical.html>.

46. "Redefining IT's Role" *InfoWorld* (October 4, 1999): 35.

47. Bob Evans, "Forged By IT," *InformationWeek* (September 21, 1998): 8.

48. Intranets are local networks, often running the Internet's TCP/IP protocol and largely concerned with an organization's internal communications.

49. Tim Berners-Lee, *Weaving the Web: The Original Design and Ultimate Destiny of the World Wide Web by Its Inventor* (San Francisco: Harper, 1999): 117.

50. Among the computer manufacturers who have announced thin client machines are Sun Microsystems, IBM, Compaq, Hewlett-Packard, Microsoft, and Oracle.

51. The Gartner Group specializes in providing "advice and targeted insights to support competitive decision making across the IT spectrum." It supports "research, analysis, consulting, measurement, decision evaluation, and product and vendor selection." See <http://www.gartnergroup.com/> for its web site. Many institutions purchase subscriptions to the Gartner Group's reports database.

52. C. Anderson, and A. Apfel, "The Arrival of the Network Computer: Past Predictions," Gartner Group, Inc., (31 October 1997) Document # PTP-103197-03.

53. Mike Koller, "Amazon Adds Thin Clients To Its Shopping Cart," *InternetWeek Online* (November 24, 1999) at <http://www.internetwk.com/story/INW19991124S0002>.

54. Cynthia Morgan, "PC Vendors Boost Thin-Client Lineups," *ComputerWorld* (September 27, 1999): 76.

55. Berners-Lee, "*Weaving the Web*," 158.

56. See <http://www.sun.com/products/sunray1/> for Sun Microsystems product information on the Sun Ray. The Sun Ray may also be considered a "network computer" (NC) which in the Fall of 1997 was hyped by the information systems print and non-print media for its promise of providing, at the individual or enterprise level, affordable computing devices at less cost to buy and maintain than PCs.

57. Wireless Application Protocol Forum Ltd., "WHAT IS WAP AND WAP FORUM? " at <http://www.wapforum.org/what/index.htm>.

58. Computing Services, Carnegie Mellon University, "Handheld Andrew" at <http://www.cmu.edu/computing/handheld/>.

59. Michael L. Dertouzos, "Foreword," to Berners-Lee, *Weaving the Web*, xi.

60. U.S. Department of Labor, *Futurework: Trends and Challenges for Work in the 21st Century* at <http://www.dol.gov/dol/asp/public/futurework/execsum.htm>.

61. Ellsworth Mason, "The Great Gas Bubble Prick't; or, Computers Revealed–by a Gentleman of Quality," *College & Research Libraries* (May 1971): 184.

62. Ibid., 188.

APPENDIX

Alerting Services

Subscribing to a selected group of alerting services is one way for administrators to keep abreast of new developments and help their staff find new opportunities to use technology to further the organization's service mission. The following are recommended for library administrators:

CIT Infobits (formerly **IAT Infobits**) is an electronic service of the University of North Carolina at Chapel Hill Academic & Technology Networks' Center for Instructional Technology. Each month the CIT's Information Resources Consultant monitors and selects from a number of information technology and instructional technology sources that come to her attention and provides brief notes for electronic dissemination to educators. Current issues, an archive to past issues and subscription information to receive the alerting service via e-mail may be found at URL: http://www.unc.edu/cit/infobits/infobits.html.

Edupage is a service of EDUCAUSE, and provides short synopses extracted from the mainstream media regarding information technology. It is distributed via e-mail three times a week to subscribers. See http://www.educause.edu/pub/edupage/edupage.html for subscription information.

InformationWeek Daily An e-mail news service from InformationWeek magazine. To subscribe, go to http://www.information week.com/magazine

InternetWeek Newsletter a service of CMP Media Inc. Visit *InternetWeek*'s homepage at URL: http://www.internetwk.com/ and follow the link to **E-Mail Newsletter** to subscribe.

NewsScan Daily To subscribe, go to http://www.newsscan.com/

ZDNet AnchorDesk Berst Alert
http://www.zdnet.com/anchordesk/whoiswe/subscribe.html

CIO Insider To subscribe, go to http://www.cio.com/CIO/cioinsider.html

Selected Technology News Services & E-zines

CIO.COM–The Leading Resource for Information Executives http://www.cio.com

Macworld Online *URL: http://macworld.zdnet.com/*

Knowledge Industry Publications *URL: http://www.KIPInet.com/*

PC Computing URL: http://www.zdnet.com/pccomp/

PC World URL: http://pcworld.com/
Wired News URL: http://www.wired.com/news/
ZDNet URL: http://www.zdnet.com/

E-Newspapers & E-Media With Technology Sections

Arizona Daily Star URL: http://www.azstarnet.com/
Boston Globe URL: http://www.boston.com/
CNN.com URL: http://www.cnn.com/
Chicago Tribune URL: http://www.chicago.tribune.com/
Electronic Telegraph URL: http://www.telegraph.co.uk/
Los Angeles Times URL: http://www.latimes.com/
MSNBC URL: http://www.msnbc.com/
New York Times on the Web URL: http://www/nytimes.com
SF Gate URL: http://www.sfgate.com/
Seattle Times URL: http://www.seattletimes.com/
The Times URL: http://www.Sunday-times.co.uk/
Washington Post URL: http://www.washingtonpost.com/
Also visit **U.S. News Archives on the Web** http://metalab.unc.edu/slanews/internet/ForArchives.html **and Non-US Newspaper Archives on the Web** URL: http://metalab.unc.edu/slanews/internet/archives.html to identify on-line newspapers in your region.

Financial Resources and What Leaders Should Know

Kate Donnelly Hickey

SUMMARY. A review of the literature suggests that credibility and communication are keys to expanding library funding beyond the traditional budgetary constraints. Library leaders must be aggressive in forging connections both within their institutions and among their communities at large. Such leaders recognize that fiscal responsibility is only the important first step on the path to achieving adequate resources and that development work, far from being an occasional unpleasant task, can bring both satisfaction and rewards. *[Article copies available for a fee from The Haworth Document Delivery Service: 1-800-342-9678. E-mail address: <getinfo@haworthpressinc.com> Website: <http://www.HaworthPress.com> © 2001 by The Haworth Press, Inc. All rights reserved.]*

KEYWORDS. Leadership competencies, financial management, library funding, development, college and university libraries

<Leadership> and <finances> and <libraries>–a surprisingly difficult database search! When asked to write on this topic I had no idea how little my first search would reveal. Much of the literature of library finances deals with issues of management, not leadership. Such titles as Madeline Daubert's *Financial Management for Small and Medium-Sized Libraries*[1] focus on the fiscal cycle of planning, budgeting, controlling, reporting, and evaluating. She notes that few libraries are independent legal entities and therefore have little control over the limited resources they have been allocated. This situation, combined with the professional librarian's service ethic, contributes, Daubert believes,

---

Kate Donnelly Hickey is Director of the Carol Grotnes Belk Library, Elon College.

[Haworth co-indexing entry note]: "Financial Resources and What Leaders Should Know." Hickey, Kate Donnelly. Co-published simultaneously in *Journal of Library Administration* (The Haworth Information Press, an imprint of The Haworth Press, Inc.) Vol. 32, No. 3/4, 2001, pp. 81-93; and: *Leadership in the Library and Information Science Professions: Theory and Practice* (ed: Mark D. Winston) The Haworth Information Press, an imprint of The Haworth Press, Inc., 2001, pp. 81-93. Single or multiple copies of this article are available for a fee from The Haworth Document Delivery Service [1-800-342-9678, 9:00 a.m. - 5:00 p.m. (EST). E-mail address: getinfo@haworthpressinc.com].

© 2001 by The Haworth Press, Inc. All rights reserved.

to a fairly low level of financial accountability for libraries. She, and others, attempt to correct this deficiency by presenting excellent insights into managing budgets, determining allocation formulas, and the like–but they speak only tangentially of leadership issues–i.e., how to expand resources, how to motivate both administration and staff, how to influence donors and politicians, how to use consortial relationships to advantage.

Then I thought of Herb White. Throughout my career I have admired his many articles focussed on obtaining resources for libraries. To paraphrase one of his basic messages–resources are earned, not given; leaders must convince administrators that the resources are necessary to obtain mutually desirable goals and that the lack of these resources will result in curtailment of services. We cannot rely on what we see as the obvious assertion that "libraries are good" and therefore should be supported.

In his recent article on outsourcing in *American Libraries,* White reiterates a familiar but easily forgotten theme:

> The keepers of the purse strings (who are usually not firsthand library users) can't make an informed decision about the cost-effectiveness of replacing you . . . if they don't even know who you are or what you can do for them.
>
> Does your senior management know what you do? Do they know what service cutbacks will result if they deny your requests for staff increases or cut your budget? Or do your reports pretend that everything is just fine?
>
> The key is communicating up the chain of command, not only what you have done . . . but what you can accomplish on their behalf with adequate resources. As management guru Peter Drucker noted long ago, the essence of effective management communication is exception reporting–what went badly, what didn't happen at all, and why it's bad for management.[2]

White rarely uses the word "leadership," but that is what he is describing.

Justification, credibility and imagination must work together in the achievement of fiscal success–we must "create, not merely consume, revenues."[3] Success is always, in the broad sense, political–it is not enough just to need or want something; we must sell the idea to others.

As with leadership in general, financial leadership must operate up, down, and sideways to be effective–up in dealing with higher administration, politicians, and donors; down in motivating, mentoring, and modeling staff; and sideways in working with professional organizations, peer institutions, and consortia. All are crucial to success. These relationships are not linear but web-like; people may play multiple roles.

FISCAL LEADERSHIP AND UPPER ADMINISTRATION

Financial resources can be considered "necessary" in several ways. Most important is the most obvious–to improve desired library services. But other, more political needs may surface–the need to meet accreditation standards, the desire to shine in comparison with others, the wish for academic or intellectual prestige. The skilled leader will be able to take advantage of these motives and funnel the resources gained into worthy outcomes.

To achieve this, library leaders must convince the administration (be it academic, public, school, or corporate) of their credibility, honesty, insight and vision.

Credibility is achieved first by demonstrating responsible stewardship of the resources already owned.

> Successful claims for new resources require clear evidence of the efficient and responsible use of existing resources, including internal reallocation as new program priorities emerge and older priorities weaken. Central administrators are most likely to commit new resources to units that not only stand high in institutional priorities but also have a demonstrated capacity for making hard decisions and using resources wisely.[4]

Such credibility is built on more than balancing the bottom line, important though that is, but on honestly conveying the realities of our situations. Information is rarely, if ever, free. Some may refer to the World Wide Web as "free," but anyone enmeshed in the world of T-1 lines, sophisticated modems, virus-scan software and firewalls can dispel that myth instantly. Even the proverbial "free" government documents require shelves to hold paper volumes, hardware to access databases, and librarians to select, catalog, and instruct.

Hiding the costs of information can be tempting but usually backfires in the long run. Administration needs to know the reality of having 15% journal inflation in a budget with a 3% increase. Silently reallocating funds to cover the shortfall only decimates other resources and avoids the hard decisions in which the entire community should participate. Put succinctly by White, "we can shift and transfer priorities, but quite simply a cut in budgets means a cut in something, and the ultimate responsibility for that rests with the people who decreed the budget cut."[5] But if we do not loudly and clearly communicate true costs, no one will assume this responsibility.

Budget transfers can be another way of hiding costs by dispersing them across an organization. Frequently popular with business offices, a charge-back system is often used for such services as photocopying, media production, even interlibrary loan. Proponents argue first that the system is "fair" because it only charges actual users and secondly that the system will reduce costs by damping demand. However, if the service in question is generally needed and contributes to the library's mission, we want to *increase,* not decrease, demand and users! We want our services–and their costs–to be visible, measurable, and agreed upon by our institution. We do not want our services available only to the highest bidder, nor do we want our priorities and policies determined by the same. A charge-back, or transfer system could conceivably lead to such dilemmas as having to handle hundreds of interlibrary loans for one person because "well, I'll pay for it!" On a more practical note, the costs of managing such a transfer system frequently exceed the so-called revenue gained (actually it is only institutional money being moved about). And the system may contribute to an unfortunate image of our staffs as detail-oriented nit-pickers. This shortsighted measure at best only succeeds in masking the true expense of library services, and at worst results in a loss of autonomy and control.

In short, library leaders must be pro-active in documenting the costs of programs and resources and in explaining the consequences of under-funding. Skillful use of statistics, cost studies and analytical models demonstrate accountability and therefore credibility. Also critical is assessment–we must convincingly justify the value and cost-effectiveness of our expenditures, both for resources and for people. Wise hiring is in fact one of the quickest ways to gain respect from administration, who should be receiving regular briefings on staff accomplishments. Contrary to popular lore, not all upper administrators want their employees to come cheap, but all want them to be cost effective! Assessment is relatively easy at the statistical level: Do the books circulate?

Are the librarians consulted? Are the databases accessed? More challenging is documenting actual results or outcomes: Is anything learned? Did the user actually find the information that led to a more successful term paper, auto repair, or medical decision?

After earning a reputation as a responsible steward, the library leader next must convince administration that he or she can see the big picture of organizational goals and objectives–and be willing to step back when confronted with a higher priority. The leader must be able to conceptualize and prioritize for the organization as a whole and to contribute valuable insights to institution-wide problems. While it is true that the computer technology department probably has supplanted the library as the proverbial "black hole" of fiscal resources, librarians must avoid being stereotyped as never satisfied. Acceptance as a valued senior manager rests upon the ability to put one's own concerns into perspective.

Wiemers argues succinctly:

> We should aim at gaining credibility within universities, not money. Not that money is unimportant, but in the long run, we need credibility more. We should listen to the priorities and categories of analysis in the institutions around us and try to be responsible to them. We should not give up trying for mutual understanding with institutional administrators on fiscal matters. We have more to gain from a shared understanding of the progress we do make in keeping up with the information revolution than we can gain in any single crisis budget year, because there will always be another budget crisis. We need to make clear the choices we are making among information products and services and the consequences of financial constraints rather than argue that the constraints should be lifted.[6]

Recognizing the many conflicting, worthwhile goals, how can the library manager get the library placed high on the list of its institution's priorities? Academic libraries must compete with scholarships and fiber optic cabling; public libraries with municipal sewage plants and law enforcement; school libraries with textbooks and asbestos removal; corporate libraries with management software and ad campaigns. All are necessary. In such a political environment, people skills are critical. If library managers have achieved credibility, established personal ties with decision-makers, and become known as team players, they will garner their share of the rewards.

In his superb article on reasserting the centrality of libraries in our institutions of higher learning, John Howe emphasizes both the difficulty and the importance of building constituencies:

> First of all, there is the essential task of constituency building, something basic to any political process. For libraries it presents special problems, for everyone is the library's constituency and yet no one is. Unlike instructional colleges, libraries do not award degrees and, thus, do not have alumni. Nor do they have influential associations dependent on them for professional training as, for example, medical or law schools do.
>
> The library's task of constituency-building, therefore, must be internal to the college or university and must focus on faculty, college deans, and central administrators. The task is not any easy one, for the central themes of institutional life in American higher education over the last half century have been growth and fragmentation, expansion and a weakening of common identity and purpose. We find unmistakable evidence of this centrifugal force in the proliferation and fragmentation of fields of knowledge; the chaotic structure of the curriculum and bitter encounters over the content and purpose, even the very viability, of commonly shared liberal education; the organizational fracturing of our colleges and universities as departments, centers, and research institutes proliferate; and in the face of this, the all-too-common emphasis on political brokering rather than creative, integrative vision among educational leaders. In such an educational and organizational environment, it is not surprising that our libraries also should have lost focus, or that library administrators should have difficulty knowing how to reach out and build political support.
>
> And yet, though the university environment is complex and often contentious, the library is one of the few agencies that is universal in its domain, that reaches across collegiate and divisional lines and supports the work of virtually everyone.[7]

Vision is a word often linked with leadership issues but sometimes difficult to define. We have watched national political figures struggle with "the vision thing"–to convince voters of their ability to be more than bureaucrats but still possessing substance beyond their public facades. We librarians often struggle similarly to shift our image from that of a detail-oriented, competent manager to that of a creative-far-thinking leader.

Vision in library-land rarely manifests itself as wild-eyed, charismatic idealism–particularly in financial circles. Instead, vision is clear communication of consistent goals, backed by the flexibility to respond effectively to unexpected problems and opportunities. Vision sees possibilities everywhere–in colleagues, in staff, in patrons, in donors–and has the sense to reprioritize and reposition as needed without losing sight of the library's main mission.

Outstanding leaders go a step further, positioning their personal vision with that of their larger institution. It is not always self-evident to others (although it usually is to us!) how the library's mission–and its related budget–enhances the broader organization. We must speak eloquently to this issue, often and to many audiences.

FINANCES AND STAFF

Howe reminds us that staffs are valued allies in the competition for resources. While a prime task of the library director, strategic constituency building presupposes and rests directly upon the active outreach of instruction and reference librarians, circulation staff and student assistants. Effective, innovative, outreaching service is essential for securing meaningful support.[8]

Staff must work in an environment where they feel comfortable bringing forward both good news and bad. Such an atmosphere is built through communicating problems and collaborating on goals, through soliciting opinions and truly listening to the responses, and through involving staff directly in the implementation of solutions. Like it or not, to many users, anyone who works in a library is a "librarian" and speaks with an official voice. Therefore, the whole staff should understand the budgeting process, campus priorities and realities, and the factors affecting financial resources. Extending this information to clerical and student workers, and to our patrons as well, can be particularly helpful.

Once knowledge is shared, leaders may emerge from unexpected places. A recent *C&RL News* article sings the praises of student advocates at Southwest Missouri State University who were the key to the success of a major building project.[9] Led by a student member of the Library Planning Committee, the SMSU student government passed resolutions, circulated petitions, and even visited the state capital to meet with legislators. Carefully coordinated and focussed, these actions added the critical voice necessary to raise SMSU's library expansion to priority funding level. Such advocacy, recognized and enhanced by library administrators, is leadership at its finest.

LOOKING OUTWARD

In today's economic world, all the internal politicking, hard work and good deeds may not be enough. We see a dramatic shift from public funding to private, particularly for private colleges and universities but increasingly for public ones as well. At the corporate and research level industrial funding often replaces federal money. The trend from public to private funding includes public libraries, and on occasion, school libraries as well. Consider the recent initiatives of the Gates Foundation in supplying technology to both public libraries and schools.

Over twenty years ago Breivik and Gibson[10] noted that leadership means both planning for funding alternatives and recognizing the unexpected. They suggested such alternatives as traditional capital campaigns, special events, government grants, and foundation funding. More recently, Corson-Finnerty and Blanchard bring these same themes into the digital world in *Fundraising and Friend-Raising on the Web*.[11] All agree that, whether campaigning for funds internally or externally, the basic tenets of credibility and communication remain the same. Nutter notes in her foreword to the classic *Becoming a Fundraiser* by Steele and Elder:

> The increasing diversity of library services will require library leaders to define and articulate to the communities they serve the mission and priorities of their libraries. If they cannot communicate a clear message about who they are, what they do, and why their health and growth are absolutely essential to the health of the community and the culture of which they are part, libraries will face institutional identity crises, both internally and externally. A fundraising-oriented development program provides a vehicle for explaining the nature and function of the library to the community in order to obtain the support needed to realize the full potential of the library of the future.[12]

While much has been written for librarians on the subject of grant writing, a challenging but often straightforward task, the art of development work requires additional leadership skills. Many librarians are uncomfortable asking for money, especially outside of regular budget channels; the cultivation of major donors can be daunting. "The biggest fundraising problem libraries face is that of being taken for granted. It is assumed that they will be available, well-stocked, and ready to serve on a weeklong, year-round basis–and without a direct charge to their customers."[13]

The library community excels at building partnerships and networking within itself; successful fund-raising requires transferring these skills to a broader arena. How well do we know our campus development officer, or the county planner? Who in our institutional world is known for money-raising skills, and how can we join with them? The plus side of libraries often being seen as essentially passive entities is that others will allow us a "piece of the action" without feeling threatened. While rarely garnering large sums, a budget line for "library resources" in a college history department grant or municipal planning program can effectively augment regular funds.

Less obvious partnerships are equally desirable although more rare. The leadership of football coach Joe Paterno in both personal giving and heading capital campaigns for Penn State Libraries is as legendary as his winning record. First Lady Barbara Bush's personal passion lent considerable weight to the literacy movement. Not all of us know celebrities, but such examples remind us to look beyond the obvious.

Successful development work is a constant–not a one-time event–and requires the energy for creative thinking, followed by assertive action once an opportunity is recognized. Dollars are not the only goal; development contacts may result in collection gifts, prestigious speakers, or resource sharing opportunities as well.

For the latter, an often valuable source of external funding are consortia and associations, which allow the advantage of recognizing–in fact, seeking out–partners with whom we have mutual goals. Wiemers challenges the assumption that cooperative activities are an add-on; in fact, "our ability to depend upon partners is fundamental to our success, not something we do once our basic needs are met at home."[14]

Examples abound of cooperative successes. In North Carolina, the NC LIVE project, brokered by the State Library and dozens of librarians working cooperatively, provides basic database services to all public and academic libraries across the state. Soon the project will expand to offer access to digitized special collections housed in state research libraries. The scope and cost of the project challenged the leadership skills of the State Librarian and her staff, of the sponsoring legislators, and of the many volunteer librarians who lobbied lawmakers, negotiated with vendors, and coordinated hardware and software purchases. Ongoing maintenance and enhancement of the project will bring additional challenges.

In areas as diverse as Massachusetts, Illinois, and Washington, shared automated systems bring sophisticated services to libraries unable to afford them alone. Often when such cooperative projects begin there is doubt and resistance to the idea of cooperation; only superb negotiation and cheerleading skills–i.e., leadership–prevail over the nay-sayers. Once mature, such cooperative projects may be taken for granted and languish; it is necessary for librarians at all levels to remain vigilant and cost-conscious. As with other activities, consortial costs must be justified regularly.

In the OCLC publication *Libraries and Leaders,* symposium speakers highlight cooperative success stories. In Colorado, the State Library partnered with SuperNet, an Internet service provider, obtained funding from private foundations and federal grants, and established ACLIN, Access Colorado Library and Information Network. Initially designed to provide state-wide telnet access to major library catalogs, the project has been upgraded to web access, has added a statewide contract for OCLC FirstSearch service, and established the state's first multi-type Governance Board. ACLIN's project director, Susan Fayad, summarizes:

> Librarians are not powerless people, and libraries are not powerless entities. However, our level of cooperation in providing service is unique and generally a source of surprise to those outside our ken. This is what makes information systems integration at various levels and from various aspects so important to how we function. It's a source of power we need to leverage and should probably exploit more by extending our cooperative efforts and alliances outside the library community. One thing ACLIN has taught us is that there are many (educators, social service agents, health workers, government employees) who share our values and goals.
>
> Finally, I think a cooperative endeavor is important as librarians move into the new networked information technology and examine how this can be applied to providing information services. The traditional role and mission of the library has not changed in the environment, but the need to explore the applications of these tools has created new stress and new possibilities for the library community. One of the most important leadership issues we face

> is how much of our resources we will redirect to this effort. We will certainly do better, as past experience has taught us, if we don't go it alone.[15]

At the same symposium, Kate Nevins describes similar activities on a regional level.[16] SOLINET, the Southeastern Library and Information Network, Inc., sought grants on behalf of its many members to pilot a project entitled "Linking Distributed Regional Resources," a decentralized online system which will provide uniform access to state, federal and local information for both library and government communities. The use of centralized expertise and funding has the potential for unlocking the mysteries of government information in all its diversity and complexity–and, not incidentally, to offer these benefits to member libraries at a fraction of the cost and effort needed to go it alone.

CONCLUSION

Every librarian at every level should have ready an answer–multiple answers–to the ubiquitous questions: Why do we still need libraries when everything is free on the web? How can you justify an expanding budget in the Internet Age?

Once again Howe summarizes the importance of leadership skills, "The politics of the budgetary process, in most of our institutions, is more complex and time-consuming than ever before. Often it seems to pull our energies away from what we want to do most of all. And yet, it sets the terms of institutional discourse and, in the final analysis, determines who will prosper and who will not. We ignore it at our own peril."[17]

To progress from competent fiscal manager to admired financial leader is not easy, and the path may not be obvious. Working from a base of honesty and integrity, leaders must forge imaginative and convincing links with their official funding agencies and with alternative sources of revenue. We must look to our mayors and college presidents, to our patrons and students, and especially to our colleagues as we seek to meet today's information challenges.

There is much to be learned. Several issues not investigated in depth in this article are the cultivation of major gifts and endowments, specific skills needed to work effectively with legislators on fiscal matters, and effective usage of Friends groups as fund-raising entities. All are worthy of in-depth review articles. Further research in positioning the library amidst the conflicting priorities of its larger organization–be it city government, a corporation or an educational institution–would be of benefit. Pursuing this topic in relation to public school libraries, often the most resource-poor of our colleagues, would be particularly valuable.

Finally, in an article entitled "Love Makes the World Go Round (but Money Makes Libraries Go Round)," the omnipresent White reminds us that in a political, bureaucratic environment, the most direct source of authority and power is money. He ends with cheerful words of wisdom, "Do what is doable, relax about what can't be done, and know which is which! . . . Get some money and spend it! Help make the world go round!"[18]

NOTES

1. Madeline J. Daubert, *Financial Management for Small and Medium-Sized Libraries* (Chicago: American Library Association, 1993).
2. Herbert S. White, "Why Outsourcing Happens, and What to Do about It," *American Libraries* 31 (January 2000): 66, 68, 70-71.
3. Meredith A. Butler, Thomas Galvin, and Suzanne Orlando, "Preparing Entrepreneurial Leaders for Tomorrow's Academic and Research Libraries," in *Continuity & Transformation: The Promise of Confluence: Proceedings of the Seventh National Conference of the Association of College and Research Libraries, Pittsburgh, Pennsylvania, March 29-April 1, 1995*, ed. Richard AmRhein (Chicago: Association of College and Research Libraries, 1995), 160.
4. John Howe, "Libraries and Funding: The Politics of the Budgetary Process in an Era of Decreasing Resources," in *Collection Management for the 1990s*, ed. Joseph J. Branin (Chicago: American Library Association, 1993), 48.
5. Herbert S. White, "Hiding the Cost of Information," *The Bottom Line.* 4 (Winter 1990): 15.
6. Eugene L. Wiemers, "Financial Issues for Collection Managers in the 1990s," in *Collection Management and Development: Issues in an Electronic Era*, ed. Peggy Johnson and Bonnie MacEwan (Chicago: American Library Association, 1994), 120.
7. Howe, 46-47.
8. Ibid., 47.
9. Karen L. Horny and Paul Seale, "Student Advocates: The Key to Successful Funding for a New Building," *C&RL News* 60 (1999): 899-902.
10. Patricia Senn Breivik and E. Burr Gibson, ed., *Funding Alternatives for Libraries* (Chicago: American Library Association, 1979).
11. Adam Corson-Finnerty and Laura Blanchard, *Fundraising and Friend-Raising on the Web* (Chicago: American Library Association, 1998).
12. Susan K. Nutter, "Foreword," in *Becoming a Fundraiser: The Principles and Practice of Library Development*, by Victoria Steele and Stephen D. Elder (Chicago: American Library Association, 1992), v-vi.
13. Corson-Finnerty and Blanchard, 3.

14. Wiemers, 119.

15. Susan Fayad, "Librarians as Leaders: The Statewide Perspective," in *Libraries as Leaders: Integrating Systems for Service: Proceeding of the OCLC Symposium, ALA Midwinter Conference, February 14, 1997* (Dublin, Ohio: OCLC Online Computer Library Center, Inc., 1997), 6.

16. Kate Nevins, "Order from Chaos: Libraries and Electronic Government Information," in *Libraries as Leaders: Integrating Systems for Service: Proceeding of the OCLC Symposium, ALA Midwinter Conference, February 14, 1997* (Dublin, Ohio: OCLC Online Computer Library Center, Inc., 1997), 16-19.

17. Howe, 49.

18. Herbert S. White, "Love Makes the World Go Round (but Money Makes Libraries Go Round)," *Library Journal*, 15 October 1989, 61.

Diversity and Leadership: The Color of Leadership

Camila A. Alire

SUMMARY. The author focuses on racial/ethnic diversity and the role leadership plays for emerging library leaders of color. The article covers the need for minority library leadership and the differences between white and minority leadership. Additionally, the author provides her five leadership categories followed by ten leadership realities of which readers should be aware. *[Article copies available for a fee from The Haworth Document Delivery Service: 1-800-342-9678. E-mail address: <getinfo@haworthpressinc.com> Website: <http://www.HaworthPress.com> © 2001 by The Haworth Press, Inc. All rights reserved.]*

KEYWORDS. Leadership, diversity, minorities, leadership traits, leadership development

When trying to present a spectrum of colors, a Crayola box full of yellow crayons is not a good box of crayons even if the yellow is the most beautiful color. If one could use this analogy as the theme for this whole article, then leadership and all its attributes become our professional box of crayons. If the library profession is concerned only about leadership as it relates to the predominant group of library leaders (white), then they have not achieved a leadership box of diverse colors. And if, in that profession, they want to fill their leadership box with various colors to sit side by side with and to complement their white leaders, then they need to strive for the development and placement of library leaders of color. Not until they can aggressively increase the numbers of minority leaders can they affect dramatic change in libraries and other library organizations.

This article focuses on diversity and leadership. The author recognizes the entire realm of diversity, such as gender, race, ethnicity, sex-

---

Camila A. Alire, PhD, is Dean of the University Libraries, Colorado State University, Fort Collins, CO.

[Haworth co-indexing entry note]: "Diversity and Leadership: The Color of Leadership." Alire, Camila A. Co-published simultaneously in *Journal of Library Administration* (The Haworth Information Press, an imprint of The Haworth Press, Inc.) Vol. 32, No. 3/4, 2001, pp. 95-109; and: *Leadership in the Library and Information Science Professions: Theory and Practice* (ed: Mark D. Winston) The Haworth Information Press, an imprint of The Haworth Press, Inc., 2001, pp. 95-109. Single or multiple copies of this article are available for a fee from The Haworth Document Delivery Service [1-800-342-9678, 9:00 a.m. - 5:00 p.m. (EST). E-mail address: getinfo@haworthpressinc.com].

© 2001 by The Haworth Press, Inc. All rights reserved.

ual orientation, creed, disabilities, et cetera. However, this article deals specifically with racial/ethnic diversity. Specific emphasis is placed on the *visible* racial/ethnic minorities–African Americans, Asian/Pacific Islanders, Latinos, and Native Americans. That is not to say that much of what is written here cannot be applied to the broader definition of diversity and leadership, in general, no matter the profession.

This article is written for those emerging library leaders of color and for those who want to understand the complexities of minority leadership. The author will cover topics related to why minorities need to be in library leadership positions; the differences between white and minority leadership; leadership traits, to include the author's five leadership categories and 10 leadership realities for emerging leaders of color; and a lesson on marginal leadership.

WHY MINORITIES AS LEADERS?

Around the mid-90s, it was reported that one out of every four people in the United States was a minority. It is predicted that around 2000 or soon after, one out of every three people in this country will be a minority. These kinds of data reflect on the service communities of libraries no matter the type of library being considered–public, academic, school, and to some extent, special libraries. These data reflect on whom we should be hiring to serve such diverse communities and who should be *leading* these efforts.

So why should there be such a push to develop minorities as leaders? First, there should be recognition of a basic premise that institutions need to commit to achieving diversity. Minority librarians, who find themselves in leadership positions within a library or other organization, can advocate for organizational change. They can serve as role models, leaders, and spokespersons and provide the necessary linkages to minority communities (however the community is defined), as the minority population grows and as the demographics of this country shift. Who best to articulate diversity and provide the necessary platform to enable library organizations to align their missions with the unique realities of our growing multicultural society than library leaders of color?

Minorities can fit well into those changing organizations because of their knowledge, skills, and experiences. Minority leaders bring cultural competencies to their positions, states Isaura Santiago Santiago.[1]

What falls into the category of cultural competencies? Santiago continues to state that the minority leaders' "ability to carry out their jobs is largely dependent on the extent to which they have the respect of those they seek to lead."[2] So many times people within an organization will have the perception that a leader of color was selected because of preferential treatment. However, many who hold that perception fail to realize that the minority leader's cultural competencies enhance the valid scope of his/her qualifications. What the minority leader brings to the position is knowledge of minority history and culture; evidence of supporting services to minorities; and possible linguistic abilities.[3]

Dr. Chang-Lin Tien, the renowned Chancellor Emeritus of University of California at Berkeley, truly believes that leaders of color should rely on their traditional cultural heritages and the extent of their life experiences, as minorities, to help them lead. Tien states that relying on one's cultural competencies provides minority leaders with extra resources, enriched insights, and lessons in confronting challenges.[4]

There are other reasons why we need diversity in library leadership. Leaders of color are instrumental in recognizing the value of diversity within their library organizations. These leaders can create an environment where no one is disadvantaged (or preferred) because of race, ethnicity, creed, gender, sexual orientation, et cetera. Who better to lead the efforts in looking for obstacles in achieving diversity in the library organizational policies and procedures? And why is that? It's because minority leaders have the natural awareness and sensitivity to know for what to look. In addition, minority leaders have to heighten sensitivity to diversity within their rank and file and must get organizations to expend their energies in looking for the benefits of diversity. This includes leading the old guard within the libraries to accept the value of diversity and to cope with the dynamics of change diversity brings. With this comes the responsibility of minority leaders to provide the necessary staff development that will inform and help employees along.

Eugenia Prime, the manager of corporate libraries for Hewlett-Packard, said when interviewed that, with all the challenges and obstacles minorities face growing up in a white society, they have learned/developed the courage to act.[5] This, in itself, is an important leadership trait leaders of color would bring to any organization.

If there are legitimate reasons for minorities to assume leadership positions in our library and information management profession, then are there perceived differences between minority leadership and white leadership? The author says yes.

DIFFERENCES BETWEEN WHITE AND MINORITY LEADERSHIP

Minorities themselves view differences between white and minority leadership. These include factors such as a two-pronged leadership agenda, dispelling stereotypes, and proof of self.

Minority leaders can find themselves developing a two-pronged leadership agenda. This includes leading in a predominantly white society and doing what is necessary to lead other minorities. White leaders perceive themselves as leading all followers no matter who they are. Minority leaders assume that same position but also assume the additional responsibility of identifying and developing emerging minority leaders. It is a type of self-perpetuating phenomenon. That is, to prepare to lead in a country of an emerging majority, leaders of color need to insure that they are preparing more minorities to assume leadership positions. Does this mean that minority leaders should not be involved in the leadership development of all people? Absolutely not. What it means is that minority leaders have to use added energies to lead and develop other minorities.

Another difference between white and minority leadership concerns leaders of color dispelling negative stereotypes when white leaders do not have to do so. What are some of those stereotypes? One is the perception of preferential treatment in hiring that was discussed earlier. Another stereotype involves the perception of minority leaders as only successful in leading other minorities. This separate but equal approach is far from the truth. One leadership quality that prevails in most minority cultures is respect. This cultural trait comes from emphasis on the tradition of respecting one's elders. Because of this, minority leaders have learned that if they treat all people with respect then this allows them to handle conflict with respect. It is because of this that minority leaders are as effective leading white followers as minority followers.

Another stereotype that affects minority leaders relates to communication skills, particularly the perception of their not being able to communicate effectively because of strong accents. Dr. Tien says it so eloquently when he states that people in this country tend to perceive European accents to be more prestigious. However, people with Latino and Asian accents are perceived to be ignorant, uneducated, and unequal. This can be no further from the truth, and Tien maintains that accents can make some people feel more comfortable especially if they have relatives with accents.[6]

Minority leaders are ineffective because the major stakeholders in higher positions are predominantly white. This stereotype implies that leaders of color do not have the standard leadership traits (such as vision, excellent communication skills, excellent human relations skills, integrity, respect, decision-making abilities, and many more) that can influence leaders and stakeholders who hold leadership positions higher than the minority leaders. Very effective leaders are successful because of the leadership qualities and skills, traits they employ, no matter their color and/or their level of importance. However, *if* leaders of color, who are successful at leadership everywhere else within and outside of their organizations, find themselves ineffective with the stakeholders, then it may be due to individual and/or institutional racism. Institutional racism denotes that the values, beliefs, and traditions of one race are so imbedded in the institution that minorities who come in with a different set are not accepted because of those differences.

One last stereotype to mention is that organizations cannot achieve excellence through diversity or that promoting diversity denotes substandard leadership behavior. Again, members of diverse populations are quite capable of successful or unsuccessful leadership. What determines commendable leadership is the ability of leaders to perform using all of their leadership traits successfully.

Once the stereotypes of diversity leadership are exposed, how do we then dispel them? The answer is simple: through the actions of minority leaders. If the counterpoints to all the stereotypes of diversity leadership mentioned earlier are true, then all leaders of color have to do is act on them. Action is louder than words and to try to dispel those stereotypes by talking about them would take too much time and be very ineffective.

The third difference of minority leadership recognized by leaders of color is the concept of proof of self. Are minority leaders expected to perform at a higher level than their white counterparts? For the most part, minorities think that they are held to a higher standard. This may be more the case with emerging minority leaders. They are scrutinized from the beginning of their time in a leadership position by people anticipating failure and waiting to say, "I told you so; that's what happens when you hire someone based on preferential treatment." Those library leaders of color who are well-established as leaders locally, statewide, and nationally, may not experience the same attitudes and scrutiny at that point in their careers.

If there are perceived differences between white and minority leadership, then are there differences in the leadership traits among the two groups? The next section covers this topic.

LEADERSHIP TRAITS OF MINORITIES

In order for minorities to be successful, are their leadership qualities and traits different than those of white leaders? The answer is no. However, that is not to say that emerging minority leaders ought not to concentrate on specific leadership traits to help them become more successful as leaders.

Appendix A is the author's list of leadership qualities, traits and skills. This list was compiled from experience, discussions, and observation of library leaders of color and other leaders, and reinforced in the literature. In Appendix B, the author categorizes the same leadership qualities and traits into five major areas–charismatic, visionary, personal, organizational, and leadership development. Many of these qualities and traits can fit into more than one area but were categorized based on what was considered the best fit.

These five categories and some of the qualities within each category are the emphasis of this section. According to the author, the qualities emphasized are particularly relative to guiding emerging library leaders of color, with the intent of diversifying the leadership box of crayons. Additionally, the author's ten leadership realities for emerging leaders of color are presented and discussed.

CHARISMATIC: Much has been written about transformational leadership wherein this quality lies.[7] Charismatic leaders usually serve as change agents who are enthusiastic, inspirational, and motivational in implementing their vision. They have excellent communication skills in articulating their thoughts, persuading others, and listening to others. These communication skills are what make minority library leaders successful in building teams and working collaboratively.

Reality #1 for emerging minority leaders: *First of all, they do not have to have a certain personality to be charismatic leaders.* When they read all of the qualities under the charismatic heading in Appendix B, they may think that they describe a certain personality type. Not true; this is a common misperception. When looking at established library leaders of color at all levels, they will find a multitude of personalities, as they would find among white library leaders.

For the emerging minority leaders, they need to pay attention to the qualities leaders exude and not necessarily to their personality styles. They should not assume that because they do not have a similar personality that they can not be leaders.

One of the more charismatic, renowned, and most respected minority leaders in the field of library and information management is E. J. Josey. Dr. Josey has a reserved, quiet personality, in the author's estimation. Yet, he is one of the most inspirational, empowering, and influential leaders ever in our profession. Emerging minority leaders who most mirror his personality can be as successful as a charismatic leader as can emerging minority leaders who have more outgoing, extroverted personalities.

VISIONARY: Visionary leaders know not only where they are leading their library organizations, but they also work diligently using their charismatic qualities to implement that vision collaboratively with others. The author strongly contends that leaders must also be effective administrators/managers. That is, leadership is more than vision; good leaders need to translate their vision into action by working to make their ideas become real. Quinn confirms that it is not enough to have vision. Leaders also have to provide hands-on administration necessary to set goals to achieve that vision, to work on problem-solving relative to implementation, and to monitor the progress.[8]

Emerging minority leaders need to feel comfortable with delegating or *letting go* and allowing their followers to assist aggressively in implementing the organization's vision. This can be difficult for many emerging leaders, regardless of race, because once they achieve that level of leadership, there is a tendency to keep tight reins on their vision, ideas and activities. The old adage, "if you want something done well, do it yourself," does not fit well with leaders effectively delegating responsibilities and activities.

Visionary leaders need to be adaptable, versatile, flexible, and tolerant of ambiguity. Leaders, as those who strive for implementation and progress and who have delegated to others, must adopt these traits to allow the shared process of vision implementation to proceed.

Reality #2 for emerging leaders of color: *Having vision is one of the most misunderstood leadership qualities.* Many emerging library leaders, in general, tend to think of visionaries as the likes of Dewey, White, Lancaster, Josey and others. It can be mind-boggling for emerging leaders of color who think that they need to be in that same category of leaders to have vision.

First, the demystification of being visionary needs to happen. Yates wrote that vision is no more than an outline of where you want your organization to be in the future.[9] Thus, there is nothing mystical about creating vision.

Reality #3 for emerging leaders of color: *They do not have to create their organizations' vision alone.* Shared vision makes sense; it follows the team-building and collaborative concepts of leadership. This allows others to brainstorm and create other ideas and possibilities, along with those of the minority leaders. Additionally, it allows others to take ownership and buy-in in the process and results.

Reality #4 for emerging leaders of color: *As is the case in many other professions, library leaders of color usually find themselves leading in mostly white organizations.* They should not make this an issue. As emerging leaders of color, they need only to help create their vision and to possess some of the various qualities mentioned in this and other articles to lead, no matter their race or ethnicity. They should not fall for any self-fulfilling prophecies of failure and then blame the organization. Effective, charismatic leaders of color can lead in any situation. Granted they may have to prove themselves first; however, that should not be hard to accomplish.

PERSONAL: The leadership qualities and traits that the author has placed in this category may deal more with personal traits. However, they are equally as important.

"Once you lose your integrity, everything else is a piece of cake." This is a saying posted in the author's office. Leaders will find themselves facing dilemmas–many times ethical and moral dilemmas. How they handle those dilemmas will be a true measure of their integrity. Integrity should be one of the first personal, guiding leadership principles of all emerging leaders of color. There is never room to compromise one's integrity. When followers see leaders with integrity, they become even more respectful and trusting of them and their leadership abilities.

Another personal quality that minority library leaders bring to leadership (one could say, almost naturally) is cultural sensitivity. In our ever-changing demographics of this country, this can be quite advantageous. Emerging leaders of color need to know how to market their own cultural competencies and their sensitivity to other cultural differences and how to make those strong leadership qualities.

Reality #5 for emerging leaders: *One of the best lessons leaders of color can learn when growing and advancing within their profession is how to face and handle adversity.* It is not easy being a minority, in almost every aspect of daily life except within one's family. It makes one develop the tough skin that is necessary for many leaders of color to lead. Better said, emerging leaders should not take adversity and conflict personally.

Unfortunately, for some minorities, adverse experiences are so damaging that they never overcome them. Emerging leaders of color, however, need to turn such negatives into positives. People learn more from their bad experiences than their good experiences. Learning to overcome adversity helps to develop minority leaders' self-confidence and sense of worth. It may also provide an adequate, if not ideal, way to prepare them in this regard.

Reality #6 for emerging leaders of color: *It is okay to be ambitious.* That tends to be one personal leadership trait of which minorities need not be ashamed. Webster's dictionary defines ambitious as "having a desire to achieve a particular goal." Ambition is not recognized as a positive trait in many cultures. Rarely are minorities taught or coached in *ambition*. If wanting to lead a library organization is the goal of many emerging minority leaders, then it is okay to be ambitious.

ORGANIZATIONAL: Two qualities surface here–decision-making abilities and political savvy. Although many of the other traits listed in Appendix A could fit under this area, these two are the best fit. Minority leaders must be decisive; this can make or break any emerging leader. Deciding not to make a decision is decision-making, albeit poor or wrong, and the results may be damaging. In general, followers expect a leader to make the hard decisions.

The other quality–political savvy–is very important to library organizations. For emerging leaders of color, this is best learned by observing those leaders who are excellent at it. Political savvy can range from deciding which battles the leader wants to fight (given all the political ramifications) to determining what coalitions must be built to achieve specific results. Emerging minority leaders have to pay particular attention to this leadership quality. It can affect the organization in a positive or negative way.

Reality #7 for emerging leaders of color: *They need to remember that it is more important to be respected for the decisions they make than to be popular or liked for making them.* No matter what decisions they make, leaders will be supported by some and opposed by others. They should use caution not to make decisions because they might be the most popular; they should make decisions based on what is best for their organizations. Followers will respect leaders more for making the hard decisions and respect them less for making the popular decisions.

Reality #8 for emerging leaders: *Political faux pas will happen in their leadership careers.* They can learn from those experiences to determine what to do or not to do to prevent them from happening again. They must view the mistakes as setbacks and not as failures. Leaders do not fail; they just experience setbacks.

LEADERSHIP DEVELOPMENT: A professional obligation of a seasoned leader of color is leadership development. This should be taken seriously. If minority leaders want to make a difference in the library profession, they must take the time to develop emerging minority leaders. The leadership qualities that fall under leadership development are effective networking, role modeling, and mentoring.

As minority leaders expand their spheres of influence, they develop a vast network of other library leaders, as well as librarians and other professionals. These networking activities are a part of leadership involvement that not only help the seasoned leader of color but also help emerging minority leaders with appropriate connections. Getting emerging leaders involved in professional activities, as well as referring them for better positions that can help develop their leadership capabilities, are all part of this networking process.

Another aspect of leadership development is the emphasis placed on seasoned minority leaders' role-modeling. As they perform, lead, and handle themselves under favorable and adverse conditions, they are being observed whether they like it or not. Consequently, serving as role models for emerging leaders provides a constant reminder that should mold their leadership behavior.

Mentoring as a leadership development activity is the most time-consuming of the three. Again, as a professional obligation, seasoned leaders of color need to provide the necessary time and effort to mentor emerging leaders. Mentoring is passing the gift of what one has learned and experienced to others. There are different ways to mentor; however, in a mentoring relationship, the parties need to be flexible in adjusting to what fits with the individuals involved. The author maintains that if leaders do not mentor (formally or informally), then they are not truly leaders.

One other concept to mention with regard to leadership development concerns leadership being learned. There is no genetic predisposition for leadership abilities. People who claim that all leaders are born have not experienced the blossoming of individuals into leadership positions, given the right opportunities, timing, and training. Some people may take to leadership skills almost naturally while others may have to work harder to learn how to be good leaders.

Reality #9 for emerging leaders of color: *They need to be serious about their leadership development because their performances will be a reflection on the seasoned leader(s) who mentor(s) them.* If seasoned minority leaders are working to advance emerging leaders of color in their leadership development and careers, the new leaders need to make sure that they work hard at these endeavors. Their reputations, either as hard workers or individuals who don't act and/or follow through, will soon precede them.

There is one general reality that should be mentioned before moving on to the idea of marginalized leadership:

Reality #10 for emerging leaders of color: *They should not discriminate.* This is to say that emerging minority leaders can learn from *all* seasoned library leaders. Even though the multicolored crayons enhance the diversity in the box of Crayolas, the yellow crayons are still important. There is a multitude of white library leaders who are also very committed to increasing the leadership of color within the library and information management profession. Emerging leaders of color should observe and learn from them; benefit from their networks; and, be receptive to mentoring relationships with them. Regardless of color, people can learn from each other.

The next section discusses the concept of marginal leadership. This is usually the first type of leadership circumstance in which emerging leaders find themselves.

A LESSON IN MARGINALIZED LEADERSHIP

What happens to the emerging minority leaders when they don't find themselves at the same level of leadership as their white counterparts–in lower level positions and with lesser spheres of influence? They become marginalized as leaders; another reality of professional life.

Valverde does an excellent job of describing the concept of *leading from the margins.* This concept is common relative to the development of minority leaders. If emerging minority library leaders are marginalized, then they need to know how to influence in non-traditional ways:

- They need to excel in their positions, such that they earn respect and build a following.
- They need to draw attention to their efforts by promoting new ideas, concepts, programs, and/or services.
- They need to beat the bushes to recruit more librarians of color into the organization.
- They need to be assertive in trying to secure external funds to start new projects.[10]

Overall, marginalized minority leaders need to develop a "support base that empowers them when they speak and produces the perception that they can command respect."[11]

Marginalized leadership is library leadership without authority, formal power, and/or status. In the library profession, leaders with power usually are library directors, associate directors, department heads, and highly-positioned librarians within the professional associations. However, there are advantages associated with leading from the margins. Unlike the formal leaders, marginalized leaders of color can raise questions and focus hard on one issue. They can adopt different strategies because the opportunities and constraints differ from those for the formal leaders. For example, formal leaders do not have the luxury of focusing on one issue. Additionally, formal leaders will have many stresses that a multitude of issues generates. Marginalized leaders can learn how to understand their formal leaders' efforts to reduce stress. This can be advantageous for marginal leaders down the road.

If marginalized leadership is the way for minorities to get started, then they should do it. They can generate energy and enthusiasm as marginalized leaders. However, they need to pay careful attention to the organizational barometers and not become the focus for attacks. Marginalized leaders, through their experiences learned from trial and error, can determine how far or fast they can push their organizations.

Valverde discusses three connecting leadership strategies to move minority leaders out of the margins. These include mentoring (the marginalized leaders as proteges), networking, and ad hoc leadership development that includes partnerships and collaborations.[12]

CONCLUSION

It is the intention of this article particularly to assist emerging leaders of color. Ideas such as why minorities need to be in library leadership positions; the differences between white and minority leadership; leadership traits to include the author's five leadership categories and ten leadership realities for emerging leaders of color; and, thoughts on marginal leadership were addressed. Everyone benefits from diverse leadership and leadership styles. Thus, those in the library profession need to act aggressively to increase the numbers of minority leaders in order to affect dramatic change in libraries, other library organizations, and the respective communities. In so doing, they create the opportunity for library leadership to represent the spectrum of diversity, as does the multicolored box of crayons.

NOTES

1. Isaura Santiago Santiago, "Increasing the Latino Leadership Pipeline: Institutional and Organizational Strategies," in Raymond C. Bowen and Gilbert H. Muller, eds., *Achieving Administrative Diversity.* (San Francisco: Jossey-Bass Publishers, 1996): 25-38.

2. Ibid., 32.

3. Ibid., 31.

4. Chang-Lin Tien, "Challenges and Opportunities for Leaders of Color," in Leonard A. Valverde and Louis A. Castenell, eds., *The Multicultural Campus: Strategies for Transforming Higher Education.* (Walnut Creek, CA: Altamira Press, 1998): 33-34.

5. Evan St. Lifer, "Prime Leadership," *Library Journal* 123 (September, 1998): 36-38.

6. Tien, "Challenges and Opportunities," 39.

7. Brian Quinn, "Librarians' and Psychologists' View of Leadership; Converging and Diverging Perspectives," *Library Administration and Management Quarterly* 13 (Summer 1999): 147-157. John Ramsden, *Learning to Lead in Higher Education* (London: Rutledge, 1998): 113-115. David Orenstein, "Developing Quality Managers and Quality Management: The Challenge to Leadership in Library Organizations," *Library Administration and Management Quarterly* 13 (Winter 1999): 1-10. Shirley A. Kirkpatrick and Edwin A. Locke, "Direct and Indirect Effects of Three Core Charismatic Leadership Components on Performance and Attitudes," *Journal of Applied Psychology* 18 (May 1995): 37-38.

8. Quinn, "Librarians' and Psychologists' View of Leadership," 150.

9. Albert C. Yates, "Presidential Leadership and Diversity: The First Step," in Suzanne Benally, Jere J. Mock, and Morgan Odell, eds., *Pathways to the Multicultural Community: Leadership, Belonging, and Involvement.* (Boulder: Western Interstate Commission on Higher Education): 10.

10. Leonard A. Valverde, "Future Strategies and Actions: Creating Multicultural Higher Education Campuses," in Leonard A. Valverde and Louis A. Castenell, eds., *The Multicultural Campus: Strategies for Transforming Higher Education.* (Walnut Creek, CA: Altamira Press, 1998): 27-28.

11. Ibid., 28.

12. Ibid.

APPENDIX A

LIST OF LEADERSHIP QUALITIES, TRAITS AND SKILLS

Adaptable
Advocating for change
Ambiguity-tolerant
Ambitious
Charismatic
Collaborative
Communicating effectively

Creative
Culturally sensitive
Decision-making
Delegating
Enthusiastic
Flexible
Human interacting
Implementing
Influential
Innovative
Inspirational
Integrity
Mentoring
Motivational
Networking
Optimistic
Persuasive
Politically savvy
Powerful (empowering)
Respectful
Risk-taking
Role-modeling
Self-confident
Sense of humor
Sense of self-worth
Team-building
Trusting
Versatile

APPENDIX B

CATEGORIES ON LEADERSHIP QUALITIES, TRAITS, AND SKILLS

Charismatic
Advocating for change
Collaborative
Communicating effectively
Enthusiastic
Inspirational
Motivational
Optimistic

Powerful (empowerment)
Risk-taking
Team-building

<u>Visionary</u>
Adaptable
Ambiguity-tolerant
Creative
Delegating
Flexible
Implementing
Innovative
Versatile

<u>Personal</u>
Ambitious
Culturally sensitive
Integrity
Respectful
Self-confident
Sense of humor
Sense of self-worth

<u>Organizational</u>
Decision-making
Politically savvy

<u>Leadership Development</u>
Mentoring
Networking
Role modeling

Women and Leadership

Betty J. Turock

SUMMARY. The evolution of thought about women and leadership is set against the background of feminist research and theory. The past content and scope of leadership and the dimensions that shaped it are compared with and contrasted to current concepts to determine ways to better prepare women for library leadership in the future. Four interactive phases of perception and change are described to illuminate the forces continuing to keep women from contributing to library leadership to their maximum potential. Empowerment strategies are denoted and processes and programs suggested to assist in developing leadership equity. A model for the creation of a national educational program for leadership empowerment is recommended. *[Article copies available for a fee from The Haworth Document Delivery Service: 1-800-342-9678. E-mail address: <getinfo@haworthpressinc.com> Website: <http://www.HaworthPress.com> © 2001 by The Haworth Press, Inc. All rights reserved.]*

KEYWORDS. Feminist theory, feminist research, women leaders, empowerment, change

Over time scientists have recognized that a true technological revolution, arising from the synergistic impact of many simultaneous innovations, precipitates radical alterations not only in the economy, but also in social institutions, their governance, and the requirements for their leadership.[1,2] For librarians, pressed by fast-changing technology

---

Betty J. Turock, PhD, is Professor at Rutgers University, School of Communication, Information and Library Studies.

The author wishes to acknowledge the assistance of Jennifer Dunne, PhD candidate at Rutgers University, in locating the resources, preparing the list of references, and editing this manuscript.

[Haworth co-indexing entry note]: "Women and Leadership." Turock, Betty J. Co-published simultaneously in *Journal of Library Administration* (The Haworth Information Press, an imprint of The Haworth Press, Inc.) Vol. 32, No. 3/4, 2001, pp. 111-132; and: *Leadership in the Library and Information Science Professions: Theory and Practice* (ed: Mark D. Winston) The Haworth Information Press, an imprint of The Haworth Press, Inc., 2001, pp. 111-132. Single or multiple copies of this article are available for a fee from The Haworth Document Delivery Service [1-800-342-9678, 9:00 a.m. - 5:00 p.m. (EST). E-mail address: getinfo@haworthpressinc.com].

© 2001 by The Haworth Press, Inc. All rights reserved.

brought about through the convergence of computers, video and telecommunications and the effects of increased global connections on local service, it has become more crucial than ever to move to new leadership paradigms that will result in libraries remaining powerful social forces throughout the twenty-first century.

To that end, since ours is a profession in which women have constituted a near constant figure of 85%, this article will concentrate on issues relevant to women and leadership. The point is not to debate whose style provides better leaders, men or women–a divisive stance at best–but to develop more inclusive patterns for leadership that will provide new understandings and directions for the future.

At the same time, a landmark study from the Hudson Institute, *Workforce 2000,* cannot be ignored. It reports that one of the most significant changes affecting twenty-first century leadership across all organizations is that members of the available workforce will come from more dramatically diverse backgrounds.[3] Although another article in this collection deals in depth with the examination of minorities and leadership, to maintain the most comprehensive framework possible within the limitations of this paper's focus, it is important to emphasize that many of the issues raised in this discussion of women and leadership have implications for multiculturalism, the aging of the workforce and increased openness about sexual orientation.

Greater diversity in leadership has become more than a social and moral question; it is a necessity for the economic growth and progress of our nation. Increasing diversity will not only capture unique leadership talents, it will also yield benefits in innovation and creativity that arise as a result of divergent perspectives brought to problems from those with different backgrounds and life experiences. Noting parallels between women and leadership and leadership in diverse groups can also expand the perspective developed here on the necessity for and the effects of changing leadership paradigms.

In one of the few recent articles written about the relationship between gender and library leadership, Paula Kaufman contends, "In the last two decades women have made notable strides in reaching leadership positions."[4] Data from the Association of Research Libraries, 1988 to 1999, demonstrate that women have moved from leading 28% of the largest libraries in the country to leading 47% and have attained parity in salary.[5] The Public Library Association's Statistical Report shows a similar progression continuing into the 1990s.[6] But none of these figures reflect women in leadership ranks in proportion to their numbers in the profession.

According to a survey conducted across professions by the Women's Research and Education Institute, the lack of women leading organizations continues to be the case in large part because of gender misconceptions and stereotypes indicating that women do not possess the characteristics necessary for top leadership roles.[7] Systematic discrimination, through occupational segregation–that is, a concentration of men and women in occupations that occurs when 70% or more of the jobholders are of one sex–also remains a serious social problem that has not been solved by either legislative or judicial action.[8] Jobs statistically dominated by men have higher status and pay better than those in which women are concentrated. Kaufman's conclusion, that the trend toward more women in leadership positions will continue, overlooks the necessity of rooting out the discrimination and occupational segregation that are still prevalent in librarianship.

THE FEMINIST PERSPECTIVE

In a profession numerically dominated by women, but until recent history led almost exclusively by men, it is appropriate to consider the feminist perspective in addressing the evolution of research and scholarship regarding the issue of women and leadership. In fact, it is surprising that to date so little attention has been paid to the illumination of women and leadership found in feminist literature. Perhaps the early negativism attached to the term feminism has dissuaded us from its pursuit. A recent definition supplied in Margaret Karsten's *Management and Gender: Issues and Attitudes* is apropos to the feminist approach taken here, i.e., that feminism does not claim women are superior to men nor does it esteem masculine or feminine behaviors at the expense of the other. It does reject negative cultural images of women as weak or incompetent and affirms their ability to be strong, intelligent and ethical leaders.

Feminist leadership attends to advocating fair opportunities for women and demanding the respect to which women's abilities and intellect entitle them. It includes personal agency not only to remember where we are in time in terms of women's rights, but also to take on what we must to bring society to a place where all women will be treated fairly.[9] On this basis anyone, not just women, can be a feminist. The term refers to a belief system rather than to traits that have been labeled as feminine. It is anchored in the conviction that we cannot develop ourselves unless we are committed to the development of others.

Among the more fruitful feminist works on which librarianship can draw is that of Margaret McIntosh,[10] who has identified interactive phases of perception and change, both personal and theoretical, which can be adapted to the study of women and leadership within the library profession. Her framework enables us to answers the questions:

- What was the past content and scope of leadership theory?
- What were the dimensions that shaped it?
- What is the present content and scope of leadership theory?
- How does our approach to leadership need to change to prepare library leaders better for the future?

The phases of perception, as adapted from McIntosh, are:

> Phase I. *Womanless Leadership* in which women are invisible, leadership is exclusively the province of men and only a few exceptional women become part of history.
>
> Phase II. *Women as a Leadership Anomaly* in which women are perceived as having problems that must be corrected to enter the ranks of effective leaders.
>
> Phase III. *Women as Leaders* in which women take the initiative to propose new views of leadership and to lead in ways that arise from a different base of assumptions.
>
> Phase IV. *Leadership Redefined* in which reconstruction leads to the inclusion of all in the leadership patterns crucial for future success.

In her model, issues identified in the initial phases do not disappear over time or as other phases appear, rather they remain to form a more inclusive body of knowledge that allows us to see the dominant modes of thought and behavior which we need to continue to challenge and change.

PHASE I. WOMANLESS LEADERSHIP

McIntosh refers to womanless leadership as an exclusive phase, where lack of common knowledge of the history of women and cultural expectations of them made women invisible as leaders. We seldom learned about the contributions of women over the course of human history or looked at what kept women out of visible leadership positions.

Little more than one hundred years ago women accepted the ideal of the "true woman" and confined their role to the private and domestic domains. Men, on the other hand, operated in the public domain, where they played powerful roles as leaders in formulating policy, populating government, and shaping institutions.[11] While early feminists accomplished their purpose of securing the right to vote for women, that was the only radical stance they took. Admitted to the ranks of voters, they were not expected to speak with authority; that was to remain the province of men. Nor were women to raise their voice against authority.[12] It is imperative to remember that, even now, finding the voice of authority on which to anchor leadership is not easy for many librarians. Deep-seated belief in the old norms persist, giving rise to two sets of coexisting standards. Some follow the old script even as they struggle to resolve contradictions with the new one. That struggle too frequently compromises the development of the voice of authority needed for leadership.

Berger and Luckmann's *The Social Construction of Reality* reminds us that the world of knowledge was constituted by cultural authority figures.[13] Men not only defined leadership, they also determined what was incorporated in knowledge about it. Looking at the American Library Association (ALA), the largest professional library organization in the world, validates this perspective of library leadership over time. In the early years of ALA, men dominated its leadership and only a few exceptional women were accorded a place in the historical record. The data show that of the fifteen Executive Directors from 1890 to 1972, fourteen men served in that position alone except for one year–1890 to 1891–in which a man and a woman occupied it jointly. The record of elected officers documents a similar picture. From the inception of the Association in 1876 until 1984, no woman was elected to the four-year post of Treasurer. And of the 86 elected to the presidency from 1876 to 1970, only fifteen, or 17%, were women.[14]

Since 1972, Executive Directors have been evenly balanced in gender, with three women and three men holding the position. Of five Treasurers, four, or 80%, have been women. Of thirty-one Presidents, twenty, or 65% have been women.[15] The picture has changed, but not so radically that the contributions of women to the leadership of the profession are reflected in their fullest. Too many women labor quietly behind the scenes, while the leadership successes of men are more broadly broadcast throughout the profession.

PHASE II. WOMEN AS ANOMALIES OR PROBLEMS IN LEADERSHIP

Research in the 1950s focused on understanding men's leadership behavior. Women who did not conform to masculine models were eliminated from studies that invariably concluded leadership was predominantly a male endowment. Through the social turbulence of 1960s and into the 1970s the focus shifted and concentrated on the differences between men and women as leaders. Research continually reiterates that internal barriers kept women from being right for leadership roles. These studies began from a male standard and assumed that if women didn't fit the model, they were deficient. Difference was seen as deprivation. Women were depicted as either deprived or problematic. Feminist literature tells us that women internalized the view that they were deviants, and questioned their ability to lead without significant work on themselves and their skills. Stereotypical differences between male and female leaders were frequently given a nonstereotypical slant; that is, female leaders were depicted in ways opposite to stereotypes. The assumption was that women leaders had to be exceptional to compensate for early socialization experiences that were different from men.[16]

Mary Hartman has enlightened us about this period by observing:

> Mainstream literature discovered women as subjects, although it began not by asking what was wrong with leadership that so few women were singled out as leaders, but rather what was wrong with women that they had not achieved more leadership positions. It then provided different versions of the same bleak answer: certain rooted female behaviors are antithetical to successful leadership.[17]

For some time the single thing that came out of these studies was that women should act more like men.

Betty Lehan Harragan's *Games Mother Never Taught You* urged women to recognize that organizations were modeled on the military, making them alien cultures to women.[18] In *The Managerial Woman,* Margaret Hennig and Anne Jardim advised studying football to master the male concept of a "personal strategy," which meant "winning by achieving a goal or reaching an objective."[19] Without training in team sports, they concluded, "women get bogged down in definitions of process; in planning, and in finding the best way." Women, they said, saw a career "as personal growth, as self-fulfillment, as satisfaction, as making contributions to others" and "lacked men's focus on the question, 'What's in it for me?' "[20] Because they were not accustomed to playing on a team for a coach, women made the mistake of trying to measure up to their own standards, whereas men recognized the need to "center on their bosses' expectations." Men had a larger capacity to dissemble and veil their feelings, which the authors denoted as a crucial ingredient to leadership success.[21]

Although neither of these books urged women to become like men in order to achieve success as leaders, they did exhort them to learn to play the game according to men's rules if they hoped to advance and claim a leadership position. Hartman explains it well once again, saying, "By the time the 1970s began it was no longer mandatory to blend in with the men. It was merely wise."[22]

Typical of the research of its time, a 1973 study conducted by Schein reported that when most people thought of a leader, they thought of a man. In his article on the relationship between sex role stereotypes and requisite leadership characteristics, Schein opined that men, and particularly men who were successful leaders, but not women, were considered decisive, firm, unemotional and logical. He concluded that men had the leadership ability that women lacked.[23]

Research in the 1980s and 1990s refuted this approach by illustrating the inadequacies of investigations that judged women's ability to lead from a patriarchal perspective. Grant's 1988 study criticized organizations for encouraging "she-males," women who were upwardly mobile because they patterned their behavior after the male model of leadership success. She found that the "she-male" was often received with hostility by her male colleagues.[24] Fierman explained that complaints about women as leaders were often centered on comments like, "She's too shrill. She's too aggressive. She's too hard-edged." The author concluded that women were caught in a Catch-22 by these perceptions. If their communication style was "too feminine" they were referred to as soft; if they adopted a masculine approach they were considered abrasive.[25]

But studies of communication style, like those of Kramer, who concluded that the higher pitch of woman's voice was associated with the undesirable trait of timidity,[26] have counterparts in the last decade. Tannen's research on the use of correct and forceful speech differentiated between the private and public talk of women and men and reported that women would be more effective leaders if they used more direct and stronger forms of speech.[27] As late as 1997, Shephard advised that the high-pitched quality of women's voices was not associated with serious topics or considered credible.[28] One consequence, according to Drummond, was that 80% of media voice-overs were done by men.[29] All of these studies relied on a simplistic interpretation of findings and reiterated that women should develop skills more akin to those of men. The same dictum was espoused 30 years ago earlier.

McIntosh's model prepares us for this carryover by cautioning that even though we have passed through one phase and moved on to the next, earlier attitudes from preceding phases have not completely disappeared.[30] They still deserve our attention, if we are to assure equal opportunity for women to become leaders.

PHASE III. WOMEN AS LEADERS

McIntosh refers to Women as Leaders as the initial, albeit rudimentary, phase of inclusive leadership theory. Here feminists began to think and write of women as valid leaders and develop new paradigms based on their unique leadership skills. Women's differences were seen as an asset rather than a liability. Mary Hartman tells us that, "women can now be effective leaders not in spite but because of being women–or more precisely, because of the experiences they are likely to have shared as women and the sensibilities that they are likely to have developed."[31]

Two feminists, Rosabeth Moss Kanter and Sally Helgesen, produced studies that continue to yield enlightening research about women and their leadership acumen. Disillusionment with the "women as different" argument, where different meant inferior, led to Kanter's landmark, *Men and Women of the Corporation*,[32] which concluded that it was not gender but opportunity, power and proportional distribution of diverse people that explained the differences between men and women as leaders. Those low in opportunity for advancement, growth and challenge emerged as unlikely to develop their full potential as leaders, regardless of participation in the repair programs for women that had grown to constitute a profitable industry. These programs merely confirmed the old notion that money and time were best spent remaking women who aspired to leadership.

Kanter, Power and Powerlessness. Arguing that women's problems had more to do with unequal opportunity for power than with any biological or psychological factors, Kanter differentiated between leaders with power and those who were powerless by distinguishing power from domination and equating it with the ability to mobilize the resources necessary to reach organizational goals and objectives.[33] She found that powerful leaders got more for the people they led. Since power is likely to bring more power in ascending cycles and powerlessness to generate powerlessness, the powerful can risk more and can afford to allow others their freedom, whereas the powerless behave in a more directive, authoritarian way.

Women who take on leadership positions in hierarchical organizations are often caught in these cycles of powerlessness. Their struggle for power is what leads to controlling styles. The image of women as rigid, rules-minded, territorial leaders, deemed bossy, springs into focus as the result of powerlessness. Leaders who use coercive tactics provoke resistance and aggression, which prompts them to become even more coercive, controlling and behaviorally restrictive. Kanter was an exponent of the notion that women encountered difficulties not because they were women, but because they lacked power comparable to that of their male counterparts.

According to Kanter, studies showing a preference for men as leaders indicated a preference for leaders with power. She saw effective leadership as a response to opportunities for power and proposed that both men and women exercised leadership more productively when they had power. In another standard organization cycle, power breeds effectiveness at getting results, which enhances power. Leaders perceived to have power will always be sought after regardless of their gender, Kanter concluded.[34]

Tokens. Women also encountered difficulty as leaders when they were isolated tokens. In a study with Diane Fassel, Kanter discerned that women in leadership positions were so few that their behavior was shaped by an absence of power combined with tokenism. Relative numbers–the social composition of groups–affected the relationships between the group members. When women leaders were in short supply, they tended to be more peripheral and less likely to be accepted as one of the group.

Women who did break into men's territories found themselves in the classic positions of the few among the many. They were seen as both representatives and as exceptions. Symbolic of how women led on one hand, they were also seen as unusual examples, especially when they were successful. They were seldom regarded as independent individuals. Their existence as tokens led to social segregation and stereotyping. For their part the tokens often overcompensated by over-achievement, hiding success, or turning against people like themselves. Numbers were important not only because they symbolized the presence or absence of discrimination but also because they perpetuated powerlessness.[35]

Empowerment Strategies. Kanter believed that empowerment was the answer to the limitations inflicted on women through powerlessness and tokenism. Empowering more women generated more autonomy, more participation in decisions and more access to resources, which increased the organization's capacity for effective action. Strategies that Kanter recommended to accumulate power included acquiring mentors[36] and role models[37] and forming alliances, both internally and externally to the organization, with successful peers as well as leaders.[38]

If mentors are important for the success of men, they are doubly important for the success of women. But when there are few women leaders of higher leadership status, it is harder to find a mentor. Regretfully, few senior women are available to help pave the way and shepherd talented women. Even more regretfully, men don't instinctively or intentionally shepherd women in the same manner they do other men.

Mentors make it possible for their mentees to bypass the hierarchy, to get inside information, to short-circuit cumbersome procedures, and to cut red tape. (Although the word mentee does not appear in the dictionary, it is in common usage in verbal communication. It is selected here as a more fitting concept than the usual term protegee, which has acquired a more elitist connotation. The connotation implied here is a relationship between partners.) Karsten, building on the work of Kanter, defines mentors as more experienced organizational travelers who serve as trusted advisors and who provide constructive criticism when necessary, along with advice. Mentors serve in many roles. They:

- orient mentees to organizational culture and politics;
- assist mentees in determining, seeking out and obtaining assignments that result in growth and development;
- rescue mentees from mistakes when they take risks that could lead to failure;
- remove obstacles and make sure mentees get credit for their contributions;
- recommend mentees for key assignment and help them get the resources needed to succeed in them; and
- nominate mentees for leadership positions.[39]

Mentors should have the ability to assist in a positive, constructive way and be willing to invest the necessary time and energy to the task. They often serve as positive role models. But role models may or may not be mentors or known first hand by those being mentored. When role models are in short supply, women are advised to pick someone they admire, to study that person and adapt their career and personal growth patterns, where and when feasible.

Mentors also often introduce mentees to the process of networking, in helping them to develop and nurture external contacts that provide social support, career advice and feedback. Organizational bonding requires participation in rituals both during and outside of working hours. A lone woman may feel ill at ease or may be given less encouragement and opportunity for network participation. Besides assisting in the mentoring process, providing a sense of belonging to a group and helping mentees learn the behavioral norms and expectations of the profession, networking encourages sharing the hints others learned that enhanced their entry into leadership positions. Ultimately when mentees are ready, they can branch out from the network with which they have become familiar and form their own networks, where new mentor-mentee relationships emerge.

The advantages social support networks can supply for mentees should not be minimized. Internal as well as external network connections can serve as buffers against the stress that is inherent in a woman's career. Some have argued that this buffer enhances wellness. Socializing patterns which emphasize support and intensive contacts may actually give a health advantage to those who participate in them. Women operating as tokens are at particular risk for stress-related illnesses. Supportive relationships and alliances cultivated through networking are especially important to them. Without them women could be excluded from formal exchanges and alliances in day-to-day work that participation in networks tends to solidify.

Internal networking can provide strong alliances among peers that help women to advance, particularly when peers teach them the way things are done in the organization. Networking has become one of the best strategies for women to overcome barriers in the workplace.[40]

HELGESEN AND THE WEB OF INCLUSION

With Sally Helgesen's *The Female Advantage: Women's Ways of Leadership,*[41] interpretations of the differences between men and women leaders turned around; the gender advantage now accrued to women. To contrast her examination of women in leadership positions with that of men, Helgesen adapted the research approach of Henry Mintzberg, who in 1968 had described leadership by investigating men's success as leaders in the workplace. He followed five executives through their days, keeping a minute by minute record of their activities as the basis for his 1973 book *The Nature of Managerial Work,*[42] which emphasized the roles of a leader and what he actually did, including the tasks he performed.

Helgesen described the men pictured in Mintzberg's results as feeling pressured by unscheduled and conflicting demands, having a persistent sense of their own importance in the world, and taking an instrumental view of others in their organization. She offered the interpretation that men did not seem to enjoy "the texture of their days."[43] While men liked having high-status positions and took pleasure in accomplishing many tasks in one day, she noted that they were focused on the completion of tasks and achievement of goals, rather than on the pleasure of doing the tasks themselves. Men's instrumental view of their work was congruent with their view of people–that is, working with them was a means to an end. Men defined their personal strategies in terms of winning, of achieving a goal or reaching an objective.[44]

In her study of women leaders, Helgesen found that they had more differences from men than similarities. Women made deliberate efforts to be accessible. While men saw interruptions as a usurpation of time, women saw them as a means of keeping the organization in good repair. These traits were characteristic of women's emphasis on relationships.

Men spared little time for activities not directly related to their work, including time with family, or for outside interests. Women, on the other hand, participated in activities outside their jobs, particularly with their families, whom they declared were their top priority. Helgesen referred to the approach of women to leadership as having an integrated life, in which everything–home and work–flowed together.

None of the women appeared to suffer from the intellectual isolation Mintzberg noted in men. Women frequently characterized themselves as voracious readers and considered reading a way of broadening their views and keeping them more informed. Both men and women maintained a complex network of relationships with people outside their organizations and gathered copious amounts of information. Hoarding that information, however, was considered the male leader's chief weakness. Unlike men, women scheduled time to share information.

Most importantly, women saw themselves as leading from the center of the organization, rather than from the top as men did.[45]

Helgesen posited women as moving organizational structures from the hierarchy to the web, which affirmed relationships, principles of caring, making intuitive decisions, and having a sense of work as being part of life, not separate from it. Women serving as leaders were concerned with the means used to achieve their ends. That is not to say that men did not share these values; some shared many, others a few. Helgesen's research was groundbreaking in that it was conducted from the viewpoint of women as opposed to previous studies, all conducted from the viewpoint of men.

The Web of Inclusion. Helgesen conceptualized an organizational structure in which leaders were at the center of an interconnected web, rather than the traditional organizational chart which placed the leader at the top, removed and virtually disconnected from "the frontlines" of the organization. The cornerstone of the model was a circular, web-like structure. In the center of the web was the leader–reaching out to every part of the organization. She was not alone at the top but was connected to all parts of an orbital organization. From the center, the leader was simultaneously the informer, the listener and the constant and easily accessible voice of the organization's vision. In this structure the leader used persuasion rather than coercion, and great care was taken to maintain relationships.[46] As Waggoner put it, "A web cannot be broken into single lines or individual components without tearing the fabric of the whole."[47] The web's design brought the opportunity for Kanter's empowerment to all within the organization, enabling them to learn more, make decisions and become connected. The model of the web became an instrument for greater equity for women.

PHASE IV. LEADERSHIP REDEFINED OR RECONSTRUCTED

The final stage of McIntosh's model is the most inclusive. Over time the history of leadership overlooked or obscured the contributions of women, considered women leaders problems or anomalies, and led to women developing new paradigms appropriate to their values and skills. Finally, with the help of feminist theorists, our understanding of history has matured sufficiently to reconstruct leadership theory and practice to include all who aspire to lead.

Women's Values Enter Leadership Paradigms. It is clear that notions of leadership have gone through a period of enormous change. Much of that change is the result of the research and application of feminist principles. Leading theorists, including Robert Greenleaf and Peter Senge, have made significant contributions to current thinking. Their work shows a connection to many of the ideas set out by Kanter, Helgesen and other feminists whose studies have been fruitful in stimulating research that continues to reconstruct our knowledge of leadership.

Kanter was the first feminist to refuse to accept that problems women encountered as leaders were of their own making. The fate of women, like that of men in organizations, she declared, was inextricably bound to organizational structure, and their behavior was a rational response to the culture of hierarchical organizations. For her, too few people, both men and women, were empowered. Her solution was to modify the hierarchical framework of the organization, share power more widely, open opportunity, broaden participation in decisions and increase diversity.[48] Brown and Irby, building on Kanter's work, identified the foremost task of the leader as acknowledging, creating and empowering more leaders.[49]

Kanter's thinking might best be embodied in a later critique offered by Bennis and Goldsmith, who agreed that bureaucracy was a "splendid social invention in the nineteenth century, but organizations should consider the control-and-command mentality intrinsic to this model as an increasingly threadbare mode for organizational operations."[50]

While Kanter suggested a divergence from the traditional bureaucratic model of leadership, it was Helgesen who named it and developed the form it would take. Her web of inclusion set a structure in which the leader was conceived of as the facilitator of a shared sense of organizational vision and purpose. The female values of responsibility, connection, and inclusion, described and discussed in the research of Helgesen, had been devalued in our culture, but bias diminished as society's problems–family instability, drugs and random crime–forced recognition that a sense of community and its connectedness was needed in modern culture. Women's values have emerged as highly needed leadership qualities for men as well as women, without the need to deny men's comparable, but often different, values and skills. As an enhancement to Helgesen's web, Carol Leland introduced the link between feminist theory and the ascendancy of collaboration as a product of the inclusivity, connectedness and process orientation of women in leadership positions. She counters arguments that collaboration means no leaders with the argument that collaboration means more leaders who create organizational synergy.[51]

Both Greenleaf and Senge incorporate these values into their models. Helgesen contends that women have demonstrated their capacity for using power to enhance society through the centuries by providing service for the benefit of the common welfare, which, for her, is the ideal power motive. The Servant-Leader Model of Robert Greenleaf is similar to Helgesen's viewpoint in that she also identifies service as a fundamental value in leadership. Helgesen defined the value of service found in her research as feminine because, as she put it, it was nurtured in the private, domestic sphere to which women were restricted for so long. Servant leadership emphasizes increased service to others, a holistic approach to work, a sense of community and shared decision-making–all features which Helgesen ascribed to women's values.[52]

In Senge's Learning Organization Model, we find notions shared with both Kanter and Helgesen. The idea of eliminating a hierarchical structure and the web of inclusion are mirrored in Senge's circle theory of learning.[53] According to Senge, the work of leadership is to:

> Build learning organizations through the ability to build shared visions, to bring to the surface and challenge the prevailing mental models and to foster more systematic patterns of thinking, where people are continually expanding their capabilities to shape their future, that is, leaders are responsible for learning.[54]

The end result of the learning organization is greater responsiveness to the needs of the people the organization is chartered to serve.

From Deficient to Better to Equal. Although in the past deficiencies were the theme of work about women and leadership, the difference pendulum swung to viewing women as better leaders and now is coming to rest with differences having a neutral connotation.

Powell joined Kanter in laying the responsibility for the development of leaders at the doorstep of the organizations that employ them. He admonished them to make sure that their policies, practices, and programs minimize the creation of gender differences and experiences on the job. For him there is little reason to believe that either women or men make superior or different types of leaders. Instead, it is likely that there will be excellent, average, and poor performers in both genders. Organizations have the responsibility to make the best use of the talent available to them.[55]

Greater balance is needed on the part of both genders, according to Songer, who tells us that there is a broad spectrum of useful leadership qualities needed and no group has a monopoly on all of them. "Being aggressive, independent, individualistic and task-oriented can make an excellent leader. But so can humility, a sense of collaboration, process orientation and intuition."[56] Men would benefit from learning to incorporate the strengths of women and women from learning to incorporate the strengths of men.

Discrimination: Has It Passed? The redefinition of leadership and its reconstruction to include women has occurred over three decades. It is safe to say that the results of the research reported here represent a product of their time in history. While it would be uplifting to believe that all biases against women have passed, research does not support that assumption.

A conference held in Spring, 2000 at Rutgers University's Douglass College by the Institute for Women's Leadership focused on workplace inequities, which were cited as reasons for dropping out of the workforce by many women. A recent study helped make this case. Chief Executive Officers (CEOs) were interviewed and asked why so few women were breaking through to leadership positions. The CEOs cited problems in the pipeline. When women leaders in the same organizations were asked that question, they noted that talented women were leaving because of a host of subtle acts of exclusion and devaluation.[57] This was not much different from research conducted by Taylor in 1988, which found that women were dropping out not because of home and family, but because of career frustrations.[58] In 1990, Schein repeated his 1970 study, described previously, and found to his surprise that we still have a long way to go before women have the same opportunity to be leaders as men. Views had changed little in 20 years. For many, women still do not possess the qualities and attitudes needed for leadership[59] and, as the conference sponsored by the Institute for Women's Leadership demonstrated, women still face an abundance of micro-inequities in the workplace.

CONCLUSIONS AND IMPLICATIONS FOR LIBRARIANSHIP

Although librarians and the library workforce are largely women, the parent organizations of which they are a part are not. Nor are libraries completely free of attitudes and behaviors which slow or even eliminate the development of women's potential for leadership. But the library can become, if it is not already, the model for the parent organization. Increasing the awareness of feminist models and approaches to leadership on the part of the library workforce and implementing the recommendations inherent in the methods cited in feminist literature can help many more emerge as leaders.

Feminist Values and Global Leadership. Rapidly evolving technological change has installed libraries in the center of the global information society. Successful libraries are no longer merely the product of local leadership. Old-culture values, still holding sway in many of America's libraries, must be cast aside along with old modes of thought and behavior if libraries are to continue to provide the best possible service in a world where electronic information proliferates. Once derided for bringing emotions to decision making, women's values, with their attention to caring, supportive leadership and the use of intuition, are encouraged by Goleman's research findings which emphasize the necessity for successful leaders to possess emotional intelligence.[60] Goleman has demonstrated that emotional intelligence enhances thinking and decision making. Feminist values that combine inclusiveness and connectedness with empathic reasoning and the ability to maintain relationships provide a framework for collaboration in designing and offering services for and with people and nations that may have vastly different values.

New values, identified in the feminist literature, have also highlighted the unique contributions of women to leadership. If libraries are to continue to make their maximum contribution to society, current-day library leaders are responsible for creating enabling conditions that fully embrace these contributions and create synergy between the ways men and women contribute, combining them to form new and powerful leadership paradigms.

Inclusive Structures and Tenets of Conduct. Old-culture structures also remain the prevalent mode in libraries where hierarchical organizations predominate. It is time for the hierarchy to give way to the web of inclusion that is the basis for the orbital organization with its participative style of leadership. Orbital organizations and matrix, or project management, offer more opportunities for autonomy, shared power, and participation in decision making, all of which provide more experience in leading.

If the foremost task of leaders is to acknowledge, create and empower more leaders, then all libraries must assume responsibility for the development of policies as well as values and structures that encourage a climate conducive to helping women realize their full leadership potential. Effective policies, reducing the gap in leadership based on gender as their aim, must be promulgated throughout libraries. It is important to make clear that esteem for women's values and women's contributions is a nonnegotiable tenet of acceptable behavior. There can be no doubt left about the behavior and processes that libraries will reward.

As Schein and others have shown so clearly, beliefs and attitudes are difficult to modify. A better course is to focus on changing behavior. Libraries need to initiate policies that distribute rewards for incorporating equity in organizational performance, in this case, for being gender blind in decision making and for reflecting that gender blindness in performance appraisals and recognition systems. Research has shown that this combination will not only influence conduct, but also will frequently result in those rewarded coming to believe in what they are doing.[61]

Education for Leadership. Broadly held knowledge of how to stimulate inclusive leadership will ultimately yield a better environment for the library's workforce as well as better services for library constituents. Libraries that are learning organizations can create educational experiences focusing on how to empower more workers as leaders by providing them with access to resources, which is tantamount to replacing powerlessness with power. These learning experiences can incorporate familiarity with the countless acts of exclusion and devaluation that occur for women in the day-to-day world of work, and teach the strategies of empowerment to both leaders and those who aspire to leadership.

Empowerment–A National Agenda. With the proliferation of demands on library budgets, the ability to provide education for empowerment in each library is limited. This is an area in which nationwide attention is imperative. National models exist for successful empowerment programs. The Oregon chapter of the American Leadership Forum has launched a pilot project in mentoring and the United States Small Business Administration has set up a program specifically geared to women.

But closer to home two successful models, which were recently put into action by the American Library Association, are worthy of emulation. During her term of office as ALA President, Mary Somerville created the Emerging Leaders Institute, in which a national call went out for the identification and nomination, including self-nomination, of emerging leaders. The goal was to select thirty-five participants, with follow-up Institutes held at Midwinter and Annual conferences. Over three hundred nominations were received from which the thirty-five were selected. That response was a signal from members of the need they felt for education as leaders.

Unfortunately, although successful, the Emerging Leaders program was discontinued after only one year. The model remains, however, as a point of departure for the development of a more comprehensive leadership empowerment program. The Library Institute at Snowbird and the Association of Research Libraries' Leadership and Career Development Program and Senior Fellows Program serve this purpose on a smaller scale. ALA could make leadership development available to a wider audience. It is a fitting presidential initiative and ALA's Diversity Council is a fitting place for its development.

In addition to the Emerging Leaders model, another longstanding ALA model exists for the way in which leadership education could be promoted nationally, that is, Advocacy Now! This program began with an initial call for participation in advocacy training sessions at Midwinter and Annual Conferences, led by consultants from outside ALA with established reputations for excellence. Each trained participant pledged to go back to his or her state and offer a similar workshop, using materials made available by the Association. This training was done largely through programs offered at state library association conferences. The participants there pledged to take the program and materials back to their libraries and continue the training. Advocacy Now! also developed a Speakers Network comprised of member-experts who were willing to travel around the country to offer or assist in offering programs at ALA divisional conferences, state association conferences, library schools, and in libraries.

The work of this program has met with outstanding success, exemplified by the 30,000 advocates it has trained thus far.[62] The spin off from the national model has resulted in the creation of state advocacy programs and the introduction of the idea of advocacy as a professional responsibility in courses offered in several of the ALA accredited programs of library and information science education around the country. The model is cast for all chapters, libraries, and library schools to have a role to play. If followed, it could afford the same kind of success for an Empowering Leadership program.

EQUITY IN LEADERSHIP

Although the trend is toward more women in leadership posts, the need for concerted efforts directed to attaining equity that results in a fair, just and equitable distribution of leadership, is still with us. To date, while issues in leadership have been approached on the basis of gender, little has been done to discern the issues vis-à-vis ethnic and other nonmajority women and leadership. While some women have made progress in leadership ranks, it is predicted that it may take an additional 75 to 200 years to overcome the inequities of African American women in gaining and retaining leadership positions. Surely that must be one of the most important areas to focus on at the beginning of the twenty-first century. The issues surrounding occupational segregation remain equally acute and equally in need of action. The work to ensure equity for all who aspire to leadership is far from over.

NOTES

1. Colin Cherry, *The Age of Access: Information Technology and Social Revelation: The Posthumous Papers of Colin Cherry,* ed. William Edmondson, (London: Croom Helm, 1985).
2. Melvin Kranzberg, The Information Age: Evolution or Revolution. In *Information Technologies and Social Transformation,* ed. Bruce R. Guile, (Washington, DC: National Academy of Engineering Press, 1992).
3. Lea P. Stewart, Gender Issues in Corporate Communication. In *Women and Men Communicating: Challenges and Changes,* ed. Laurie P. Arliss and Deborah J. Borisoff. (Belmont, CA: Waveland, 2000, in press).
4. Paula T. Kaufman, "Library Leadership: Does Gender Make a Difference?" *Journal of Administration* 18 (3,4): 109-128 (1993).
5. Martha B. Kyrillidou, Julia Blixrud, and Ken Rodriguez, "Table 15: Number and Average Salaries of ARL University Librarians, 1989-1999." *ARL Salary Survey* (Washington, DC: Association of Research Libraries, 1999).
6. Public Library Association, *Statistical Reports 1992-1999* (Chicago: American Library Association, 1999).
7. Stewart, op. cit.
8. B.A. Lee, The Legal and Political Realities for Women Managers: The Barriers, the Opportunities, and the Horizons Ahead. In *Women in Management: Trends, Issues, and Challenges in Managerial Diversity,* ed. Ellen. A. Fagenson (Newbury Park, CA: Sage, 1993), 246.
9. Margaret Foegen Karsten, *Management and Gender: Issues and Attitudes* (Westport, CT: Greenwood, 1994).
10. Margaret McIntosh, Interactive Phases of Curricular Re-Vision: A Feminist Perspective. Working Paper No. 124 (Wellesley College, Center for Research on Women, 1983), 1-33.
11. Jean Bethke Elstain, *Public Man, Private Woman* (Princeton, NJ: Princeton University Press, 1981).
12. Nadya Aisenberg and Mona Harrington, *Women of Academe* (Amherst, MA: University of Massachusetts Press, 1988).
13. Peter L. Berger and Thomas Luckmann, *The Social Construction of Reality: A Treatise in the Sociology of Knowledge* (New York: Irvington, 1980).
14. American Library Association, ALA Handbook of Organization 1999-2000. (Chicago: American Library Association, 1999), 148-9.
15. Ibid.

16. Gary Powell, One More Time: Do Female and Male Managers Differ? *The Academy of Management Executives* 4 (3): 68-75, (1990).
17. Hartman, op. cit., 10.
18. Betty Lehan Harragan, *Games Your Mother Never Taught You* (New York: Warner Books, 1977), 42-5.
19. Margaret Hennig and Anne Jardim, *The Managerial Woman* (New York: Pocket Books, 1976), 39.
20. Ibid., 33.
21. Ibid., 51.
22. Hartman, op. cit., 10.
23. Virginia E. Schein, "The Relationship Between Sex Role Stereotypes and Requisite Management Characteristics," *Journal of Applied Psychology* 57: 95-100, (1973).
24. J. Grant, "Women as Managers: What Can They Add to Organizations?" *Organizational Dynamics* 16 (3): 56-63, (1988).
25. J. Fierman, "Why Women Still Don't Hit the Top," *Fortune.* 30 July 1990, 46.
26. C. Kramer, Women's Speech: Separate but Unequal? In *Language and Sex: Difference and Dominance,* ed. Barrie Thorne and Nancy Henley, (Rowley, MA: Newbury Howe, 1975).
27. Deborah Tannen, *You Just Don't Understand,* (New York: Ballantine, 1990), 76-7.
28. L.S. Shephard, Women as School District Administrators: Past and Present Attitudes of Superintendents and School Board Presidents, In *School Administration: The New Knowledge Base,* ed. Louis Wildman, (Lancaster, PA: Technomic, 1997), 114-122.
29. M.E. Drummond, "Seven Things We Do That Keep Us From Getting Ahead," *Women Managers* 97 (4), 1997, 1,4.
30. McIntosh, op. cit., 2.
31. Hartman, op. cit., 11.
32. Rosabeth Moss Kanter, *Men and Women of the Corporation* (New York: Basic Books, 1977).
33. Ibid., 166.
34. Ibid., 164-205.
35. Ibid., 206-242.
36. Ibid., 181-184.
37. Ibid., 280, 282.
38. Ibid., 184-186.
39. Karsten, op. cit., 116-123.
40. Karsten, op. cit., 127-130.
41. Sally Helgesen, *The Female Advantage: Women's Ways* of *Leadership* (New York: Doubleday, 1990).
42. Henry Mintzberg, *The Nature of Managerial Work* (New York: Harper and Row, 1973).
43. Helgesen, op. cit., 15.
44. Helgesen, op. cit., 10-16.
45. Helgesen, op. cit., 19-29.
46. Helgesen, op. cit., 45-60.
47. F. Irene Waggoner, Leadership Skills in the Balance, in *Women and Leadership: Creating Balance in Life,* ed. Genevieve Brown and Beverly I. Irby (Commack, NY: Nova Science, 1998), 80.
48. Kanter, op. cit., 276-277.

49. Genevieve Brown and Beverly I. Irby, (eds.), *Women and Leadership: Creating Balance in Life,* (Commack, NY: Nova Science, 1998).

50. Warren G. Bennis and Joan Goldsmith, *Learning to Lead: A Workbook on Becoming a Leader* (Reading, MA: Addison-Wesley, 1997).

51. Carol Leland, Talking Leadership, lecture given at Princeton University, 8 February 2000.

52. Robert K. Greenleaf, *Servant-Leadership: A Journey into the Nature of Legitimate Power and Greatness* (New York: Paulist Press, 1977).

53. Peter M. Senge, *The Fifth Discipline: The Art and Practice of the Learning Organization,* (New York: Currency-Doubleday, 1990).

54. Peter M. Senge, "The Leader's New Work: Building Learning Organizations," *Sloan Management Review* (fall 1995).

55. Powell, op. cit.

56. N. Songer, "Work Force Diversity," *Business and Economic Review* 37 (3), 1991, 3-6.

57. Brigid Moynahan, "The Devastating Impact of Micro-Inequities," *Eliminating Workplace Micro-Inequities,* conference sponsored by The Center for Women and Work and the Institute for Women's Leadership, Douglass College at Rutgers University, 13 April 2000.

58. A. Taylor, "Why Women Managers are Bailing Out," *Fortune*, 18 August 1986, 16-23.

59. Karsten, op. cit., 94.

60. Daniel Goleman, *Emotional Intelligence,* (New York: Bantam, 1995).

61. Karsten, op. cit., 92.

62. Wallace, Linda, Director of the Public Information Office of the ALA. Telephone conversation with author, 1 June 2000.

The Concept of Leadership in Technology-Related Organizations

George Needham

SUMMARY. Technology-related organizations have several important leadership roles to play in creating an environment to nurture a successful transition of libraries into the new roles they will play. Among these roles are helping to create standards and protocols, advocacy, mentoring, creating heroes, and underwriting leadership training for new members of the profession. The willingness to take a leadership role presents several potential traps, which must be avoided diligently, through humility and vision. *[Article copies available for a fee from The Haworth Document Delivery Service: 1-800-342-9678. E-mail address: <getinfo@haworthpressinc.com> Website: <http://www.HaworthPress.com> © 2001 by The Haworth Press, Inc. All rights reserved.]*

KEYWORDS. Leadership, technology, advocacy, leadership training, non-profit organizations

INTRODUCTION

That libraries are at an intersection of great danger and even greater opportunity is no secret. The rise of networked systems and the ubiquity of the World Wide Web offer the promise of vast amounts of hitherto unavailable information. At the same time it has also forced librarians to question their most basic assumptions about their roles, even their professional survival, in the coming years and decades.

George Needham is Vice President for Member Services, OCLC.

[Haworth co-indexing entry note]: "The Concept of Leadership in Technology-Related Organizations." Needham, George. Co-published simultaneously in *Journal of Library Administration* (The Haworth Information Press, an imprint of The Haworth Press, Inc.) Vol. 32, No. 3/4, 2001, pp. 133-144; and: *Leadership in the Library and Information Science Professions: Theory and Practice* (ed: Mark D. Winston) The Haworth Information Press, an imprint of The Haworth Press, Inc., 2001, pp. 133-144. Single or multiple copies of this article are available for a fee from The Haworth Document Delivery Service [1-800-342-9678, 9:00 a.m. - 5:00 p.m. (EST). E-mail address: getinfo@haworthpressinc.com].

© 2001 by The Haworth Press, Inc. All rights reserved.

Librarians have already realized that for libraries to make the leap into this new world, to continue to contribute to the intellectual growth of our communities, their institutions must change. Librarians need to develop new approaches and new tools to attract and retain an audience of users whose expectations have changed drastically.

Many companies and associations have stepped up to help librarians meet these challenges.

In the commercial world, established companies such as H. W. Wilson, the Gale Group, and UMI (now Bell & Howell Information and Learning) seem to have successfully weathered the transition from a paper-based product line to one in which electronic information, both on- and offline, is the norm.

The association/not-for-profit world has many players in this arena. Some, such as the American Library Association (ALA) and the Association of Research Libraries (ARL), have been around for many years, staying relevant by adding new units or services to deal with technological issues. Others, like OCLC Online Computer Library Center Inc. and the Research Libraries Group, are somewhat younger but developed early in the Information Era to exploit the nascent technology for libraries. Still others, like JSTOR[1] and The Open Archives, are recent collaborative endeavors intended to address newly delineated issues.

To harness and exploit this rapidly evolving environment, a positive strategic alliance must develop among all of the participants. Librarians need the assistance of technology-related organizations for software, hardware, training, and a connection to the larger, tumultuous world of information technology. Technology-related organizations need libraries to prosper in order to ensure their corporate survival.

And, all of the participants need to be constantly mindful of the end users of our institutions, to understand their needs and find the most effective way to meet those needs.

LEADERSHIP AND THE TECHNOLOGY RELATED ORGANIZATION

The late Rear Admiral Grace Hopper, the inventor of the first computer compiler program in 1952 and later the developer of COBOL, once said "You manage things, you lead people."[2] Technology-related organizations are seen as being involved with things (software or hardware, for example) rather than people. For this reason, they've tended to be left out of the leadership equation.

A review of the library literature shows very little has been published on the topic of leadership from the technology-related organization's point of view.

The issue of leadership in technology in libraries has been discussed frequently, and dozens of articles have been written about identifying electronic solutions for various library challenges. But these articles haven't looked at the role of the technology provider once the contracts have been signed and the machinery is in place. A good example of this may be found in Greg Kearsley and William Lynch's article "Educational Leadership in the Age of Technology: The New Skills" which calls for an (almost) inclusive approach to getting the affected parties involved in technology selection and implementation:

> . . . leadership does not come only from individuals. Committees, development groups, support groups, subject-centered teams, and associations may all play leadership roles.[3]

Leadership within the library community is sometimes seen as the ability to inspire people and institutions to work together in a cooperative rather than competitive way.[4] This has led to the remarkable growth of new library cooperation, as seen in the proliferation and variety of consortia, in the United States. In some cases, libraries are cooperating to facilitate group purchases of electronic resources (GALILEO, AccessMichigan, the Committee on Institutional Cooperation, INSPIRE). In others, they work to create union catalogs and statewide access to library collections for improved resource sharing (OhioLink, Georgia's PINES, the Library of California).

Occasionally, this "urge to merge" could be seen as a defensive maneuver. There has been a widespread perception that some vendors are out to squeeze the maximum number of dollars out of their library customers with the minimum amount of service. Deserved or not, this reputation has been the 800-pound gorilla in the middle of many a negotiation.

From the for-profit vendor's point of view, the world is a very different place. Most library vendors have stockholders who expect to profit from their investments. These companies may also have parent corporations that expect a certain level of revenue from their subsidiaries. The purpose of any commercial enterprise, after all, is to maximize the return on these investments.

Leadership in corporate terms may be expressed as becoming the number one purveyor of a certain product or service, or the leading corporation in its field. This competitive attitude leads to the development of new products and new approaches to service. The front-running company raises the bar higher, differentiating itself from its competitors. This type of leadership helps push the library world ahead: if these innovations survive the cauldron of the market, they can become the standards in the industry.

For non-profit organizations, or in the newer jargon of the field, "for cause" organizations, leadership is expressed in a third way. The goal of a "for cause" is, logically enough, to further the organization's cause. OCLC, the Research Libraries Group, JSTOR, and similar groups are mission-driven organizations that exist to achieve the goals delineated by their members.

These organizations provide leadership by harnessing their own resources and those of the collective experience, creativity, and intelligence of their members to further a specific solution or set of solutions. Because they aren't beholden to stockholders or parent companies, they can undertake activities that may not have a proven track record of profitability. This allows the organization to experiment in new areas to support their memberships and the profession as a whole.

This does not mean that for-cause organizations have carte blanche to pursue whatever chimera the director or staff selects. Boards of trustees act as the membership's check and balance, and survival is not guaranteed. The library landscape is littered with the husks of organizations which have disappeared or merged into other groups, or have taken on a completely different mission as the needs of the profession change.

One way to understand the differences between for-profit and for-cause organizations is to take a close look at the web sites or the annual reports they offer. Most for-cause organizations prominently feature their mission or vision statements, couched in language that reflects dedication to its cause. For-profit companies tend to write such statements in terms of their product or service offerings.

THE EVOLVING ROLE OF TECHNOLOGY PROVIDERS

Technology providers have several possible leadership roles in the library world.

The simplest role of any provider is to offer products and services to the library community. This role requires the company to assiduously study the library market, getting to know the needs of librarians and library users, and finding ways to improve processes or fill gaps in services.

Next, the company may move on to create the environment in which innovations can be accepted. This could include demonstrating the product at an ALA conference (or at another division, national association, or state conference), purchasing advertising in appropriate library and education journals, and putting together a sales force to explain the innovation to the librarian.

This step frequently involves creating demand for a product that no one but its inventor knew was needed. This means advertising not only the product but also the intended benefits. Why does a library need a cooperative cataloging system or a self-check out system? Although they may be painfully apparent to the innovator, it is in the company's best interest to inform the audience of the intended benefits to be derived from its innovations.

More innovative producers will take the next step, scouting the horizon for the ideas that will change the library landscape. This involves keeping abreast of current literature, not only within the library world but also in the computer and technology fields.

The most innovative companies do all of these things but they refuse to stop at these largely reflexive steps. These innovators help shape the future environment in which they and their clients will operate. They do this by underwriting research, working with industry and government committees which develop standards and protocols, sponsoring specialized programs and focus groups, and convening high level think tanks to try to get a sense not only of where the library world is going, but where it could go.

LEVELS OF LEADERSHIP

Besides the roles outlined above, there are multiple levels of leadership to which a technology organization can aspire.

At the most basic level, a company can simply stake out its place in the market and then do this job exceedingly well. There is a valuable leadership lesson to be taught in doing one's work sublimely well.

The next level of leadership is to push the envelope, to introduce new ways to accomplish the traditional roles of the institution. For example, the first electronic checkout systems simply automated the functions of a circulation department. The application of the computers was new; the functions would have been familiar to Melville Dewey.

A higher level of leadership is to redefine the paradigm. In other words, the innovator looks at the situation as it currently stands and creates an entirely new point of view from which to approach it. For example, Charles Robinson, the longtime director of the Baltimore County (Maryland) Public Library, introduced the concept of a public library collection intended for the people who support and use it, not as an extension of what the librarian thought the public should want. This created a new way of thinking about the role of the public library. However, the public library world didn't simply roll over and accept the idea: the support, criticism, controversy, and discussion which Robinson and the Baltimore County Public Library sparked are frequently associated with innovative leadership.

Finally, an innovator can create a whole new paradigm. When Frederick Kilgour accepted the commission from the Ohio College Association to look at ways to simplify the sharing of information among the academic institutions of the Buckeye State, his patrons didn't realize he would develop a whole new understanding of what cataloging, or for that matter, the catalog is. He and his colleagues in the original Ohio College Library Consortium defined a new paradigm for both cataloging and resource sharing.

LEADERSHIP FOR THE FUTURE

What should library technology organizations be doing now to help create the preferred future?

The one issue that invariably arises in the various forums we hold at OCLC is the role of the library in the years to come. Technology-related organizations cannot tell libraries what they should be in the future. But they can provide the tools and the resources that allow libraries to shape their own futures. This is a collaborative process that will take many forms in the years to come, but the following examples of what organizations are doing now may provide some clues.

Standards and Protocols. One of the biggest frustrations librarians and library users face is trying to get all the various systems they use to work together. Migrating from one system to another, creating unified front-end systems, and effectively searching across multiple databases are all technological minefields.

To minimize this confusion and frustration, leading technology-related organizations have become active in the various agencies that develop and implement standards for electronic services. The International

Organization for Standardization (ISO), the National Information Standards Organization (NISO), the World Wide Web Consortium (3WC), and Internet2 are among the organizations that count library-oriented, technology-related organizations among their memberships.

The MARC (Machine-Readable Cataloging) format is the progenitor of many of the technological standards librarians use today. The MARC standard was introduced in 1966 as a way to define the structure, content designators, and content of cataloging records so that computers could use them.[5] This standard allowed libraries to share automated records, leading to the development of the online union catalog, consistency in cataloging from one institution to another, and eventually sophisticated resource-sharing systems.

The more recent Z39.50 standard (adopted in 1988, revised in 1995) specifies a protocol to allow an application on one computer to query the database of another computer.[6] Another set of ISO standards, 10160 and 10161, provides ways to simplify the interlibrary loan process in a multi-system environment.

Staff from several leading technology-related organizations, including OCLC, serve on and chair key NISO committees. Data Research Associates (DRA)[7] has become the only library automation vendor to become a member of the World Wide Web Consortium, the organization that "develops common protocols that promote (the web's) evolution and ensure its operability."[8]

These standards are always the result of a major investment of time and intellectual capital on the part of librarians, their employing institutions, and the various organizations that help formulate the standards. Frequently the battles are hard fought and seem endless. Compromises–some inspired, some bitterly resented–are required.

The leadership role of the technology-related organization is to provide the smoothest possible integration and implementation of the new standards. These organizations can also provide political cover for the librarian who must return to her home institution and explain why a favored local feature was deleted in the final agreement.

Leadership Institutes. Technology-related organizations have been among the most consistent supporters of the library leadership institutes that have arisen over the past decade around the country.

Dynix (later Ameritech Library Services and recently spun off to become epixtech) was the primary financial and technical supporter of the first of these institutes, the Library Leadership Institute at Snowbird.[9] A collaboration between Dynix founder Paul Sybrowsky and Salt Lake City Public Library Director Dennis Day, Snowbird has helped scores of people relatively new to the library profession develop leadership skills.[10]

In other parts of the country, the Texas Library Association, which receives support from Baker & Taylor, Brodart, Demco, Highsmith, Ingram, SIRS, and Southwestern Bell, sponsors the TALL Texans Leadership Development Institute,[11] while DRA and Kapco have supported Ohio's Library Leadership 2000 program.[12]

In 1999, Ameritech Library Services announced a $30,000 grant to the Urban Libraries Council to underwrite the costs of planning and implementing a New Leaders Conference. The purpose of the conference, in the words of Urban Libraries Council President Joey Rodger, is "to identify and support new leaders in America's urban libraries."[13]

In addition to the actual training that participants in leadership institutes receive, the mentoring that goes on is also extremely beneficial. The mentors share their experiences and insights into their profession, and the participants share the enthusiasms that brought them to librarianship. For a technology-related organization, this sort of contact with the coming leaders of the profession is vital.

Advocacy. The political issues libraries will face in the years to come are complex and involve huge sums of money. Battles over copyright, creation and use of internet domain names, access to the web and cable television, internet filtering, corporate consolidation, and software licensing have serious repercussions for libraries. However, since most libraries are the creatures of governmental agencies, they are circumscribed in the amount and variety of political activities they can undertake.

Technology-related organizations, and especially for-cause organizations, can take a leadership role in these battles. Such groups as ALA's Office for Information Technology Policy have already had a key role in this fight, but only the initial skirmishes have been fought to date.

Unfortunately, some of these battles will pit publishers against librarians. Organizations established to serve libraries cannot stand on the sidelines as these fights are waged. The existence of libraries, and their ability to share the information wealth of the United States, is at risk. This is no time to adopt a policy of neutrality.

Creating Heroes. Another important role technology-related organizations (and other organizations that serve libraries) play is in the creation of library heroes. They do this by sponsoring library award programs and then publicizing the winners of these awards. A few examples:

- SIRS (founded in 1973 as Social Issues Resources Series, now known as SIRS Mandarin, Inc.) sponsors more than thirty state, regional, and national association intellectual freedom awards, going back to 1981 when it established its first award with the North Carolina Library Association.[14]
- The H. W. Wilson Company has sponsored the John Cotton Dana Award for library public relations activities through the Library Administration and Management Association, a division of ALA, since 1946.[15]
- OCLC has announced a project to sponsor four fellows from developing countries annually to travel to the U.S., attend OCLC Institute programs, visit key research libraries, and learn more about the directions of library and information science here.[16]
- GEAC sponsors the Public Library Association's New Leaders Travel Grants. These grants provide recipients with $1,500 to attend a major professional development activity.[17]

Scholarships and Fellowships. Many technology providers provide funds for scholarships and fellowships for librarians.[18] For example, OCLC recently announced a joint program with the International Federation of Library Associations to provide four fellowships to allow librarians from the developing world to come to the United States for thirty days. During this time, the visitors will attend programs of the OCLC Institute, visit key research libraries in the U.S. and Canada, and talk with library leaders about the directions of library service here.[19]

THE TRAPS OF LEADERSHIP

An old adage in business goes, "You can always tell the pioneers. They're the one with the arrows in their backs."[20] Technology-related organizations face a number of potential obstacles and traps as they attempt to take a leadership role in the library field.

One obstacle is the distrust of leadership that seems to manifest itself in librarians whenever someone asserts such a role. In several organizations that for obvious reasons will remain unnamed for purposes of this article, the attempt to provide leadership among librarians has been compared to herding cats. Generally, this assertion comes from other librarians.

This distrust appears to be linked to the concerns of librarians about organizations with a profit motive. Is this organization undertaking a leadership role in order to help libraries achieve their missions, or are they doing it to maximize profits? The concept that such motivations do not need to be mutually exclusive has not achieved widespread acceptance in the library community.[21] Thus, the technology-related organization's leadership role can be precarious.

Another trap is losing touch with the audience. In an article on the history of the H. W. Wilson Company, Diane Panasci noted:

> By 1903 the foundation for the company's eventual worldwide reputation was solid. One reason for this was (company founder Halsey William) Wilson's policy to seek advice of librarians before publishing anything new. Through the years, each new service has been launched with the advice of the profession it was meant to serve.[22]

An organization that loses touch with its audience can easily fall into the next and most deadly trap, arrogance. Once a solution has been proposed, tested, refined and accepted, it's all too easy for the innovator to believe that the work is completed and that it cannot, indeed should not, be improved.

This arrogance will handicap an organization when revisions or updates are needed to reflect changing realities in the library world or in the wider environment of information technology. Companies and other organizations that are slow to recognize these changes, or that assume their current solutions have an indefinite shelf life, risk being left behind. Being ignored is an almost karmic penalty for organizations that ignore their clients.

Technology-related organizations, especially non-profit, for-cause organizations, have a responsibility to move ahead in a way that is simultaneously humble and visionary.

To be humble, these organizations must understand that they do not have all of the solutions. At every level of the organization from the CEO to the folks who answer the phones, the best organizations understand that the freshest and most acceptable ideas are those which grow in the warmth and light of open communication between the organization and its membership.

To be visionary, these organizations must also be willing to nurture an environment that has the potential to challenge their key business lines, and to be ready to offer leadership as libraries move from traditional services and delivery methods to new paradigms. They must aggressively search beyond the library and the academic worlds for models of innovation and cooperation.

To master these roles, technology-related organizations will need librarians who are able both to develop a vision for libraries and to communicate and organize effectively around their vision. Participation in leadership institutes, underwriting scholarship programs, cooperating with library and information science education programs, and mentoring future leaders can help ensure that there will be a steady supply of such luminaries.

CONCLUSION

As important as it has been to fostering a climate of intellectual endeavor, the library community remains very small. For libraries to have a future, to grow and develop and mature, it will be even more important that all the players work together instead of at cross-purposes in the coming years.

It is also important that technology organizations, and especially for-cause organizations, work collaboratively to serve their users. Cooperatively developed standards and protocols, high level conferences to work jointly on assessing possible futures, open communications among organizations, and a constant focus on the end user will ensure that all segments of this profession will have a future as bright as its past.

NOTES

1. JSTOR was originally an acronym for Journal Storage, devised by the project's founders at the Mellon Foundation in the early 1990s. (William G. Bowen. "JSTOR and the Economics of Scholarly Communications." <http://www.mellor.org/jsesc.html> 1994). When the project was incorporated in August 1995, the name was simply JSTOR. (<http://www.jstor.org/about/background.html>).
2. "The Lemelson-MIT Prize Program: Grace Murray Hopper." <http://web.mit.edu/invent/www/inventorsA-H/hopper.html>. Web site undated.
3. Greg Kearsley and William Lynch. "Educational Leadership in the Age of Technology: The New Skills." *Journal of Research on Computing in Education*, 25:1 (Fall, 1992): 50.
4. Ann DeKlerk and Peter V. Deekle. "Perceptions of Library Leadership in a Time of Change." *Liberal Education*, 79:1 (Winter 1993): 42.
5. *Encyclopedia of Library and Information Sciences*, s.v. "Machine-Readable Cataloging (MARC) Program."

6. Walt Crawford. *Technical Standards: An Introduction for Librarians*, 2nd edition. (Boston: G.K. Hall, 1991), 262-263.

7. "Data Research Associates." <http://www.dra.com/> 1999.

8. "W3C: About the World Wide Web Consortium." <http://www.w3.org/Consortium/> November 30, 1999.

9. Nancy Tessman. "Learning to be Library Leaders." *Wilson Library Bulletin*, 65 (October, 1990): 16.

10. Teresa Y. Neely and Mark D. Winston. "Snowbird Leadership Institute: Leadership Development in the Profession." *College and Research Libraries*, 60:5 (September, 1999): 412-425.

11. "TALL Texas Library Leadership: Sponsor Gateway." <www.txla.org/html/gateway.html>. May 12, 1999.

12. "LL2000" <www.ll2000.org/sponsors.htm>.

13. "Ameritech Library Services Awards Urban Libraries Council $30,000 Grant for New Leaders Conference." <http://www.als.ameritech.com/ls/press/1999/urban_lib.htm>. 1999.

14. "About SIRS: Intellectual Freedom." <http://www.sirs.com/corporate/freedom.htm>. 1999.

15. "John Cotton Dana Library Public Relations Award." <http://www.ala.org/lama/awards/jcd/index.html>. 1999.

16. "OCLC to Sponsor New IFLA Early Career Development Fellowship." <http://www.oclc.org/press/19990824.htm> 1999.

17. "PLA: I Want to Nominate a Star!" <http://www.ala.org/pla/awards.html>. 1998.

18. For example, the ALA Scholarship web site lists scholarships co-sponsored by EBSCO, Geac, LSSI, and OCLC. <http://www.ala.org/work/awards/scholars.html#ALL>. 2000.

19. "IFLA/OCLC Early Career Development Fellowship." <http://www.oclc.org/institute/ifla/htm>. 1999.

20. Clayton M. Christensen, *The Innovator's Dilemma: When New Technologies Cause Great Firms to Fail*. Management of Innovation and Change Series. (Boston: Harvard Business School Press, 1997), 126.

21. OCLC, despite its non-profit status, is not exempt from this concern; in my travels as an OCLC vice-president, the general reaction to the concept of OCLC as a non-profit is derision. Being a large organization does not equal being a for-profit company.

22. Diane Panasci, "An Old Fashioned American Success Story." *The Lighthouse*, Winter, 1982. Quoted at <http://www.hwwilson.com/AboutHW/history.html>. Web site undated.

Leadership Evaluation and Assessment

James F. Williams II

SUMMARY. Much of the literature on leadership assessment both within and outside the library profession points to a healthy skepticism about the true value of administrative appraisals. Such appraisals are, however, an essential ingredient for success in any library organization–an ingredient that monitors and promotes effective leadership. This article explores the topic of leadership assessment through a review of the literature, through a review of the counterbalancing arguments on the topic of performance reviews, and through an exploration of the societal and institutional context within which these reviews take place in academia. It concludes with a brief look at the library leader's portfolio and a suggested process by which to assess the performance of library leaders. The overall intent of this article is to move practice forward to a point where it matches best knowledge. *[Article copies available for a fee from The Haworth Document Delivery Service: 1-800-342-9678. E-mail address: <getinfo@haworthpressinc.com> Website: <http://www.HaworthPress.com> © 2001 by The Haworth Press, Inc. All rights reserved.]*

KEYWORDS. Leadership evaluation, leadership assessment, management, leadership portfolio

THE LITERATURE OF PERFORMANCE MANAGEMENT

"It doesn't make any sense. The higher you climb the ladder in this organization, the less chance you have of getting feedback about your performance. The working rule of thumb is: 'the farther up you go, the stranger things get,' especially in the way you are reviewed and re-

James F. Williams II is Dean of Libraries, University of Colorado at Boulder.

[Haworth co-indexing entry note]: "Leadership Evaluation and Assessment." Williams II, James F. Co-published simultaneously in *Journal of Library Administration* (The Haworth Information Press, an imprint of The Haworth Press, Inc.) Vol. 32, No. 3/4, 2001, pp. 145-167; and: *Leadership in the Library and Information Science Professions: Theory and Practice* (ed: Mark D. Winston) The Haworth Information Press, an imprint of The Haworth Press, Inc., 2001, pp. 145-167. Single or multiple copies of this article are available for a fee from The Haworth Document Delivery Service [1-800-342-9678, 9:00 a.m. - 5:00 p.m. (EST). E-mail address: getinfo@haworthpressinc.com].

© 2001 by The Haworth Press, Inc. All rights reserved.

warded. We seem to have time for everything else, but no time to give our top people the kind of reviews they need to help them develop." This quote was made by an executive-level controller in the business sector, and it is part of the critical feedback included in one of the most cited studies on executive performance appraisal in the human resources literature.[1] The authors of this study tell us that this is the type of feedback received from most of the executives in their study of the business community. In 1996 a similar story in the *Wall Street Journal* reported that "in almost every major survey, most employees who get evaluations and most supervisors who give them rate the process a resounding failure."[2] Likewise, The Society of Human Resource Management has concluded that over 90 percent of appraisal systems are unsuccessful.[3] And, a conclusive report by Lawler states that it is a well-documented fact that most performance appraisal systems do not motivate individuals nor guide their development effectively.[4] At the executive level it is even reported that there is virtually no regular performance feedback other than superficial praise or criticism, and the prevalence of this pattern suggests an apparent paradox in performance appraisal.[5] The human resources literature from the business sector is replete with other studies of similar negative results. Despite these negative results Longenecker and Gioia report that the widespread disappointment with the quality of executive appraisals, for example, is traceable to a series of dysfunctional beliefs or myths surrounding the process. Further, the following myths are fairly common:

- Executives neither need nor want structured performance reviews;
- A formal review is beneath the dignity of an executive;
- Top-level executives are too busy to conduct appraisals;
- A lack of feedback fosters autonomy and creativity in executives;
- Results are the only basis for assessing executive performance;
- The comprehensive evaluation of executive performance simply cannot be captured via formal performance appraisal.[6]

The authors go on to say that organizations with effective executive appraisal systems have implemented the following widespread practices:

- They conduct a structured, systematic executive appraisal process;
- They incorporate performance planning into the executive appraisal process;
- Performance review and appraisal is an ongoing process;

- Executive reviews focus on both process and outcomes;
- Executive reviews are both specific and thorough.[7]

In the case of the library literature, while the amount of it on this topic is not as voluminous, the results tell a different story, and perhaps reveal a different administrative culture of higher education and libraries related to performance appraisals. This is particularly so for the literature that discusses the performance appraisal of library administrators. One of the most cited studies on this topic was published by the Association of Research Libraries (ARL) in 1980.[8] The 1980 study was updated in 1997 and it concluded that formal evaluation of directors of ARL libraries "is an established and growing fixture of campus human relations programs. Like most people in the world of work, ARL directors value fair and effective performance evaluation processes that give them useful data about how they have been doing and what they might do to improve."[9] ARL has also published a useful checklist for those who are responsible for, or those who participate in the performance appraisal of academic library directors, and it should be considered a companion document to the 1997 study.[10]

A CURRENT DEBATE: THE MEASUREMENT OF EXECUTIVE BEHAVIORS OR OUTCOMES

Today's organizations are increasingly flat, with cross-functional teams, task forces, etc., performing in dynamic patterns. This mode of collaborative and fluid work occurs at the executive level as well and some parts of the world of work are beginning to value how executives perform in equal fashion to what they accomplish.[11] Thus, one of the current debates in the performance appraisal literature is related to the question of measuring executive behaviors or outcomes. Smither takes the position that while some would say that performance must be defined in terms of behaviors, the critical component of an executive appraisal system is outcomes. He prefers to rely upon results-based criteria of performance, and takes the position that the disagreement over the content of an appraisal can be reconciled through the definition of outcomes. Further, the definition of a performance outcome should include "the frequency that a performer exhibits a behavior related to some aspect of value such as quantity, quality, or cost."[12] In a review of the empirical literature on leadership competencies, one study points to a direct relationship between transformational leadership competencies and the performance of certain firms. The key characteristics of transformational leaders in this study included charisma, inspirational motivation, intellectual stimulation, and individualized consideration.[13] Yet another study of public leaders and leadership educators about the abilities of effective leaders and society's needs for public leadership is in agreement with Smither. The leaders and educators surveyed were in agreement that ability to inspire, excellent people skills, personal direction, understanding of authority and power, synergy with followers, and an ethical orientation were the most important leadership abilities from among 20 attributes. While the study found that both character and competence would be highly needed over the next 20 years, it concluded that competence would, however, be needed more.[14] While he agrees that these characteristics should be part of the process to define a particular job function, Smither takes the position that the measurement of competencies is not the same as measurement of personal performance. For example, the measurement of decision-making ability should take into account whether this is a function of the job, but performance in decision-making could be judged on the basis of quality, quantity, timeliness, cost-effectiveness, interpersonal impact, etc. Thus, Smither's prescription for effective performance management includes the following elements:

- Precision in defining and measuring performance dimensions (e.g., define performance with a focus on valued outcomes; outcome measures can be defined in terms of relative frequencies of behavior; incorporate the measurement of contextual performance into the system);
- Link performance dimensions to meeting internal and external customer requirements;
- Incorporate the measurement of situational constraints into the system.[15]

Thus, leadership competencies and behaviors, vs. outcomes, shape the debate.

The incorporation of situational constraints into the performance appraisal of senior managers is a key element in the process. Such constraints as employee absenteeism, loss of clerical support, excessive restrictions, workloads, lack of equipment, poor subordinate performance, economic conditions, etc., have been well documented in terms of their impact on performance.[16] These constraints are a particular fact of life in the library environment and thus their importance as part of Smither's prescription.

A later discussion of perceived leadership qualities of library directors will shed further light on the relative value placed on transformational leadership characteristics by those in whose service the library director works, in contrast to the administrative appraisal systems actually used to evaluate library deans/directors.

BEYOND THE BEHAVIORS VS. OUTCOMES DEBATE: WHY SHOULD LEADERSHIP APPRAISALS BE CONDUCTED?

Despite the many negative reasons sometimes offered regarding why leadership appraisals don't work and should therefore be eliminated, e.g., (a) system vs. personal factors, (b) they undermine teamwork, (c) they encourage unhealthy competitiveness, etc., there are counterbalancing arguments related to why such appraisals should be implemented on a regularized basis. Candy and Carson have summarized these arguments from the perspective of employers and employees as follows:

Employer Perspective

- Despite imperfect measurement, individual differences in performance can make a difference;
- Documentation of performance appraisal and feedback may be needed for legal defense;
- Appraisal provides a rational basis for constructing a bonus or merit system;
- Appraisal dimensions and standards can operationalize strategic goals and clarify performance expectations;
- Providing individual feedback is part of a performance management process;
- Despite the traditional individual focus, appraisal criteria can include teamwork and teams can be the focus of appraisal.

Employee Perspective

- Performance feedback is needed and desired;
- Improvement in performance requires assessment;
- Fairness requires that differences in performance levels across workers be measured and have an impact on outcomes;

- Assessment and recognition of performance levels can motivate improved performance.[17]

While these are excellent counterbalancing arguments in support of conducting performance appraisals, it bears note that one of the finer points in the *Employers'* list above is that which addresses legal defense. Documentation about performance appraisal and feedback should always be of concern to the employee when there are no expressed contract terms that govern performance appraisals. Smither points out that courts have allowed employers latitude to determine how to evaluate their employees; he cautions, however, that the *employment-at-will* relationship is not without limits.[18] Many library deans/directors are employees-at-will and the very fact that their performance is evaluated is probably a chief determinant of whether an employment relationship continues to exist between them and their institutions. Those who are at-will probably have a letter of offer stating that their employer can terminate their employment at any time for any reason, with or without cause. And, employment documents probably exist at those institutions stating that performance appraisals for at-will employees will not be considered in determining the nature of the employment relationship between the institution and at-will employees. Thus, the societal and institutional context within which such appraisals are conducted must be considered carefully by those stepping into new leadership positions. The other fine point in the *Employee's* list is the issue of fairness. Smither points out that the employee under review as well as the reviewer should always be aware of legal principles and laws that relate to performance appraisals and employment discrimination. His suggested list includes principles and laws pertaining to disparate treatment, disparate impact, the Civil Rights Act, the Equal Pay Act, the Age Discrimination in Employment Act, the Americans with Disabilities Act, and the Rehabilitation Act.[19] Thus, while the arguments for performance appraisals are strong and convincing, those assuming new leadership roles should not overlook the societal and institutional contexts within which appraisals are conducted.

SOCIETAL CONTEXT

The library dean/director's portfolio is set in an environment where the process of scholarly communication is changing at a very fast pace.

Information technology has totally altered the influence of certain components of the scholarly communication process to the point where some of those components may not be essential to the process any longer. Secondly, economic considerations (including the job market for scholars in certain fields, the cost of publishing and fluctuations in rates of exchange) have exercised considerable influence on scholarly communication, as we have known it. Thirdly, governments now influence the flow of scholarly communication through policies that affect access, changes in funding priorities for research, and by regulation of law. Academia has seen extraordinary growth in the number of scholars as well as in their output in the past quarter century. This growth has seriously overloaded the traditional systems of communication. And, the continuing flood of communication (research findings, analyses, interpretations, new theories) has affected quality control, increased the propensity to stake claims by rushing to publish, and has led, in some fields, to an emphasis on team research and multiple authorship. New information technology is contributing directly and indiscriminately to the productivity of scholars, while adding indirectly to the communications overload. Information technology has simplified the investigative process, enabled improvements in research methodology, and removed the drudgery from research. Scholars now manipulate large blocks of data or text; store, test, and revise data or text using information management systems; gain access to bibliographical, geophysical, statistical, informational databases; and communicate electronically with other scholars anywhere on the globe. In the publishing field, technology has prompted the development of electronic books, journals born digitally, and on-demand publishing services. And, in the communications field, legislation has passed to create the next generation Internet. In the midst of this dynamic environment, research library deans/directors are operating organizations that still have a heavy investment in the commercial publishing sector, but with the advent of high-speed networks we are beginning to see the end of the era of building great local research library collections. The portfolio and role of the research library dean/director today is focused, therefore, on building a demand-driven (vs. supply-driven) library system with: (a) relevant information resources, (b) effective assimilation of information technology, (c) global connections, and (d) librarians to instruct users and facilitate access.

THE INSTITUTIONAL CONTEXT FOR LEADERSHIP IN THE PROFESSION

The remaining narrative in this paper will focus mainly on leadership as it occurs in the research library environment. Research libraries (particularly those in public institutions) function within an institutional context where the academy is faced with any number of present day public policy issues: acute competition for public funds; a heightened demand for public agency oversight of finances, administration, and academic affairs; increased pressure from state and federal policy makers to increase productivity and provide access at reasonable costs; new legislation on student aid reforms, e.g., direct loans, national service, income-contingent loan repayment; constrained federal funds for university-based research, and a shift in emphasis to research supporting economic development; institutions asked to do more to address societal problems, including race and diversity; the national health care debate; heightened public scrutiny of intercollegiate athletics amid ongoing concerns about cost containment, gender equity, and the effects of reform; the academy is being asked to do more to advance public school reform; and the elimination of a mandatory retirement age will affect the finances and faculty demographics of many institutions.

Within this context, as the 21st century begins, research librarianship has entered a period of heightened accountability and visibility of its own, with increased emphasis on the need to be even more efficient, effective, and productive. This is a turbulent time of organizational restructuring, advanced information technologies, expanded or new services, with libraries responding to the effects of a current and probable near-term projection for a stable economy. For more than any other time in recent memory, performance for research libraries is therefore directly related to the leadership and management skills of their deans/directors, middle managers, and prospective managers; managers who must be able to plan with effect, organize services and resources for ready/maximum accessibility, attract, motivate and lead staff, evaluate and utilize new information technologies, and evaluate organizational performance on an ongoing, formal basis. Within the institutional context of the academy at this turning point in time, the current pressure is concentrated on the research libraries' ability to show accountability, to be more inventive, agile, responsive and effective. This, is what our colleague, Ron Dow at the University of Rochester, calls four distinct operational environments:

- the resource environment (access vs. ownership)
- the assessment environment (student outcomes, research output, funding)
- the learning environment (discovery, knowledge generation, knowledge dissemination)
- the work environment (staff recruitment & retention, skills development, competitive salaries, etc.)

It is an environment where these libraries should be evaluated against a set of eight measures that have been identified and recommended by the Association of Research Libraries' (ARL) Statistics and Measurement Program as follows:

- Ease and breadth of access;
- User satisfaction;
- Teaching and learning, e.g., impact on learning and education, learning outcomes, and overall involvement in the educational enterprise;
- Impact on research, i.e., what specific library activities have the most impact on the success of the research enterprise both locally and globally?
- Cost effectiveness of operations and services, i.e., to what degree do library service offerings facilitate use in order to meet expressed and actual needs?
- Facilities and space, i.e., is library space adequate and are facilities best used to serve the needs of users?
- Market penetration, i.e., what portion of the academic community uses the full range of library services, information resources, and available facilities?
- Organizational capacity, i.e., what is the capacity of the library to perform, change, and reinvest? Organizational capacity can include (a) performance measures for staff, (b) staff morale, (c) staffing levels that support outcomes, (d) the skills/abilities of staff as compared to the outcomes the library wants to achieve, (e) salary compensation levels for staff based on the competencies needed, (f) salaries that support outcomes, (g) capacity for risk-taking, (h) capacity to invest in research and development, (i) alignment of internal and institutional human resources support systems to leverage investments.[20]

Within this assessment environment, where the expectations are that the library organization will be continuously transformational and inventive, Leonard-Barton found that organizations that build and manage knowledge effectively must possess four core technological capabilities: physical systems, skills and knowledge, managerial systems, and values. Likewise, she found that such organizations typically display the following common characteristics:

- enthusiasm for knowledge
- the drive to stay ahead in knowledge
- iteration in all activities
- higher order learning (learning that cuts across all activities)
- leaders who listen and learn[21]

Leonard-Barton goes on to say that agile organizations are the ones that learn from their performance, failures, risks, and successes; and ones that move quickly to incorporate learning from these performance factors. As for invention, Janov says the inventive organizations are those with enhanced capabilities to imagine and create; those that lead change through a strategy that is aligned with organizational structure, policies, and practices; and those that learn how to learn, while chasing dreams instead of competition.[22]

The library dean/director who works in this environment does not work in a structured environment of organizational discipline like that of fellow deans from the schools and colleges on campus. In other words, the library has no cognate on campus, and the environment in which the dean/director will be evaluated has a completely different institutional context. For example, the library dean generally has a larger staff consisting of faculty and more paraprofessionals than do other deans; the job involves more supervision. At the macro level, academe itself has a much looser context for organizational discipline, one where personal administrative style is nurtured and encouraged. In keeping with the behaviors/competencies argument discussed earlier, successful leadership in the academy is much more likely to be based on a strong sense of self that inspires confidence in others, emotional wisdom, aggressiveness, energy level and enthusiasm, cooperativeness, ambition, sense of humor, intelligence, judgment, originality, persuasiveness, popularity, sociability, and social sensitivity. Bennis and Nanus believe that the best leaders in any setting are those who maintain "positive self-regard," and a sense of self that inspires self-confidence in others. In their analysis of 90 top executives, they found that positive self-regard is related to a maturity they call "emotional wisdom," expressed in five key skills:

1. The ability to accept people as they are, not as one would like them to be;
2. The capacity to approach relationships and problems in terms of the present, rather than the past;
3. The ability to treat those who are close to you with the same courteous attention that is extended to strangers and casual acquaintances;
4. The ability to trust others, even if the risk seems great;
5. The ability to do without constant approval and recognition from others.[23]

One of the more popular classic best-sellers in the management literature also postulates the effectiveness of a style of people-centered leadership.[24] But, situation theory contends that there is no right way to lead. Effective leaders therefore adapt their style of leadership to the needs of the followers and the situation. According to Maslow the effective manager must be aware that each staff member moves from one level of need to another as their assignment develops, i.e., psychological, safety, social, esteem, and growth.[25] To return to the outcomes arguments discussed earlier, to the extent that these factors are not constant, discerning the appropriate style in any leadership situation becomes a challenge to the leader. Aside from style, it must be remembered that leadership effectiveness is not necessarily more important than managerial effectiveness. Before Smither, studies showed that effective leadership could account for only 10 to 15 percent of the variability in unit performance.[26] In other words, good managers are often more important to unit performance than leadership. So, what are the counterbalancing views in the library environment?

In an interesting series of sketches of yesterday's library leaders (eight men and ten women between 1836 and 1944), the following were found to be common leadership characteristics among these 18 people:

- breadth of knowledge
- specialization in subject fields
- strong initiative
- a high degree of intelligence
- devotion to the spirit of librarianship
- originality

- a vision, sometimes formalized, sometimes not
- a sense of humor
- a gift for organization
- belief in policies of conciliation and compromise
- a liberal and open mind
- a fine sense of proportion
- tolerance
- belief in the library as an instrument of popular education
- emphasis on the book as a social force
- vision combined with energy, enthusiasm, and practical effectiveness
- knowledge of business methods and administrative experience
- uncanny flair for judging people
- commitment to the profession and activity in it
- never intimidated; perfectly fearless for good causes
- ability to see things in a big way and in true proportion
- giving of time and strength
- commitment to staff and colleague development[27]

It is easy to discern from this list that the expectations more than 50 years ago were that effective leadership included several aspects of good management. In research librarianship, as in other professions, people in leadership positions are either promoted or appointed to their posts. As described by Battin, prospective leaders in academic librarianship must have four traits:

1. A first-rate mind with the ability to solve problems;
2. A solid undergraduate preparation in any of a variety of disciplines;
3. Proven managerial abilities because almost every research library responsibility, even at the entry level, now requires some degree of sophisticated management of either people or resources;
4. An intellectual commitment to research librarianship.[28]

In addition to Battin's prescription, personal observation of many of today's recognized leaders in research librarianship reveals that they are individuals who have: (a) been successful in establishing sound near-term and long-term goals for the library, while developing specific workable objectives to accomplish those goals, (b) developed effective programs, (c) creatively evaluated and restructured the library organization, (d) formulated sound policies for the guidance of other administrative staff, (e) established a record of responsiveness with staff and constituents, and (f) have developed an effective group of advisors/counselors from whom to receive information.

If the library director happens to have librarians as faculty and he/she has been appointed at the level of dean, then the institutional context changes dramatically as the librarian is recognized as an officer of the institution. Within this context, the librarian discovers the following about other academic dean colleagues:

1. They approach academic administration from inside the hierarchy;
2. They have the vantage point from which to view the entire organization. It is the only line position that enjoys routine contact with the full spectrum of organizational elements, e.g., staff at all levels, students, faculty, fellow deans, vice-presidents, president;
3. They hold a faculty position;
4. Deanships are the seat of personnel administration on campus. They are the highest officers in the organization who are expected to have regular, operational contact with the faculty, who are the deliverers of the University's service.[29]

Morris also finds that the institutional expectations of deans include a high demand for collaborative, integrative skill, tolerance for chaos, a steady tattoo of criticism, measured restraint in exercising power, a sturdy ego and hearty self-confidence, and the ability to bury these attributes, if necessary, in order to bring problems to closure. For the library director who is also a dean, he or she too, has to approach academic administration from inside the hierarchy. They serve at the pleasure of the chancellor or president, and they usually have librarians with some form of faculty rank or status. They enjoy routine contact with the full spectrum of the university community, and they sometimes hold faculty rank and tenure. They are considered officers of the university, and they are the hiring authority for the library organization. The enterprise they administer has a split personality: a service-oriented organization, with a collection of faculty colleagues. Library deans must have a tolerance for chaos because they have the largest, most diverse constituency on campus, closure on most issues is protracted because of so many constituencies, fellow deans on the campus are both colleagues and constituents, library faculty are both colleagues and constituents, the library has no cognate on campus, and much of the library dean's success depends on persuasiveness, cooperation, and collaboration with other deans. This then represents the real nature of the institutional context within which the library leader functions and is evaluated.

THE LEADER'S PORTFOLIO

Peter Scholtes reminds us in his latest work on the new competencies of leadership that the pivotal factor in a leader's job is "giving vision, meaning, direction and focus to the organization."[30] He has developed a list of six new competencies based on the earlier work of Dr. W. Edward Deming in his book entitled *Systems of Profound Knowledge* (1994). Scholtes' list is derived from the belief that managers need to have a knowledge of systems thinking, and a knowledge of the interdependence and interactions between systems, variation, learning and human behavior; and, knowing how each affects the others. In the earlier discussion about research libraries being organizations that build and manage knowledge, Scholtes' article provides a good segue to a discussion of the library dean's/director's portfolio. And, how important it is for those who evaluate these library leaders to have an understanding of the kind and content of these leadership positions in the academy. ARL's Checklist on this topic reminds us that the key leadership roles of the library dean/director are:

1. Chief Representative and Spokesperson: chief external representative of the library organization;
2. Campus Administrator: active participant in the governance of the university;
3. Liaison: maintains contacts outside the library with key stakeholders both within and outside the university;
4. Monitor: remains informed about key developments in the field as they may affect users needs, as they lead to problem solving, and as they may lead to new services;
5. Negotiator and Advocate: negotiates with organizations and individuals outside the library on a variety of issues that safeguard the interests of the library organization;
6. Fundraiser: leads the effort to identify needs, and garner external funding that supports library development;
7. Leader of Planning and Operations: leads members of the library organization in developing value systems, visions, and goals of the library organization;

8. Leader of Staff: creates and supports a continuous learning environment within the library organization, and encourages all staff to participate in all of the leadership activities of the dean/director;
9. Communicator: shares and distributes information within the library organization through various means;
10. Change Agent and Entrepreneur: introduces change, seizes opportunities, encourages risk-taking, and encourages staff to develop entrepreneurial skills;
11. Resource Allocator: develops priorities for resource allocation, allocates the fiscal, human and material resources of the library organization, and authorizes major resource-related decisions.[31]

This exciting work of research library deans/directors is grounded in a new set of principles and action items to guide their libraries' efforts and establish a foundation for joint future-oriented action based on traditional research library values. These principles can be summarized as three areas requiring continuous action in the interest of research library users as we enter a new century: access to information as a public good, the need for bias-free systems and for libraries to create those systems, and the need to affirm the idea of the library as a nexus for learning and the sharing of knowledge.[32] As the research library dean/director faces performance appraisals, it is thus very important for those who manage that process to subscribe ideologically to the library leader's general soapbox; that is, the library leader's firm belief that learning will remain a very human process; that transforming information into knowledge and wisdom will remain a personal struggle; that technology's role in academe is to enrich the ways in which the academic community interacts in teaching, learning, and creating new knowledge, while making those processes more human and personal; and, that the library's role is to be a central part of the campus infrastructure that empowers the academic community to (a) have teaching, learning and creating experiences that support individual needs and styles, (b) have easy communication, and (c) have access to information and knowledge resources independent of time, place, or personal pace.

ASSESSING THE LIBRARY LEADER'S PERFORMANCE

A 1997 survey of ARL library deans/directors revealed:

> that 84% of the responding deans/directors have some form of formal performance review; that a third of the respondents found the

> five-year review cycle to be the most critical; that the provost was the review initiator in approximately 60% of the cases; that the majority of review cases involved a variety of participants; that more than 25% of the review cases were conducted with no specific process guidelines or criteria in use; that for the majority of the review cases there was no relationship between the review and compensation decisions; that half of the directors found their review process "somewhat useful"; and, that on several issues the directors were "inclined to be less satisfied with the review process. Many felt that reviews could be significantly more useful in providing them with appropriate, thoughtful input; in helping them understand institutional goals and priorities; and in enabling them to convey key messages to the parent institutions. The least satisfactory aspect of reviews for respondents was that many processes did not indicate a sufficient appreciation of the special problems and issues related to the director's library."[33]

Perhaps, the most ideal leadership assessment tool for research library leaders would be one that is developed within the societal and institutional context for libraries as discussed earlier. And it would be developed in an organization that has a high involvement style of management. There are probably few library leaders who have had the opportunity to discuss (during the interview process for their jobs) how they will be assessed in terms of performance, and by what set of expectations. Further, many have also probably not had the opportunity to engage in protracted discussions that lead to the development of a list of performance expectations that will be used (and revised as circumstances dictate) as part of the assessment process. As suggested by ARL's Checklist, the ideal process would begin with a discussion between the library leader and the person responsible for managing the leader's performance assessment. The items under discussion would form the framework for a base set of understandings between the library leader and the person responsible for managing the leader's review. The items under discussion would include the nature of the process (formal/informal), procedural guidelines (documented/undocumented), the purpose of the review, the frequency of the review, participants in the process, the nature of feedback from the review, the nature of information provided to reviewer(s), and the contextual aspects of the review.

Given the changing nature of work in research library organizations, and the need for the library leader to have an opportunity to provide substantial information about the institutional context within which that works occurs, it appears that one of the most critical parts of the assessment process is the opportunity for the dean/director to conduct a self-assessment as the first step in the assessment process. An agreement between the library leader and the reviewer that a self-assessment statement should not be an ad hoc part of the process, and that it will be a critical part of the input during the process, will accomplish several things. Assuming that the self-assessment process is accompanied by a set of performance criteria that relate specifically to the dean's/director's post (and not the generic criteria for those deans who are responsible for degree-granting programs), and assuming that the process of negotiating a set of institutional expectations of the dean/director has been successful, and assuming that the institutional context within which the dean/director works will be continuously recognized as the review progresses, and assuming that a distinction has been made in the performance criteria between the dean/director's performance and the performance of the library organization, the dean/director's self-assessment should take on the following meaning as part of the process. It tells the dean/director that the reviewer respects the full context of the dean/director's portfolio. The dean/director should thus be able to approach the self-assessment with a sense that his/her input will have value. Assuming that the appraisal process also includes a face-to-face discussion prior to the conclusion of the appraisal, that input should also provide the basis for a continuing series of discussions that the dean/director and the reviewer will have over the course of the dean/director's tenure at the institution. Whether by intent, or not, the narrative input of the self-assessment should also document the need for revisions in the expectations of the reviewer; revisions that become a point of clarification on the part of both parties. For those deans/directors who undergo comprehensive reappointment review, e.g., on a 5-year cycle, as well as annual performance review, the self-assessment should provide an excellent opportunity for reflection; reflection not so much on the past, but on the future, and, reflection on the need for personal or professional development during the next review cycle. Overall, the opportunity to provide the self-assessment allows the dean/director to focus on and distinguish those aspects of performance that are related to real outcomes, while minimizing the tendency of the reviewer to concentrate on personality traits. Of significance here is the previous discussion on the measurement of behaviors or outcomes in such reviews, and recognition of the fact that effective performance management must include precision in defining and measuring the dimensions of performance, i.e., valued outcomes, relative frequencies of behavior, and the measurement of contextual performance. Thus, if the dean's/director's self-assessment succeeds in adding value to the process while moving the focus away from personality traits, it sends a very strong message about the fairness of the process.

Self-assessments that are generated for annual performance reviews do not have to differ in format from those that are generated for comprehensive reappointment reviews, but the narrative for the comprehensive review should focus on a discussion of accomplishments that have occurred since the last reappointment. In both cases, the dean/director should also be aware of the different audiences to whom the self-assessment is addressed. In the case of comprehensive reappointment reviews, there is often an internal and external review component that includes review of the self-assessment statement by constituents, advisors, and colleagues.

The format of the self-assessment should facilitate a future discussion between the dean/director and the reviewer. Ideally, it should be structured to address accomplishments, areas or issues for improvement, and any special circumstances or matters to be noted. Its outline can vary, but at a minimum, it should provide the opportunity for the dean/director to contextualize information about, and discuss the following:

1. Leadership
    - Strategic vision and goals for the library organization
    - Campus-wide role and contributions
    - Initiative and creativity
    - Efforts to build community, maintain morale, inspire others
    - Other
2. Academic Planning
    - Instructional mission of the library organization
    - Research/creative work mission of the library organization
    - Service mission of the library organization
    - Understanding of how the library organization's mission/functions relate to that of other units, and of the campus as a whole
3. Management and Decision Making
    - Effective use and fair allocation of resources (financial, space, time, personnel, equipment, physical and virtual information resources)
    - Timely decisions; consistent follow-up on decisions
    - Management of disputes
    - Effective use of personnel; delegation of authority
    - Deserved recognition of others
    - Setting reasonable standards and expectations
    - Consultation and consensus-building
    - Investing time and energy for high quality performance
    - Other

4. Diversity
   - Commitment and record
5. External Relations
   - Representation to external constituents
   - Friend-raising
   - Fundraising
   - Other
6. Communication
   - Effective listening
   - Effective communication with and has support of:
     - Librarians
     - Staff
     - Faculty
     - Students
     - Other administrators
     - External constituencies
7. Professional Development
   - Informed of developments in the profession of research librarianship, and in higher education generally
   - Retains currency in the profession of research librarianship through scholarship, instruction, and/or professional activities
   - Mentoring leadership development
   - Other

Following submittal of the self-assessment to the primary reviewer (and prior to completion of the appraisal) it should be shared with review participants. If the basic premise behind leadership assessment is to improve personal and professional development while looking forward, the more information made available to the library leader during the assessment process, the greater the likelihood of reducing the cynicism and skepticism discussed earlier. One means to facilitate additional sharing may involve input from others in what is sometimes called a 360-degree feedback process.[34] The process can vary widely across organizations, but the basic structure is one which provides those supervised with the opportunity to evaluate the supervisor in a fashion that does not betray the identity of the reviewer. In many cases, the self-assessment statement discussed above is made available to those supervised, along with an input form that may or may not include specific questions. In those cases where specific questions are asked, they generally fall into the category of operating behaviors, institutional values, critical management skills and knowledge areas, accomplishments during the review period (and a rating of those accomplishments). If this type of multi-source feedback mechanism is formalized as part of leadership assessment, it is critical that the evaluation instrument have validity, that there is top-down administrative support for the process, that the rules of engagement for the process are developed with those doing the rating and those being rated, that retention and use of feedback is documented, and that there is some form of training associated with the process for new employees regarding how to give and receive such feedback. When 360-degree processes work, they are an excellent source of candid information for the library leader, and they provide a very meaningful way to have an open dialogue about personal and professional development. When this 360-feedback is sent to the library leader's reviewer, the concluding aspect of the process is one where the feedback is usually summarized by the reviewer as part of the assessment narrative.

Tucker and Bryant have provided a candid conclusion to the topic of self-assessments that include multi-source feedback. In answer to the question "What, then, is the ultimate purpose of the dean's self-evaluation?" They provide the following advice:

> First, the process helps to avoid surprises. The most devastating kind of surprise is to learn, after believing that one is doing well, that one's job performance is regarded by most of one's colleagues as poor. Yet, no matter how hard the dean works and no matter how scrupulously the dean heeds the advice this book offers, if the dean is not a good listener, he or she can be terribly surprised. But more important than the avoidance of surprise is the necessity for the dean to know how well he or she is doing in order to assure that the college is continuously getting better. If deans are not helping to make their colleges or divisions better, then they must either improve their performance or find something else in life to do.[35]

The importance of self-awareness as an attribute of library leaders must be underscored here as an essential element of the self-assessment process. Such awareness includes knowing one's own strengths and weaknesses and using strengths effectively while compensating for weaknesses. Self-awareness as an essential leadership trait also includes the greater willingness to accept responsibility for one's own development, based on the notions of self-motivation and a belief that development is a continuous process.

Ideally, the library leader is also working with a reviewer who is open and frank, who is directive, and who does not shy away from using the imperative voice where necessary. In the final analysis, the library dean/director's appraisal interview should provide an opportunity for the dean/director to test his/her internal perception of the personal development challenges ahead, against the views of the reviewer. And, the dean/director should receive, at a minimum, a written reply to his/her performance assessment process that acknowledges whether or not the performance has been assessed as exceeding the expectations of the reviewer, meeting the expectations of the reviewer, or is below the expectations of the reviewer.

CONCLUSION

As we approach the year 2001, academic librarianship will enter a new period of heightened accountability and visibility, with an increased emphasis on the need to be even more efficient, effective, and productive. This is a tremendous time of opportunity for library organizations to reinvent and reframe themselves as ones that can imagine and create, while building and managing knowledge effectively. Performance for these libraries is directly related to the leadership and management skills of their deans/directors, middle managers, and prospective managers; managers who must be able to plan with effect, organize services and resources for a demand-driven organization, attract, motivate and lead staff, evaluate and use new information technologies, and evaluate organizational performance on an ongoing, formal basis. The assessment process for these library leaders is quite distinct from the assessment process for the organizations they lead. An essential ingredient for success in the library organization is an assessment process that monitors and promotes effective leadership. That process works best when it is formal, when it contains documented process guidelines and criteria specific to the leadership position under review, when reviews are conducted on the basis of clear goals and jointly-developed performance expectations, when multi-source feedback mechanisms are encouraged as part of the process, and when those responsible for the review appreciate and recognize the distinct societal and institutional context within which the library leader is being reviewed. Onward towards a growing tradition where practices in the assessment of leadership match best knowledge.

NOTES

1. Clinton O. Longenecker & Dennis A. Gioia. "The Executive Appraisal Paradox." *Academy of Management Executive*, May (1992): 18-28.

2. T. Schellhardt. "Annual agony: It's time to evaluate your work and all involved are groaning." *Wall Street Journal*, November 19 (1996): A1.

3. B. Smith, J. S. Hornsby, & R. Shirmeyer. "Current trends in performance appraisal: An examination of managerial practice." *SAM Advanced Management Journal*, summer (1996): 10-15.

4. E.E. Lawler III. " Performance management: The next generation." *Compensation and Benefits Review*, 26, no. 3, (1994): 16-19.

5. Longenecker & Gioia, *Ibid.* 18-28.

6. Longenecker & Gioia, *Ibid.* 18-28.

7. Longenecker & Gioia, *Ibid.* 18-28.

8. Association of Research Libraries. Office of Management Services. *Executive Review in ARL Libraries*. SPEC Kit #72. Washington, D.C., 1980.

9. Association of Research Libraries. Office of Leadership and Management Services. *Evaluating Academic Library Directors*. SPEC Kit #229. Washington, D.C., May 1998.

10. Association of Research Libraries. Office of Leadership and Management Services. *Evaluating Library Directors: A Study of Current Practice and a Checklist of Recommendations*. Washington, D.C., May 1998.

11. A.M. Mohrman, Jr. & S.A. Mohrman. "Performance management is 'running the business.'" *Performance Management*, August (1995): 69-75.

12. James W. Smither. *Performance Appraisal: State of the Art in Practice*. (San Francisco: Jossey-Bass Publishers, 1998): 10-11.

13. B.M. Bass. "Does the transactional-transformational leadership paradigm transcend organizational and national boundaries?" *American Psychologist*, February (1997): 130-139.

14. Adam J. Goodman. *The National Survey on Public Leadership: Abridged Results*. (Boulder, Colorado: Leadership Education and Development Institute, 1999): 2-3.

15. Smither. *Ibid.* 5-6.

16. H.J. Bernardin & R.W. Beatty. *Performance Appraisal: Assessing human behavior at work*. (Boston: Kent, 1984): 149.

17. R.L. Candy & K.P. Carson. "Total quality and the abandonment of performance appraisal: taking a good thing too far?" *Journal of Quality Management*, 1(1996): 193-206.

18. Smither. *Ibid.* 51.

19. Smither. *Ibid.* 58-59.

20. For the full report on the ARL New Measures Retreat, see <http://www.arl.org/stats/program/retreatjan.html>.

21. Dorothy Leonard-Barton. *Wellsprings of Knowledge: Building and Sustaining the Sources of Innovation*. (Boston: Harvard Business School Press, 1995).

22. Jill Janov. *The Inventive Organization: Hope and Daring at Work*. (San Francisco: Jossey-Bass, 1994).

23. W. Bennis & B. Nanus. *Leaders*. (New York: Harper & Row, 1985).

24. N.M. Tichy and M.A. Devanna. *The transformational leader*. (New York: Wiley, 1986).

25. A. H. Maslow. *Motivation and personality.* (New York: Harper & Row, 1970).

26. O.C. Behling & C.A. Schriesheim. *Organizational Behavior.* (Boston: Allyn & Bacon, 1976).

27. E.M. Danton. *Pioneering Leaders in Librarianship.* (Chicago: American Library Association, 1953).

28. P. Battin. "Developing university and research library professionals." *American Libraries,* 14 (1983): 22-25.

29. V.C. Morris. *Dealing: Middle management in Academe.* (Urbana, Illinois: University of Illinois Press, 1981).

30. Peter R. Scholtes. " The New Competencies of Leadership." *Total Quality Management,* Vol. 10, No. 4/5 (1999): S704-S710.

31. Association of Research Libraries. Office of Leadership and Management Services. "*Evaluating Library Directors: A Study in Current Practice and a Checklist of Recommendations.*" *Ibid.* 1998.

32. Association of Research Libraries and the Online Computer Library Center. "The Keystone Principles." (1999). Available at <http://www.arl.org/training/keystone.html>.

33. Association of Research Libraries. Office of Leadership and Management Services. "Evaluating Academic Library Directors." *Ibid.* 1998.

34. For a description of this process, see Dick Grote. *The Complete Guide to Performance Appraisal.* (New York: American Management Association, 1996): 288-293.

35. Allan Tucker & Robert A. Bryan. *The Academic Dean: Dove, Dragon, and Diplomat.* (New York: MacMillan, 1991): 265.

Leadership: An International Perspective

Haipeng Li

SUMMARY. The definition of leadership is a complex and constantly changing concept in the global environment. While previous scholarship has focused on leadership values, styles, and experience, research on the definition of leadership from a cultural perspective has drawn little attention. In spite of some of the universal attributes pertaining to outstanding leadership some leaders share, it is difficult and risky to attempt any one universal definition of leadership across cultures. The aim of this article is to examine the differences and similarities among definitions of leadership in different cultures and how in turn these cultures shape the definitions of leadership in their own cultural environments. *[Article copies available for a fee from The Haworth Document Delivery Service: 1-800-342-9678. E-mail address: <getinfo@haworthpressinc.com> Website: <http://www.HaworthPress.com> © 2001 by The Haworth Press, Inc. All rights reserved.]*

KEYWORDS. Leadership, international perspectives, Australia, China, Russia

INTRODUCTION

As the world is entering its new millennium, the role of leadership is becoming increasingly important in the international environment. The shrinking of the global community presents various challenges to individual countries and cultures. There is no doubt that the 21st century will pose many challenges to the leaders of the world. Robert House, Chair of Organizational Studies at the Wharton School of Management

---

Haipeng Li is Reference Librarian at Oberlin College.

[Haworth co-indexing entry note]: "Leadership: An International Perspective." Li, Haipeng. Co-published simultaneously in *Journal of Library Administration* (The Haworth Information Press, an imprint of The Haworth Press, Inc.) Vol. 32, No. 3/4, 2001, pp. 169-186; and: *Leadership in the Library and Information Science Professions: Theory and Practice* (ed: Mark D. Winston) The Haworth Information Press, an imprint of The Haworth Press, Inc., 2001, pp. 169-186. Single or multiple copies of this article are available for a fee from The Haworth Document Delivery Service [1-800-342-9678, 9:00 a.m. - 5:00 p.m. (EST). E-mail address: getinfo@haworthpressinc.com].

© 2001 by The Haworth Press, Inc. All rights reserved.

at the University of Pennsylvania, and co-founder of the journal, *The Leadership Quarterly,* points out that "organizational leaders in the twenty-first century will face a number of important changes that will impose substantial new role demands. These changes include greater demographic diversity of workforces, a faster pace of environmental and technological change, more frequent geopolitical shifts affecting borders and distribution of power among nation states, and increased international competition."[1] Although House was referring to leadership at the organizational level, these challenges do apply to any type of leadership in the twenty-first century–local, regional, national or international. The twenty-first century leaders should be what James McGregor Burns describes in his book *Leadership* as "transformational leaders" rather than "transactional leaders."[2] It is important, therefore, to consider how leadership is defined and functions in each culture and how leaders from different cultures can work together in order to address the issues of international importance. This paper attempts to examine the various definitions of the concept of leadership in different cultures and how these cultures in turn shape the role of leadership, with some consideration of the issue of diversity and the ways in which the gender and ethnic composition have created leadership challenges and affected the ways in which successful leadership is defined and valued in individual countries.

RESEARCH ON LEADERSHIP

A survey of the literature reveals a large amount of scholarship on leadership from many different perspectives: psychological, managerial, ethnological and empirical. Scholars have been engaged in research on leadership from cross-cultural perspectives since the last century.[3] Hofstede, who was one of the first scholars to look extensively at leadership from a cross-cultural perspective, examined cultural patterns of work-related values in his book, *Culture's Consequences: International Differences in Work-Related Values.* Hofstede analyzed 116,000 survey questionnaires in IBM subsidiaries located in forty countries. Based on his research, Hofstede identified four dimensions of culture: individualism versus collectivism, power distance, uncertainty avoidance, and masculinity versus femininity.[4] Hofstede suggests that these dimensions influence preferences or tendencies toward certain types of organizational leadership. For example, the degree of individualism within a culture will be related to the degree of participation in organizations and the hierarchical nature of worker-manager relations. In spite of his solid empirical study, however, his research focused on a single multinational corporation, rather than taking the approach of exploring different cultures in their own cultural context.

While previous scholarship has focused on leadership values, styles, and experience, research on the definition of leadership has drawn little attention and there is still much debate regarding the importance of culture in the practice of leadership.[5] One reason for this is that it is difficult to provide a fixed definition of the concept of leadership because leadership styles vary drastically and, in particular, from culture to culture. Peter R. Sholtes, an internationally known author and consultant, discusses many aspects of leadership in his book *The Leader's Handbook: a Guide to Inspiring Your People and Managing the Daily Workflow,* including styles, values, competencies and measurements. However, when it comes to the definition of leadership, he writes, "There is no formula for leadership. Leadership consists of more than the approaches, capabilities, and attributes talked about in books such as this one."[6] He goes on to say, "Leadership is an art, an inner journal, a network of relationships, a mastery of methods, and much, much more . . . "[7] Berenice D. Bahr Bleedorn, a psychology professor at the College of St. Thomas in St. Paul, also describes: "The concept of leadership is in the process of evolution."[8] As leadership is a complex concept that is changing constantly, another psychology researcher, Cecil A. Gibb addresses the difficulty associated with this evolution.

> The concept of leadership, like that of general intelligence, has largely lost its value for the social sciences . . . There is a great variety of ways in which one individual stands out in social situations and in which the one may be said, therefore, to be 'leading' the others. So diverse are these ways that any concept attempting to encompass them all as 'leadership' does, loses the specificity and precision that's necessary to scientific thinking. [9]

In spite of the argument by some researchers that leaders share some universal attributes pertaining to outstanding leadership,[10] as it is not easy to define leadership generally, it is difficult and risky to attempt any one universal definition of leadership across cultures.

In discussing leadership issues in the multinational business management context, where there is a great need for market development in foreign countries, Mary Ann Von Glinow and others have addressed the importance of culture, arguing that although some degree of system-wide consistency in leadership style should be maintained in a multinational organization, the operational rules used throughout the organization or in the headquarters country should be carefully blended into the local cultural context.[11] In the Glinow article, the authors examine the prevalent views of leadership in three countries: the United States, Japan, and Taiwan, which are similar in economic systems, but differ significantly in many cultural dimensions.[12] Triandis, another leading scholar on the study of cross-cultural leadership, also argues that common leadership factors may exist, but depending upon the cultural value orientations of a given country or set of countries, the meaning of the leadership situation changes from culture to culture.[13] Thus, the concept of leadership may be context specific and culturally dependent.

LEADERSHIP AS DEFINED BY INDIVIDUAL COUNTRIES/CULTURES

Hofstede defines culture as "the collective programming of the mind which distinguishes the members of one human group from another."[14] This definition includes the systems of values and beliefs, which are among the basic elements of culture. It is this "collective programming" that determines the perception of people from a particular culture in defining what leadership is in that culture. Many empirical and non-empirical studies have provided support for the notion that culture has significant impact on the concept and the role of leadership. Among many others, Hofstede's widely cited study shows that in countries with similar value orientations similar leadership styles will be prominent, and individual cultures do have different impact on leadership styles.

As Glinow and others have pointed out, "Research in the area of leadership has been moving along for years without paying much attention to cultural differences."[15] In another article, Den Hartog and others have also written that "The way in which the social environment is interpreted is strongly influenced by the cultural background of the perceiver. This implies that the attributes that are seen as characteristic or prototypical for leaders may also strongly vary in different cultures."[16]

In his discussions about the effectiveness of a leader, Afsaneh Nahavandi, professor at the Arizona State University-West, states that "there are many cross-cultural differences in what a leader should do to be effective."[17] Bass also points out there are differences in the concept and meaning of leadership as one crosses national and cultural boundaries. "The differences in socialization in the various nations of the world give rise to different conceptions of leadership."[18] In their discussions of the differences of management cultures between Britain and France, Gerard Naulleau and John Harper argue that leaders' or managers' roles and practices are deeply embedded in the social and cultural environment of the actors.[19] One of the findings of Smith and others, who studied the generality of leadership style measures across cultures, also indicates that while transnational dimensions of leader type can be identified, the skill of executing each style effectively varies by cultural setting.[20] Thus, it is particularly important to examine cultural differences and implications in the discussions of leadership in a cross-cultural environment.

Because of the complex nature of the concept of leadership in a cross-cultural context, the aim of this article is not to create one uniform definition of global leadership, but rather to examine the differences and similarities among definitions of leadership in different cultures by discussing four countries as examples: Australia, China, Russia, and the United States. The rationale for choosing these countries is three-fold: first, these countries all play an important role in current world affairs; therefore, they provide a current and potential representation of what is going on throughout the world. Second, geographically, they represent four different continents–Asia, Australia, Europe, and North America, and play major roles in the affairs of their respective regions. Thirdly, these four countries possess very different cultures that subsequently shape their concepts of leadership, to one extent or another. Table 1 shows the population and land areas of the four countries to be discussed.

Australia

A country with a population of over 18 million, Australia is primarily a nation of immigrants. Although the breakdown of the major categories in population is Caucasian (92%), Asian (7%), Aboriginal and

TABLE 1

Country	Population (in thousands)	Land Area (sq. km) (in thousands)
Australia	18,311	7,682
China	1,236,260	9,571
Russia	147,100	17,075
United States	270,298	9,809

Source: The Europa World Year Book, 1999.[21]

other (0.1%),[22] the immigrant populations have always been a crucial factor throughout the history of Australia. Even today, the percentage of immigrants remains more than a quarter of the population at 26% percent.

Table 2 provides a snapshot of the former nationalities of those granted Australian citizenship between 1997 and 1998 and reveals the wide variety of country origins of recent immigrants. It provides a picture of the level of diversity in Australian society, which suggests the level of challenge this diversity might pose to Australian leadership. Historically Australia had strong ties with a number of European countries. Even before it was discovered, Australia was already divided up as a colony by the two European imperialists in the fifteenth century, Spain and Portugal. However, the British Empire was the single most important influence on Australia from 1788 to the 1950s, as Australia served as a jail for British convicts. In the 1890s, the colonies in Australia formed a federation to protect the rights of the states and in 1900, the Australian constitution was enacted. Since the inauguration of the Commonwealth of Australia in 1901, the federation of the Australian colonies has created a new political framework for Australia and has led Australians to much of its success in political and institutional history. In many ways, the Australian history is a history of struggles among the Aboriginals and non-Europeans. As life in Australia was dominated by the Europeans for many years, the Aboriginals and non-Europeans were used mostly for manual labor and were denied access to social systems. Even until today, Aboriginals remain the most disadvantaged group in Australian society.[23] Thus, it might be fair to say that Australia is a country of immigrants and a culture of cultures.

The geographical location of the country also poses many challenges in terms of isolation. For example, between 1925 and 1949, the average number of Australians who traveled overseas was only about 20,000 or about 0.5%.[25] Not until the early 1970s did it become easier for most Australians to have access to modern means of transportation such as jumbo jets and speedy ships. The size of the country also challenges most Australians. The total area of Australia is greater than all of Western Europe. The lack of a network of permanent inland navigable rivers has made transportation and communications difficult. Most land transport was horse drawn until the 1870s when rail became available, which was the main form of land transport from the 1870s to 1960s. Issues of immigration, transportation and isolation, as well as communications have been challenges to Australian leaders throughout the country's history. Based on the results of her study on gender differences in leadership, Christina Gibson argues that leaders vary in terms of the degree

TABLE 2. Selected Former Nationality of People Granted Australian Citizenship 1997-98

Name	Number	%
British or Irish	24,247	21.6
Chinese (PRC)	21,053	18.7
New Zealander	8,764	7.8
Vietnamese	4,685	4.2
Filipino	3,688	3.3
India	3,358	3.0
Yugoslav (former)	3,153	2.8
Iraqi	2,877	2.6
Bosnia-Herzogovinian	2,728	2.4
Sri Lankan	2,049	1.8
Fiji (citizen of)	1,934	1.7
South African	1,880	1.7
United States (citizen of)	1,565	1.4
Lebanese	1,364	1.2
Cambodian	1,233	1.1
Iranian	1,143	1.0
Italian	1,063	0.9
Turkish	1,029	0.9
Croatian	935	0.8
Bangladeshi	921	0.8

Source: Australian Bureau of Statistics.[24]

of direction of leadership style and states that Australians indicated less emphasis on interaction facilitation and more emphasis on a directive style, which is more autocratic and benevolent, due to Australia's geographic isolation, than did managers from the other countries in her study.[26]

Thus, it is no wonder that the Australian concept of leadership is defined on the basis of problem solvers who are able to pull different immigrant populations together as a united force, to find alternative modes of transportation, and to create better channels of communication. For example, many of the great personalities and institutions were often associated with trying to improve communications, such as the largest horse-drawn coach service in eastern Australia in its early history, Cobb and Co.,[27] known for its reliability; Charles Kingsford Smith, one of country's great navigators in Australian history;[28] and School of the

Air, which served as a leader by first providing education through a two-way radio service to children living in isolated remote areas who were unable to attend school.[29] Thus, the basis for leadership was often effectiveness in solving major social problems.

In the international arena, Australia has taken on a leadership role in many current world affairs. For example, Australia has also taken on a leadership role in the East Timor conflict, ultimately leading the United Nations' armed forces to settle the issue. In the years of Paul Keating, who was the prime minister from 1991 to 1996, Australia was gradually transformed from a country with a political system patterned after a European model to more or less an Asian country and has explored many options in dealing with both domestic and world affairs as a leader, particularly, in the Pacific region. Christina Gibson points out that as Australia increases its ties in the global market, Australian leaders may be faced with a situation in which they are the "odd one out"[30] and may need to adapt accordingly. One of the ways that Australians have been adapting recently is in raising leadership awareness and improving leadership skills by conducting workshops and institutes on leadership in different areas of the society. In librarianship, for example, the Aurora Leadership Institute, a leadership institute similar to the Snowbird Institute for American librarians, but for librarians in New Zealand and Australia, and which first started in 1995, received much positive feedback from participants.[31]

In spite of the fact that Australia has become more prominent in the Asian Pacific region, the Australian perception of leadership is still very much defined on the basis of the traditional European model and only recently focused on one of the other major social problems in the country. Although efforts have been made in more recent years to restore the social, economic, and political status of the Aboriginal people, including the elimination of anti-Aboriginal legislation, the Australian concept of leadership has not completely addressed the social problem of achieving full integration of Aboriginals into Australian society.

China

As the largest country in the world in terms of population, China throughout its history has consistently presented itself to the outside world as a mythical culture, and its leadership has challenged and puzzled many leaders in the Western world. With a history of more than 5,000 years, China claims to be one of the oldest civilizations on earth. For many years, China remained a closed country. Although China has realized significant economic growth and development and is poised to continue to do so, China evolved first from the Middle Kingdom, an agrarian society on the Yellow River, with a vast ocean to the east, deep jungles to the south, towering mountains to the west, and freezing deserts to the north. These factors have had a significant effect on its national culture and leadership in that it has been difficult to form a long-lasting relationship with any other country in the world. Thus, China has retained its own view of leadership as being one in which the concept of control is valued.

China is also a very diverse country with many ethnic minorities. According to the Bureau of Chinese Statistics, there are fifty-six ethnic groups in China. Table 3 shows the names and populations of major ethnic minorities in China. The ethnic composition in China has posed many

TABLE 3. Principal Ethnic Groups in China

Name	Number (in thousands)	%
Han (Chinese)	1,039,187	91.92
Zhuang	15,555	1.38
Manchu	9,846	0.87
Hui	8,612	0.76
Miao	7,383	0.65
Uygur (Uigur)	7,207	0.64
Yi	6,578	0.58
Tujia	5,725	0.51
Mongolian	4,802	0.42
Tibetan	4,593	0.41
Bouyei	2,548	0.23
Dong	2,508	0.22
Yao	2,137	0.19
Korean	1,923	0.17
Bai	1,598	0.14
Hani	1,254	0.11
Li	1,112	0.10
Kazakh	1,110	0.10
Dai	1,025	0.09
She	634	0.06
Lisu	574	0.05
Others	3,838	0.34
Unknown	753	0.07
Total	1,130,510	100.00

Source: The Europa World Year Book, 1999.[32]

challenges to the Chinese leadership, particularly, in recent years under the Communist control, including the Tibetan independence movement and the recent Muslim riots in Northwest China.

One of the oldest philosophies that has had the most significant effect on the culture is Confucianism, which is based on unequal relationships among people in the Chinese society.[33] Confucianism has advocated, for thousands of years, that people have a predetermined status in the society before they are born. A ruler is destined to be a ruler. A ruler is always the ruler of his subordinates; a father is always the ruler of his son; and, a husband is always the ruler of the wife. The ruler has the ultimate control of all under his rule. Everyone should be content with their positions in the society and should not challenge their superiors, but rather depend upon their leaders for directive actions. Such an authoritarian leadership style is usually the result of what Triandis calls "collectivism," which defines the leader as "paternalistic, taking good care of his ingroup."[34] It is true that in a collective culture like China, the term "we" is much more emphasized than the word "I," to discourage people from demonstrating their individuality. While exploring the theory of collectivism, Triandis, McCusker and Hui also state that "in collective cultures there is much emphasis on hierarchy," where "the father is the boss and men superordinate women."[35] In turn, the leader is someone who should take care of his subordinates and exercise his control over anyone who dares to disobey.

The perception on leadership related to gender in China is also significant. Since traditionally the Chinese society has been a patriarchal society, women's roles in the society tend to include staying at home and making sure that the husband and children are well fed. They are, in Wu and Minor's terms, "Secretary of the Interior," whereas men are "Secretary of Defense,"[36] responsible for affairs outside of the family. With the economic reform in China, however, women have entered the workforce in increasing numbers and more women have become managers or taken on other types of leadership positions, subsequently changing the traditional structure of the Chinese society.

China's recent history since the 1840s has also challenged the Chinese to demand a stronger and more protective leader. China became a victim of the Western imperialism after the Opium War with the British in 1840, which opened the door of China for many other imperialist invasions from countries including Japan, Germany, France and the United States. This endangered the Chinese sense of ownership of their country and, thus increased their sense of patriotism. Subsequently, a Chinese leader would take advantage of this piece of history to provoke nationalistic feelings among the Chinese and anyone who could do this would be considered a great leader. Again, the leader in turn would be seen as a "father figure" that could stand up and protect his "children."

This patriarchal "father figure" is deeply rooted in the Chinese concept of leadership and, it appears, will last for a long time, as China is seeking ways to solidify and stabilize the nation. Current Chinese leadership allows "freedom" and "individuality," as long as the state of China is not threatened. In spite of all this, given the current rate of economic growth and development, there is no doubt that China will be a powerful force in almost every aspect of world affairs in the near future. As a result, how the Chinese define their leaders is not going to be simply an issue for the Chinese. It will have significant impact on many other countries as well.

Russia

In spite of the downfall of the Soviet Republic in 1992, the Russian Federation today still has a very important role in the affairs of Eastern Europe and the rest of the world. With a population of over 147 million, Russia is unique in that it straddles the Eurasian continent from the Baltic and Black seas to the west and south and to the Pacific Ocean in the east. It occupies a territory of about 17 million square kilometers and is the largest country in the world in land area.[37] Throughout its history, Russia has experienced rulers ranging from emperors and tsars to Communists and liberals, and societal structures from tribal and feudal to socialist and democratic. For a country of this size and with such a long history, leadership has been a real challenge for the Russians.

A country with many ethnic minorities, it often appears too easy to define Russian leadership. In fact not all Russian leaders have been Russian. For example, Stalin was a Georgian and Mikoyan was Armenian. The ethnic composition in Russia is rather complex. According to *Russia & Eurasia Facts and Figures of 1998,* the Russian Federation consists of 21 republics, 6 territories and 49 regions, within each of which together live the different ethnic groups, including Russians, Ukrainians, Armenians, Tatars, and Belarusians.[38] Table 4 provides a listing of the republics and their populations, which indicates the diverse nature of the Russian population. This diversity has also challenged the Russian leaders in many ways, including making certain that all republics and various ethnic groups make peace with one another. The recent conflict with Chechnya against terrorists is only one of those challenges that Russian leaders have to face.

TABLE 4. Republics with the Russian Federation

Republic	Area (sq. km)	Population (in thousands)
Adygeya	7,600	450
Altai	92,600	202
Bashkortostan	143,600	4,097
Buryatiya	351,300	1,053
Chechnyat	n. a.	921
Chuvashiya	18,300	1,361
Dagestan	50,300	2,042
Ingushetiya	n. a.	300
Kabardino-Balkariya	12,500	790
Kalmykiya	75,900	319
Karachayevo-Cherkessiya	14,100	436
Kareliya	172,400	785
Khakasiya	61,900	586
Komi	415,900	1,185
Marii-EL	23,200	766
Mordoviya	26,200	956
North Osetiya (Alaniya)	8,000	663
Sakha (Yakutiya)	3,103,200	1,023
Tatarstan	68,000	3,760
Tyva	170,500	309
Udmurtiya	42,100	1,639

Source: The Europa World Year Book, 1999.[39]

Above and beyond the social and political factors which change over time, two factors which determine the nature of the Russian culture are relatively unchanging. These are the vastness of the Russian land area and the harshness of the climate. The boundless mass of land often projects a sense of indefensibility and vulnerability; and, the relentless harsh climate challenges the Russians to survive and seems to lead to the development of hostility toward outsiders. These factors, in some ways, demand leaders who can rule with an iron fist and apply exploitative measures to their own people.[40] This explains why over the centuries, the churches, the Tsars, and the Soviets had taken control of the Russians for so long.

Russia has gone through some truly revolutionary movements. The October 1917 Revolution under the leadership of Lenin totally destroyed the feudal system and established of the Communist society. In

1991, the Russian Republic emerged to replace the former Soviet Republic led by liberals such as Boris Yeltsen. In "Political Leadership in Post-Communist Russia," Archie Brown notes that "The task of leadership in the conditions of collapse of the Soviet Union has been a conspicuously difficult one."[41] It is evident that while the country is in a state of transition, certain features of the culture inevitably reflect the style of leadership, current and future, and thus further define the concept of leadership in Russia. Serebriny discusses the changing role of the Russian culture and points out that since the disintegration of the Soviet Union, "Russian culture now lives through a period of crisis and painful experience."[42] Like China, Russia opened itself recently to the outside world and is undergoing many changes in a new market economy. For example, the new Russian entrepreneurial leadership involves an opportunistic style, risk-taking, and often a short-term profit orientation in this new market economy.[43] As a result, many aspects of the Russian culture, including beliefs, morals, and customs, are also changing. Indeed, this cultural change, along with the current unstable political and economic situation in Russia, determines the unstable nature of the Russian leadership. As culture may change over time, leadership changes accordingly, as well.

United States

The United States is a world leader in many aspects of current world affairs. Its international leadership is demonstrated through world markets and trade policies, political involvement and military exercises. In addition to its crucial role in the Gulf War, the Kosovo conflict, and the World Trade Organization affairs in recent history, the United States has the world's largest economy and claims many of the firsts on earth. America is first in volume of trade, first in industry, first in food output and first in aid to others.[44] Not only is America first in many production areas, but it is also first in consumption of energy, oil, coffee and cocoa.

As one of the largest nations on earth, America is also the most diverse country of cultures in the world, with a vast variety of immigrant populations. Even at the time of the birth of this country, America was already a diverse place, with a large immigrant population from Europe (including Germany, France, England, Scotland) and a large number of African Americans. According to the 1990 census, responses from Americans to the question "What is your ancestry or ethnic origin?" were tabulated for 215 ancestry groups.[45]

Table 5 shows the projected ethnic composition of the American population in the years 2000 and 2050, which indicates a time period of rapid growth in the diversity in the United States population.

TABLE 5. Percent of Projections of the Resident Population by Race for Years 2000 and 2050

Year	White	Black	American Indian, Eskimo, Aleut	Asian, Pacific Islander	Hispanic Origin
2000	82.1	12.9	0.9	4.1	11.4
2050	74.8	15.4	1.1	8.7	24.5

Source: Statistical Abstract of the United States.[46]

Individual freedom has been a central theme in the life of Americans since the very beginning of the country. It is always important to remember why the first Europeans came to the Americas. Persecuted because of their religious beliefs in their home country, Puritans came to this land to seek religious freedom and escape religious bondage. Many other immigrant groups came because of the freedom and opportunities this country provided in order to live a better life. The belief in freedom in American culture over the years has enhanced the concept of individualism, which in turn creates and ensures more freedom and individuality. Such a circular causation is evidenced almost everywhere in American history and society, and certainly in the U.S. Constitution. Individualism is centrally rooted in the well-known statement that "Everyone is created equal," and the concept of freedom is also much reflected in the Bill of Rights. While these concepts of equality and freedom have been espoused by leaders in the U.S. since the formation of the country, not all members of the diverse society have been afforded such circumstances. However, it is generally the case that those who are and have been praised as leaders have been successful in promoting these ideals to one extent or another. In the workplace people are encouraged to perform their best in their own unique and personal way. Thus, a leader in the American mind should be someone who is not only able to protect citizens' individual rights and freedom but also possesses his/her own unique individuality that can move the country forward.

Another important aspect of American leadership is the risk-taking, adventurous, and entrepreneurial spirit, which is a part of the American pioneering and frontier tradition. In the workplace, employees in American corporations are encouraged to try new things and rewarded for their individuality in getting the job done well. This risk-taking concept is something that is hard for people from other cultures to comprehend, and Asian cultures in particular, because individuality is not encouraged and appreciated as much. In their empirical study on leadership traits, lifestyles and role perceptions of female managers in Japan, Taiwan and the United States, Wu and Minor found that in addition to the fact that American female managers see their work role as more important than their counterparts in the other two countries, they "tend to be more aggressive, practical, and risk taking."[47] It is clear that this entrepreneurial spirit is an important part of the American concept of leadership.

Americans are fully aware of their roles in continuing to create and define the concept of leadership. It is not exaggerating to say that in many aspects of the American society, leadership is promoted and appreciated. In corporate enterprises and educational institutions, much promotion of leadership has been conducted in recent years. For example, there have been an increasing number of leadership programs designed to focus on leadership development for individual participants in various professions, including librarianship, such as the Library Leadership Institute at Snowbird, the Association of College and Research Libraries/Harvard Leadership Institute, and the Association of Research Libraries Leadership and Career Development Program.[48] As society changes, leadership in America has been and will continue to be defined and redefined in the years to come.

CONCLUSION

The examination of the concept of leadership in the above four countries provides a glimpse into the study of leadership from an international perspective. Given the background information about the four countries, the similarities and differences in their cultures are presented to contribute to the understanding of the concept of leadership in these countries. This discussion further shows that although leaders in different countries or cultures share some basic values and qualities of leadership, the ways in which these countries define the concept of leadership are different, sometimes drastically and sometimes to a lesser degree. For example, since Australia and the United States are both immigrant countries to a large extent, these two countries share much in common in defining their leadership historically and futuristically. However, even these two countries define their leaders differently in a number of ways. Because of its geographic isolation, Australia defines its leaders as those who are not only capable of solving problems and creating solutions with communications, transportation and immigration, but also are able to lead Australia forward in the global arena politically and economically, and in the Asian Pacific region in particular. The United States, on the other hand, won its independence much earlier and has a longer history of individualism, which places on the leader the role of not only protecting individual freedom and rights, but also placing the country in a leadership position in the world. For China, in spite of its history of authoritarian rule, many changes have taken place in recent years and have challenged the traditional leadership since the nineteenth century. With challenges coming from both within and outside China, the Chinese still have much dependency on their leaders to take them into the new millennium. Russia has been struggling since the collapse of the former Soviet Union and will need much stronger leaders to sort out the chaos and to be able to lead the many different republics and regions.

FUTURE RESEARCH

As evidenced in the literature review, much has been written on the topic of leadership in terms of leadership styles and qualities. Although some research has been done on leadership from cross-cultural perspectives, the study of leadership along cross-cultural dimensions has received little attention.[49] Further empirical and non-empirical research needs to be carried out in the study of the concept of leadership, rather than limiting to a few countries. Since culture varies from place to place, further country-to-country study on leadership is needed for the purpose of comparison. While engaging in the research on the topic of leadership, it is also important to keep in mind the ways in which research is conducted. Since most of the research on leadership is conducted in Western countries and in the United States, in particular, there might be a tendency that research on the concept of leadership is somewhat colored by what Peterson and Hunt call the "American academic colonialism."[50] This argument makes research on the definition and concept of leadership from international perspectives even more significant.

NOTES

1. Robert J. House, "Leadership in the Twenty-First Century: A Speculative Inquiry," in Ann Howard, ed., *The Changing Nature of Work* (San Francisco: Jossy-Bass Publishers, 1995), 411.

2. James McGregor Burns, *Leadership* (New York: Harper and Row, 1978), 4.

3. Roya Ayman, "Leadership Perceptions: The Role of Gender and Culture," in Martin M. Chemer and Roya Ayman, eds. *Leadership Theory and Research* (New York: Academic Press, Inc. 1993), 153.

4. Greet Hofstede, *Culture's Consequences: International Differences in Work-Related Values* (Newbury Park, California: Sage Publications, Inc. 1980), 11.

5. George A. Marcoulides et al., "Reconciling Culturalist and Rationalist Approaches: Leadership in the United States and Turkey," *Thunderbird International Business Review* 40: 6 (November/December 1998): 264.

6. Peter R. Scholtes, *The Leader's Handbook: A Guide to Inspiring Your People and Managing the Daily Workflow* (New York: McGraw-Hill, 1998), 372.

7. Ibid.

8. Berenice D. Bahr Bleedorn, *Creative Leadership for a Global Future: Studies and Speculations* (New York: Peter Lang, 1988), 7.

9. Cecil A. Gibb, "Leadership," in David L. Sills, ed. *International Encyclopedia of the Social Sciences*. (New York: Macmillan, 1968), 91.

10. Den Hartog et al., "Culture Specific and Cross-Culturally Generalizable Implicit Leadership Theories: Are Attributes of Charismatic/Transformational Leadership Universally Endorsed?" *The Leadership Quarterly* 10:2 (Summer 1999): 219.

11. Mary Ann Von Glinow et al., "Leadership Across the Pacific Ocean: A Trinational Comparison," *International Business Review* 8 (1999): 1.

12. Ibid.

13. Harry C. Triandis, "The Contingency Model in Cross-Cultural Perspective," in Martin M. Chemers and Roya Ayman, ed. *Leadership Theory and Research* (New York: Academic Press, Inc. 1993), 181.

14. *Culture's Consequences: International Differences in Work-Related Values*, 25.

15. Von Glinow et al., "Leadership Across the Pacific Ocean: A Trinational Comparison," 2.

16. Den Hartog et al., "Culture Specific and Cross-Culturally Generalizable Implicit Leadership Theories: Are Attributes of Charismatic/Transformational Leadership Universally Endorsed?" *The Leadership Quarterly* 10, 2 (Summer 1999): 227?

17. Afsaneh Nahavandi, *The Art and Science of Leadership* (Upper Saddle River, NJ: Prentice Hall, 1997), 6.

18. Bernard M. Bass, *Bass and Stogdill's Handbook of Leadership: Theory, Research, Managerial Applications* (New York: The Free Press, 1990), 760.

19. Gerard Naulleau and John Harper, "A Comparison of British and French Management Cultures: Some Implications for Management Development Practices in Each Country," *Management Education and Development* 24:1 (Spring 1993): 15.

20. Peter B. Smith et al., "On the Generality of Leadership Style Measures Across Cultures," *Journal of Occupational Psychology* 62 (1989): 108.

21. *The Europa World Year Book* (London, England: Europa Publications Limited), 1999.

22. CIA, "Australia," *The World Factbook*, [on-line] Available: www.abs.gov.au/ausstats/ABS%40.nsf/94713ad445.

23. James C. Docherty, *Historical Dictionary of Australia* (Lanham, Md.: Scarecrow Press, 1999), 23.

24. Australian Bureau of Statistics (2000). "A Statistical Profile" [Australian Bureau of Statistics Homepage] [On-line]. Available: http://www.statistics.gov.au/websitedbs/c311215.NSF/Australia+Now+-+A+Statistical+Profile/69B354D7B1602F35CA2567220072EB13/ [last updated 6 January 2000].

25. Docherty, *Historical Dictionary of Australia*, 5.

26. Christina B. Gibson, "An Investigation of Gender Differences in Leadership Across Four Countries," *Journal of International Business Studies* 26:2 (London; Second Quarter 1995): 19.

27. Docherty, *Historical Dictionary of Australia*, 71.
28. Ibid., 145.
29. Ibid., 213.
30. Gibson, "An Investigation of Gender Differences in Leadership Across Four Countries," 19.
31. Andrew Shiells, "Aurora Leadership Institute: An Australian Participant's Perspective," *The Australian Library Journal* 45 (1996): 23-27; Joanne Tuffield, "Aurora Leadership Institute: A New Zealand Perspective," *The Australian Library Journal* 45 (1996): 28-32.
32. *The Europa World Year Book*, 933.
33. Lewis, *When Cultures Collide: Managing Successfully Across Cultures*, 276.
34. Triandis, "The Contingency Model in Cross-Cultural Perspective," 175.
35. Harry C. Triandis, Christopher McCusker and C. Harry Hui, "Multimethod Probes of Individualism and Collectivism," *Journal of Personality and Social Psychology* 59 (1990): 1007.
36. Wann-Yih Wu and Michael S. Minor, "Role Perceptions, Personal Traits, Lifestyles and Leadership: An Empirical Study of American, Japanese, and Taiwanese Female Managers," *International Business Review* 6:1 (1997): 19.
37. Boris Raymond and Paul Duffy, *Historical Dictionary of Russia* (Lanham, MD & London: The Scarecrow Press, Inc. 1998), 1.
38. Lawrence R. Robertson, ed., *Russia & Eurasia Facts and Figures* 24 (Gulf Breeze, Florida: Academic International Press, 1998), 21-29.
39. *The Europa World Year Book*, 2975.
40. Lewis, *When Cultures Collide: Managing Successfully Across Cultures*, 231.
41. Archie Brown, "Political Leadership in Post-Communist Russia," in Amin Saikal and William Maley, ed., *Russia in Search of its Future* (1995), 28.
42. Serebriany, Sergei, "Culture in Russia and Russian Culture," in Amin Saikal and William Maley, ed. *Russia in Search of its Future*. (1995), 160.
43. Daniel J. McCarthy et al., "Case Study–Olga Kirova: A Russian Entrepreneur's Quality Leadership," *International Journal of Organizational Analysis* 5:3 (Jul 1997): 267.
44. Lewis, *When Cultures Collide: Managing Successfully Across Cultures*, 165.
45. Rudolph J. Vecoli, "Introduction," in Rudolph J. Vecoli et al., ed., *Gale Encyclopedia of Multicultural America* (New York: Gale Research Inc., 1995), xxii.
46. *Statistical Abstract of the United States* [On-line]. Available: http://www.census.gov/prod/www.census.gov/startab/www/.
47. Wu and Minor, "Role Perceptions, Personal Traits, Lifestyles and Leadership: An Empirical Study of American, Japanese, and Taiwanese Female Managers," 31.
48. Teresa Y. Neely and Mark D. Winston, "Snowbird Leadership Institute: Leadership Development in the Profession," *College & Research Libraries* 60:5 (Sept. 1999): 413.
49. Rabindra N. Kanungo and Mabuael Mendonca, *Ethnic Dimensions of Leadership* (Thousand Oaks: SAGE Publications, Inc. 1996), 106.
50. Peterson and Hunt, "International Perspectives on International Leadership," *The Leadership Quarterly* 8:3 (1997): 203.

Index

Page numbers followed by "n" indicate notes.

© 2001 by The Haworth Press, Inc. All rights reserved.

Integrating Total Quality Management in a Library Setting, edited by Susan Jurow, MLS, and Susan B. Barnard, MLS (Vol. 18, No. 1/2, 1993). *"Especially valuable are the librarian experiences that directly relate to real concerns about TQM. Recommended for all professional reading collections." (Library Journal)*

Leadership in Academic Libraries: Proceedings of the W. Porter Kellam Conference, The University of Georgia, May 7, 1991, edited by William Gray Potter (Vol. 17, No. 4, 1993). *"Will be of interest to those concerned with the history of American academic libraries." (Australian Library Review)*

Collection Assessment and Acquisitions Budgets, edited by Sul H. Lee (Vol. 17, No. 2, 1993). *Contains timely information about the assessment of academic library collections and the relationship of collection assessment to acquisition budgets.*

Developing Library Staff for the 21st Century, edited by Maureen Sullivan (Vol. 17, No. 1, 1992). *"I found myself enthralled with this highly readable publication. It is one of those rare compilations that manages to successfully integrate current general management operational thinking in the context of academic library management." (Bimonthly Review of Law Books)*

Vendor Evaluation and Acquisition Budgets, edited by Sul H. Lee (Vol. 16, No. 3, 1992). *"The title doesn't do justice to the true scope of this excellent collection of papers delivered at the sixth annual conference on library acquisitions sponsored by the University of Oklahoma Libraries." (Kent K. Hendrickson, BS, MALS, Dean of Libraries, University of Nebraska-Lincoln) Find insight discussions on the impact of rising costs on library budgets and management in this groundbreaking book.*

The Management of Library and Information Studies Education, edited by Herman L. Totten, PhD, MLS (Vol. 16, No. 1/2, 1992). *"Offers something of interest to everyone connected with LIS education–the undergraduate contemplating a master's degree, the doctoral student struggling with courses and career choices, the new faculty member aghast at conflicting responsibilities, the experienced but stressed LIS professor, and directors of LIS Schools." (Education Libraries)*

Library Management in the Information Technology Environment: Issues, Policies, and Practice for Administrators, edited by Brice G. Hobrock, PhD, MLS (Vol. 15, No. 3/4, 1992). *"A road map to identify some of the alternative routes to the electronic library." (Stephen Rollins, Associate Dean for Library Services, General Library, University of New Mexico)*

Managing Technical Services in the 90's, edited by Drew Racine (Vol. 15, No. 1/2, 1991). *"Presents an eclectic overview of the challenges currently facing all library technical services efforts. . . . Recommended to library administrators and interested practitioners." (Library Journal)*

Budgets for Acquisitions: Strategies for Serials, Monographs, and Electronic Formats, edited by Sul H. Lee (Vol. 14, No. 3, 1991). *"Much more than a series of handy tips for the careful shopper. This [book] is a most useful one–well-informed, thought-provoking, and authoritative." (Australian Library Review)*

Creative Planning for Library Administration: Leadership for the Future, edited by Kent Hendrickson, MALS (Vol. 14, No. 2, 1991). *"Provides some essential information on the planning process, and the mix of opinions and methodologies, as well as examples relevant to every library manager, resulting in a very readable foray into a topic too long avoided by many of us." (Canadian Library Journal)*

Strategic Planning in Higher Education: Implementing New Roles for the Academic Library, edited by James F. Williams, II, MLS (Vol. 13, No. 3/4, 1991). *"A welcome addition to the sparse literature on strategic planning in university libraries. Academic librarians considering strategic planning for their libraries will learn a great deal from this work." (Canadian Library Journal)*

Personnel Administration in an Automated Environment, edited by Philip E. Leinbach, MLS (Vol. 13, No. 1/2, 1990). *"An interesting and worthwhile volume, recommended to university library administrators and to others interested in thought-provoking discussion of the personnel implications of automation." (Canadian Library Journal)*

Library Development: A Future Imperative, edited by Dwight F. Burlingame, PhD (Vol. 12, No. 4, 1990). *"This volume provides an excellent overview of fundraising with special application to libraries. . . . A useful book that is highly recommended for all libraries." (Library Journal)*

Library Material Costs and Access to Information, edited by Sul H. Lee (Vol. 12, No. 3, 1991). *"A cohesive treatment of the issue. Although the book's contributors possess a research library perspective, the data and the ideas presented are of interest and benefit to the entire profession, especially academic librarians." (Library Resources and Technical Services)*

Training Issues and Strategies in Libraries, edited by Paul M. Gherman, MALS, and Frances O. Painter, MLS, MBA (Vol. 12, No. 2, 1990). *"There are . . . useful chapters, all by different authors, each with a preliminary summary of the content–a device that saves much time in deciding whether to read the whole chapter or merely skim through it. Many of the chapters are essentially practical without too much emphasis on theory. This book is a good investment." (Library Association Record)*

Library Education and Employer Expectations, edited by E. Dale Cluff, PhD, MLS (Vol. 11, No. 3/4, 1990). *"Useful to library-school students and faculty interested in employment problems and employer perspectives. Librarians concerned with recruitment practices will also be interested." (Information Technology and Libraries)*

Managing Public Libraries in the 21st Century, edited by Pat Woodrum, MLS (Vol. 11, No. 1/2, 1989). *"A broad-based collection of topics that explores the management problems and possibilities public libraries will be facing in the 21st century." (Robert Swisher, PhD, Director, School of Library and Information Studies, University of Oklahoma)*

Human Resources Management in Libraries, edited by Gisela M. Webb, MLS, MPA (Vol. 10, No. 4, 1989). *"Thought provoking and enjoyable reading. . . . Provides valuable insights for the effective information manager." (Special Libraries)*

Creativity, Innovation, and Entrepreneurship in Libraries, edited by Donald E. Riggs, EdD, MLS (Vol. 10, No. 2/3, 1989). *"The volume is well worth reading as a whole. . . . There is very little repetition, and it should stimulate thought." (Australian Library Review)*

The Impact of Rising Costs of Serials and Monographs on Library Services and Programs, edited by Sul H. Lee (Vol. 10, No. 1, 1989). *". . . Sul Lee hit a winner here." (Serials Review)*

Computing, Electronic Publishing, and Information Technology: Their Impact on Academic Libraries, edited by Robin N. Downes (Vol. 9, No. 4, 1989). *"For a relatively short and easily digestible discussion of these issues, this book can be recommended, not only to those in academic libraries, but also to those in similar types of library or information unit, and to academics and educators in the field." (Journal of Documentation)*

Library Management and Technical Services: The Changing Role of Technical Services in Library Organizations, edited by Jennifer Cargill, MSLS, MSed (Vol. 9, No. 1, 1988). *"As a practical and instructive guide to issues such as automation, personnel matters, education, management techniques and liaison with other services, senior library managers with a sincere interest in evaluating the role of their technical services should find this a timely publication." (Library Association Record)*

Management Issues in the Networking Environment, edited by Edward R. Johnson, PhD (Vol. 8, No. 3/4, 1989). *"Particularly useful for librarians/information specialists contemplating establishing a local network." (Australian Library Review)*

Acquisitions, Budgets, and Material Costs: Issues and Approaches, edited by Sul H. Lee (Supp. #2, 1988). *"The advice of these library practitioners is sensible and their insights illuminating for librarians in academic libraries." (American Reference Books Annual)*

Pricing and Costs of Monographs and Serials: National and International Issues, edited by Sul H. Lee (Supp. #1, 1987). *"Eminently readable. There is a good balance of chapters on serials and* *monographs and the perspective of suppliers, publishers, and library practitioners are presented. A book well worth reading." (Australasian College Libraries)*

Legal Issues for Library and Information Managers, edited by William Z. Nasri, JD, PhD (Vol. 7, No. 4, 1987). *"Useful to any librarian looking for protection or wondering where esponsibilities end and liabilities begin. Recommended." (Academic Library Book Review)*

Archives and Library Administration: Divergent Traditions and Common Concerns, edited by Lawrence J. McCrank, PhD, MLS (Vol. 7, No. 2/3, 1986). *"A forward-looking view of archives and libraries. . . . Recommend[ed] to students, teachers, and practitioners alike of archival and library science. It is readable, thought-provoking, and provides a summary of the major areas of divergence and convergence." (Association of Canadian Map Libraries and Archives)*

Excellence in Library Management, edited by Charlotte Georgi, MLS, and Robert Bellanti, MLS, MBA (Vol. 6, No. 3, 1985). *"Most beneficial for library administrators . . . for anyone interested in either library/information science or management." (Special Libraries)*

Marketing and the Library, edited by Gary T. Ford (Vol. 4, No. 4, 1984). *Discover the latest methods for more effective information dissemination and learn to develop successful programs for specific target areas.*

Finance Planning for Libraries, edited by Murray S. Martin (Vol. 3, No. 3/4, 1983). *Stresses the need for libraries to weed out expenditures which do not contribute to their basic role–the collection and organization of information–when planning where and when to spend money.*

Planning for Library Services: A Guide to Utilizing Planning Methods for Library Management, edited by Charles R. McClure, PhD (Vol. 2, No. 3/4, 1982). *"Should be read by anyone who is involved in planning processes of libraries–certainly by every administrator of a library or system." (American Reference Books Annual)*

RECEIVED
OCT 28 2002
MEMORIAL LIBRARY